Willa Cather and Aestheticism

THE FAIRLEIGH DICKINSON UNIVERSITY PRESS SERIES ON WILLA CATHER IN MEMORY OF MERRILL M. SKAGGS

This series is dedicated to publishing outstanding scholarship on the life, writings, influence, and legacy of this acclaimed American writer, whether single-author volumes or essay collections.

Series Editor: Dr. Laura Winters, College of St. Elizabeth

Watson, Sarah Cheney, and Ann Moseley (editors), *Willa Cather and Aestheticism: From Romanticism to Modernism* (2012)

Kephart, Christine, *The Catherian Cathedral: Gothic Cathedral Iconography in Willa Cather's Fiction* (2011)

Marks, Lucy, and David Porter, *Seeking Life Whole: Willa Cather and the Brewsters* (2009)

Perriman, Wendy K. (editor), *Willa Cather and the Dance: "A Most Satisfying Elegance"* (2009)

Murphy, John J., and Merrill M. Skaggs (editors), *Willa Cather: New Facts, New Glimpses, Revisions* (2008)

Urgo, Joseph, and Merrill M. Skaggs (editors), *Violence, The Arts, and Willa Cather* (2008)

Skaggs, Merrill M., *Willa Cather's New York: New Essays on Cather in the City* (2000)

Harvey, Sally Peltier, *Redefining the American Dream: The Novels of Willa Cather* (1995)

Middleton, Jo Ann, *Willa Cather's Modernism: A Study of Style and Technique* (1990)

Willa Cather and Aestheticism

From Romanticism to Modernism

Edited by Sarah Cheney Watson
and Ann Moseley

Fairleigh Dickinson University Press
Madison • Teaneck

Published by Fairleigh Dickinson University Press
Co-published with The Rowman & Littlefield Publishing Group, Inc.
4501 Forbes Boulevard, Suite 200, Lanham, Maryland 20706
www.rowman.com

10 Thornbury Road, Plymouth PL6 7PP, United Kingdom

"The Nude had Descended the Staircase": Katherine Anne Porter Looks at Willa Cather Looking at Modern Art," reprinted from Stout, Janis P. 2011. "The Nude Had Descended the Staircase." Cather Studies, Volume 9, edited by Melissa J. Homestead and Guy J. Reynolds, 225-43. Lincoln: University of Nebraska Press.

Willa Cather's Sheltering Art: Cather's Cathedral and the Adams Factor, by John J. Murphy, from the Santa Fe 400th Anniversary Worrell Lecture, St. John's College, 5 March 2010.

British Cataloging in Publication Information Available

Library of Congress Cataloging-in-Publication Data

Willa Cather and aestheticism : from Romanticism to Modernism / edited by Sarah Cheney Watson and Ann Moseley.
    p. cm.—(The Fairleigh Dickinson University Press series on Willa Cather in memory of Merrill M. Skaggs)
    Includes bibliographical references and index.
    ISBN 978-1-61147-511-1 (alk. paper)—ISBN 978-1-61147-512-8
    1. Cather, Willa, 1873–1947—Criticism and interpretation. 2. Cather, Willa, 1873–1947—Aesthetics. 3. Aestheticism (Literature) 4. Romanticism—United States. 5. Modernism (Aesthetics)—United States. I. Watson, Sarah Cheney, 1948– II. Moseley, Watson and Ann, 1947–
    PS3505.A87Z93524 2012
    813'.52—dc23   2012010592

To the Memory of Merrill Skaggs,
who encouraged us.

Studio Portrait of Willa Cather c. 1910. Black/white print by Aimé Dupont, New York, NY, 12.70 × 17.78 cm. Philip L. and Helen Cather Southwick Collection, Archives and Special Collections, University of Nebraska-Lincoln Libraries.

Contents

List of Illustrations

Preface

The inspiration for *Willa Cather and Aestheticism* originated in the late 1990s when Sarah was researching and writing her dissertation, "Servant of Beauty: Willa Cather and the Aesthetic Movement,"[1] with Ann as her faculty adviser. The inspired moment began with Sarah reading aloud the passage from *Death Comes for the Archbishop* that describes the discovery of the stone Father Latour has found and intends to use in the building of a cathedral. Latour is riding with Father Joseph Vaillant, whom he calls "Blanchet," to the Rio Grande Valley, where they come to

> a rugged wall of rock . . . a strong golden ochre, very much like the gold of the sunlight that was now beating upon it. . . . "It is curious, is it not, to find one yellow hill among all these green ones?" remarked the Bishop, stooping to pick up a piece of the stone. "I have ridden over these hills in every direction, but this is the only one of its kind." He stood regarding the chip of yellow rock that lay in his palm. As he had a very special way of handling objects that were sacred, he extended that manner to things which he considered beautiful. After a moment of silence he looked up at the rugged wall, gleaming gold above them. "That hill, *Blanchet*, is my Cathedral. . . . [When] I rode up here from the west in the late afternoon[,] this hill confronted me as it confronts us now, and I knew instantly that it was my Cathedral."[2]

In reply, Sarah's husband Jim said, "That sounds like Walter Pater in *The Renaissance*." In the preface Pater writes, "What is important, then, is not that the critic [or the educated person] should possess a correct abstract

xiii

definition of beauty for the intellect, but a certain kind of temperament, the power of being deeply moved by the presence of beautiful objects" (xxx). And in the conclusion to *The Renaissance*: "Every moment some form grows perfect in hand or face; some tone on the hills or the sea is choicer than the rest; some mood . . . is irresistibly real and attractive to us . . . ."[3] Jim continued: "Your Father Latour sounds like an aesthete in his temperament and in his treatment of beautiful things. It's almost as if it were part of his religion; for him, beauty is deeply connected to truth."

Mulling that over, Sarah read *The Renaissance* and discussed the idea with Ann. After some initial research they found that little had been published about Willa Cather's relationship with and debt to the Aesthetic movement. Even in the ensuing years, Cather's aesthetic sense has received little scholarly attention; however, we believe that Cather accepted ideas about beauty and truth from the Aesthetic movement and adapted them to her own uses. But she always believed that the artist must look at the world through a lens of aestheticism, holding her art always in the service of beauty insofar as it reflects truth.

As defined by the *Oxford English Dictionary*, aestheticism is "the quality of being aesthetic; the pursuit of, or devotion to, what is beautiful or attractive to the senses, esp. as opposed to an ethically or rationally based outlook; *spec.* adherence to the Aesthetic Movement." A close look at Cather's journalism, stories, novels, and criticism shows that she was indeed a proponent of this type of aestheticism, both as a lover of beauty and a writer who followed the Aesthetic movement. The influence on Cather of the major forerunners and representatives of the Aesthetic movement (John Ruskin, the Pre-Raphaelites, Walter Pater, Oscar Wilde, and others); the visual arts (Burne-Jones, Whistler, and others); and the material culture of the time (Arts and Crafts and Art Nouveau in design from wallpaper to jewelry) is undeniable. Yet little scholarly attention has been paid to this important influence. In addition to a 1960 statement by John H. Randall relating Cather to Pater (see our introduction) and the detailed discussion of these two writers in Sarah's dissertation, only one book;[4] one section in a book;[5] and one article[6] develop connections between Cather and Pater. As for other members of the Aesthetic movement, two essays focus on Cather and Wilde. After summarizing Cather's public criticism of Wilde in her 1890s journalism, Claude J. Summers argues that "Paul's Case" presents "a case study of the Wildean aesthete,"[7] and Eric Haralson includes a discussion of the "eternal boy" in Cather, Henry James, and Oscar Wilde.[8] And Joseph C. Murphy demonstrates how Cather adapted Ruskin's romantic typology of landscape for use in *My Ántonia, Death Comes for the Archbishop,* and *Shadows on the Rock.*[9]

Although many critics have discussed Cather's developing theory of art and several works about Cather include the word *aesthetic* or *aesthetics* as a descriptor in their titles, only a limited number of studies deal with Cather and aesthetics as it is specifically related to beauty in art—and to how this beauty grows into a truth that is not didactic or moralistic. Deborah Lindsay Williams discusses Cather's appreciation in *The Song of the Lark* and *The Professor's House* of "domestic artifacts" created by Native American women to be "beautiful, essential objects of everyday life."[10] Diane Prenatt, focusing on Cather's use of ekphrasis—"the verbal representative of a visual representation"—finds this artistic trope not only in Thea Kronborg's experience of Breton's painting *The Song of the Lark* but also in the jars, pottery, and architecture in *The Song of the Lark* and "Tom Outland's Story." However, Prenatt believes that in the first and last sections of *The Professor's House*, Cather—like other modernists—"challenges the aesthetic value of the commercial object," such as Rosamond's emerald necklace as opposed to the natural turquoises Tom found in Cliff City.[11] John Hilgart shows that Cather focuses on "privileged *objects*— enduring things of beauty and meaning" that are "the antithesis of the commodity form" that she hated and contrasts the "fully integrated" aestheticism of Jean Latour's Catholicism with her "enactment and critique" in *The Professor's House* of "the most formalist version" of her aesthetic—a version that through undermining Tom Outland and his mesa experience becomes essentially all form and no content.[12] And Chad Trevitte reads *A Lost Lady* as "an allegory of aesthetic value" that involves not only the theme of innocence and experience as related to Niel Herbert but also "social change in the decline of Marian Forrester"; to Trevitte, the idea of "aesthetic autonomy" in the novel and generally speaking "has become both more pronounced and more contradictory in the modernist era" tainted by economic and commercial values.[13]

We believe that this volume of essays on Willa Cather and aestheticism— on the understanding and pursuit of true art and beauty not just during the period of the Aesthetic movement but at all times—makes an important contribution to Cather studies. Representing a variety of critical approaches, these essays will increase our understanding of Cather's aesthetic beliefs and practices and contribute immensely to our critical understanding of her work and her life. Because painting, architecture, and material objects such as books, furniture, textiles, and jewelry were so important to Cather and such an inseparable part of the Aesthetic movement, we have also made illustrations an integral part of our volume.

We would like to express our deep gratitude to Harry Keyishian, director of Fairleigh Dickinson University Press, for his support and encouragement from the very beginning of our project as well as his sound guidance and advice as the manuscript developed; Brooke Bascietto, associate editor at the Rowman & Littlefield Publishing Group, for her help with illustrations and the production of the book; all the museum curators and others who helped us obtain the images used in the book; the Jim and Ethel Dicksen Fund for Scholarly Research and Travel (East Texas Baptist University), for the funds to procure those images; and our families for their patience and support throughout the entire process. Most of all, we thank our contributors without whom this volume would not exist.

NOTES

1. Sarah Cheney Watson, "Servant of Beauty: Willa Cather and the Aesthetic Movement" (doctoral dissertation, Texas A&M University, Commerce, 1999).

2. Willa Cather, *Death Comes fore the Archbishop,* Willa Cather Scholarly Edition (Lincoln: University of Nebraska Press, 1927/1999), 252–53).

3. Walter Pater, *The Renaissance: Studies in Art and Poetry,* ed. Adam Phillips (Oxford: Oxford University Press, 1873/1986) 152.

4. John Anders, *Willa Cather's Sexual Aesthetics and the Male Homosexual Literary Tradition* (Lincoln: University of Nebraska Press, 1999).

5. Heather Love, *Feeling Backward: Loss and the Politics of Queer History* (Cambridge: Harvard University Press, 2007).

6. John Anders, "'Something Soft and Wild and Free': Willa Cather's Sexual Aesthetics," *Cather Studies* 4 (1999): 244–63.

7. Claude J. Summers, "'A Losing Game in the End': Aestheticism and Homosexuality in Cather's 'Paul's Case,'" *Modern Fiction Studies* 36, no. 1 (1990): 103–19.

8. Eric Haralson, *Henry James and Queer Modernity* (Cambridge: Cambridge University Press, 2003).

9. Joseph C. Murphy, "Cather's Ruskinian Landscapes," *Cather Studies* 8 (2010): 228–245.

10. Deborah Lindsay Williams, "'Fragments of Their Desire': Willa Cather and the Alternative Aesthetic Tradition of Native American Women," in *Willa Cather and Material Culture: Real-World Writing, Writing the Real World,* ed. Janis P. Stout (Tuscaloosa: University of Alabama Press, 2005), 156–70.

11. Diane Prenatt, "Art and the Commercial Object as Ekphrastic Subjects in *The Song of the Lark* and *The Professor's House,*" *Cather Studies* 9 (2011): 204–224.

12. John Hilgart, "Death Comes for the Aesthete: Commodity Culture and the Artifact in Cather's *The Professor's House,*" *Studies in the Novel* 30, no. 3 (1998): 377–404.

13. Chad Trevitte, "Cather's *A Lost Lady* and the Disenchantment of Art," *Twentieth-Century Literature* 53, no. 2 (2007): 182–211.

Introduction

The "Intrinsic Beauty" of Art

Ann Moseley and Sarah Cheney Watson

Although Willa Cather declared on May 19, 1895, after the "downfall of the leader of the aesthetic movement," Oscar Wilde, that this movement was "the most fatal and dangerous school of art that has ever voiced itself in the English tongue" (Cather 1895a/1970, 153), she was actually profoundly influenced by late nineteenth-century Aestheticism and by related but diverse movements that both anticipated and followed it. Aestheticism not only affected her writing, both fiction and non-fiction, but also inspired her belief system. The background and development of Aestheticism in the verbal and visual arts also affected the art and culture of the period in which she lived and wrote. A scholarly investigation of Aestheticism, therefore, fosters a deeper understanding of Willa Cather's own aesthetic.

OVERVIEW OF AESTHETICISM

Aestheticism actually has much deeper roots than is usually thought. The term *aesthete* derives from the Greek words *aisthēta* ("things perceptible to the senses") and *aisthētēs* ("one who perceived"), but the general belief that art is its own end and is not, therefore, required to be utilitarian or didactic was developed by late eighteenth-century philosophers, including Immanuel Kant (1724–1804) in his *Critique of Aesthetic Judgment* (Abrams 1988, 2–3; Crudden 1977, 16–17).

1

The nineteenth century, however, and particularly the latter part of the century, was the era of Aestheticism, which was, according to Jonathan Freedman, represented by two different phenomena: "an austere or flamboyant Romantic fervor and social alienation" and the later "fashion and frivolity that was associated with Oscar Wilde" (1990, 2). Critical descriptions of Aestheticism and its major proponents differ widely, but, generally speaking, it was "a heterogeneous aggregate of loosely connected people whose accumulated effort moulded the culture of the day" (Mendelssohn 2007, 5). In France and England the Aestheticism of "romantic fervor" developed early in the century with an emphasis on the beauty rather than the morality of art. The most influential of the French aesthetes were Charles Baudelaire (himself influenced by the American Edgar Allan Poe), Gustave Flaubert, and Théophile Gautier. Indeed, Gautier is attributed by many with coining the term *"l'art pour l'art,"* or "art for art's sake," a concept that he discusses in his preface to *Mademoiselle de Maupin* (1835). Across the channel in England the value of art was also shifting from truth to beauty. According to Hazard Adams in *Critical Theory since Plato*, for the Romantics "beauty provid[ed] a form of knowledge that [could] not be gained by means of 'consecutive reasoning'" (1992, 492). Indeed, William Wordsworth claims that, because it reflects the general truth, "poetry is thus an acknowledgment of the beauty of the universe" (442). And John Keats points out that "What the imagination seizes as beauty must be truth" (493). Even more famously, Keats declared in "Ode on a Grecian Urn" that "'Beauty is truth, truth beauty' —that is all / Ye know on earth, and all ye need to know" (1819/1962, ll. 49-50).

Although his role as a pure aesthete is debatable,[1] John Ruskin (1819–1900) and his ideas on beauty, painting, architecture, and the dignity of craftsmanship greatly influenced Pre-Raphaelitism and the Arts and Crafts movement as well as Walter Pater and Oscar Wilde. Hilary Fraser observes that Ruskin "affirmed the significance of the aesthetic dimension in life in an age when, under the pressure of modern industrial development and burgeoning capitalism, that dimension was becoming marginal to the real business of life and perilously close to being lost altogether. He encouraged artists and laymen alike to appreciate the beauty of nature, art, and architecture and to deprecate the ugliness of all that deformed nature and human creativity" (Fraser 1986, 112). In his two most influential works, *Modern Painters* (1843 ff) and *The Stones of Venice* (1851–1853), he emphasizes the importance of the truthful representation of nature in art and architecture. Unlike most later aesthetes, however, Ruskin argues for the union of morality and art. And—although the influence of late nineteenth-century scientific theories tarnished his faith— *The Stones of Venice* clearly associates the Gothic architecture that he most admired with both aesthetics and spirituality, specifically with Christianity.

Other important movements in art and poetry in England in the middle of the nineteenth century prepared the way for Aestheticism. The original Pre-Raphaelite Brotherhood—composed of Dante Gabriel Rossetti, Holman Hunt, and John Millais—sought to portray, in Ruskin's words, "absolute, uncompromising truth in all that it does, obtained by working everything, down to the most minute detail, from nature only" (Naylor 1971, 97). The name of the group derives from their belief that Italian religious art before Raphael represented the ideals of simplicity, beauty, and truthfulness found in pure devotion and the accurate representation of nature. Other English artists associated with the Pre-Raphaelite movement—Dante Gabriel Rossetti himself, Christina Rossetti, Charles Algernon Swinburne, Edward Burne-Jones, and William Morris—developed a sensuous style employing musical effects and symbolic imagery, and several of them focused on medieval subjects and spiritual or supernatural subjects (Abrams 1988, 149; Crudden 1977, 18–19). Many of the Pre-Raphaelites were multitalented in painting, poetry, and the decorative arts.

Beginning around 1860 some of these same artists, particularly William Morris and Edward Burne-Jones, participated in the Arts and Crafts movement, which attempted to apply the quality of medieval craftsmanship to furniture, pottery, textiles, glass, metalwork, and other handcrafted objects. Finding in Ruskin's *The Stones of Venice* the idea that architecture and other crafts should "reflect man's essential" humanity and individuality (Naylor 1971, 27), these men rebelled against the trends of industry and mass production. Gillian Naylor identifies two strands in this movement—one exhibiting Ruskinian "straightforward, honest craftsmanship" in its simplicity and directness and the other more ornamental but still individualistic (102).

From the early 1890s through the first decade of the twentieth century, Arts and Crafts gave way to Art Nouveau, which manifested itself in architecture, sculpture, painting, and the applied arts such as furniture, textiles, glass, jewelry, and metalwork. Drawing on Japanese, Celtic, and Gothic art as well as the engravings of William Blake, this international movement was distinguished by a two-dimensional perspective and asymmetrical, curvilinear, and even serpentine lines, such as the whiplash design (Waddell 1977, vii–ix). Two of the best known practitioners of Art Nouveau are Louis Comfort Tiffany, who created the stained glass known by his name, and Aubrey Beardsley, who illustrated for the British periodical *The Yellow Book*, which was associated with the decadence of the fin de siècle. Both the Arts and Crafts movement and Art Nouveau strove to create unity among the arts; in particular, Albert Aurier—a supporter of "the Parisian Symbolist group the 'Nabis'—developed the idea that in order to achieve its full spiritual potential, art should have no artificial barriers separating its various spheres of activity." An important bridge to modernism, Art Nouveau was "the first self-conscious, internationally based attempt to transform visual culture through a commitment to the idea of the modern" (Greenhalgh 2000, 18–19).

During the last quarter of the nineteenth century the most important spokesperson for Aestheticism was Walter Pater (1839–1894), but Pater's own ideas outgrew the movement itself. Focusing on the Renaissance instead of the Gothic as did Ruskin, Pater attempted to establish in his preface to *The Renaissance* the goal of the true aesthete as related to the ideal of beauty: "Beauty, like all other qualities presented to human experience, is relative; and the definition of it becomes unmeaning and useless in proportion to its abstractness. To define beauty, not in the most abstract but in the most concrete terms possible, to find not its universal formula, but the formula which expresses most adequately this or that special manifestation of it, is the aim of the true student of aesthetics" (1873/1986, xxix). Discussing this quotation, R. V. Johnson explains that Pater saw beauty as "something immediately experienced" (1969, 3). Thus, Pater valorized sensations and feelings, declaring in the "Conclusion" to the first edition of *The Renaissance* that, because a "counted number of pulses only is given to us" in life, we should seek "to be present always at the focus where the greatest number of vital forces unite in their purest energy"; therefore, "to burn always with this hard, gemlike flame, to maintain this ecstasy, is success in life." Later in the "Conclusion" he declares that the best sources for the most and best "pulsations" in life are "poetic passion, the desire of beauty, and the love of art for its own sake" (1873/1986, 153). Through immediate and intense experiences, he wanted to improve the overall quality of life through what Johnson calls "our whole area of awareness, sharpening intelligence, sense-perception and powers of introspection." Indeed, his Aestheticism was one of contemplation more than action (19–20). The subtitle of *Marius the Epicurean: His Sensations and Ideas* (1885/1985) suggests the greater complexity of Pater's views, a complexity of ideas and beliefs that he strove to clarify in this story of a young pagan's philosophical and spiritual journey in second-century Rome. Although readings of this novel—and especially of its conclusion—differ widely, the novel explores both aesthetic and religious issues and, in the Christian rites provided for Marius at his death, leaves open the possibility of his Christian belief. In the novel, Pater certainly views life from an ethical—perhaps even a Christian—point of view.[2]

Two of the most flamboyant and controversial aesthetes of the period were the painter James Abbott McNeill Whistler and the writer Oscar Wilde. Born in the United States, Whistler (1834–1903) spent most of his artistic career in Paris and London. His Aestheticism is shown in the simple, nature-based forms of his portraits and in the influence of Oriental art and music on such works as his Nocturnes. Indeed, his *Nocturne in Black and Gold: A Falling Rocket* (1874) elicited Ruskin's enraged declaration that he "never expected to hear a coxcomb ask two hundred guineas for flinging a pot of paint in the public's face" (Gaunt 1945, 94). In 1877 Whistler sued Ruskin for libel; although Whistler won his case, his witty defense of art for art's sake so infuriated the jury that he was awarded damages of only a farthing and forced into bankruptcy.

Perhaps the most famous aesthete of all was Oscar Wilde (1854–1900), who seemed to take literally Pater's early advice "to burn always with [a] hard, gemlike flame" (1873/1986, 152). A flamboyant dandy and poseur, Wilde is probably best known for his involvement in civil and criminal lawsuits about his homosexuality and his imprisonment from 1895 to 1897, but he was the literal embodiment of the "art for art's sake credo" in the 1890s. Although Wilde also wrote short stories and fantasies, he is best known for his comic plays, especially for *Lady Windemere's Fan* (1892) and *The Importance of Being Earnest* (1895), and for his haunting novel *The Picture of Dorian Gray* (1891). Sadly, the controversies surrounding Wilde's life often obscured his true talent.

Finally, Henry James (1843–1916) was influenced by and contributed to Aestheticism, although his talent went far beyond that movement. According to Jonathan Freedman, much James criticism "has consisted of a series of arguments over [the critics'] vision of Henry James as a second Gilbert Osmond [in *A Portrait of a Lady*]: an effete aesthete expatriate whose works are marred by his withdrawal from the soil of social reality (an exclusively American terrain) into the consoling never-never land of art (the country of the mauve as well as the blue)" (1990, xii). Freedman traces historical and intertextual connections between James and both Pater and Wilde, but he argues that in *The Portrait of a Lady* and other works James satirizes the emptiness of the aesthete and that in his last phase he explores the decadence of the movement.

Those associated with the beliefs of Aestheticism fought valiantly against philistinism—against the moral didacticism in art that they associated with the bourgeoisie and that Cather herself criticized (1897/1970, 515). At its core Aestheticism placed the work of art—and the beauty inherent in it—above any potential message or moral, but for many representatives of Aestheticism, such as Pater, the relationship between life and art was key, as ideally one should live life in the spirit of art and beauty. Privileging the image itself, Aestheticism also privileged form, and in so doing looked forward to modernism—a direction that is especially evident in the works of Pater, Wilde, and James.

Aestheticism is also part of the larger study of aesthetics—the general philosophy of beauty and the arts, a philosophy involving imagination, emotion, understanding, and even inspiration. Artists and philosophers of every age have been concerned with aeshetics, but Cather's own aesthetic creed was formed just as Aestheticism was transforming into modernism between the 1890s and 1922, when she declared her allegiance to simplification in art in "The Novel Démeublé" (1949a/1988, 40). Whether the art object was a story, a novel, a painting, an opera, or a Gothic cathedral, Cather would have agreed with Suzanne Langer that "Art is the creation of forms symbolic of human feeling."[3]

WILLA CATHER AND AESTHETICISM

Soon after she left home in 1890 for the University of Nebraska, Willa Cather (1873–1947) began to move from her family's narrow, rather fundamentalist religious practices toward a belief that life should be a search for beauty as Pater defines it. As a student Cather read widely, and by the time she began to write for the *Nebraska State Journal* in the fall of 1893, she had "already studied a good many nineteenth-century classics . . . with some intensity: the great essayists Carlyle, Ruskin, Pater, Arnold, and Emerson, writers whose beliefs . . . touched her own" (Slote 1966a, 36). One of the first critics to recognize Pater's influence on Cather was John H. Randall, who observed that "Since it was in the nineties that Willa Cather acquired her artistic training, it is to this period we must turn if we want to understand her artistic ideas. One of the leading literary movements of the time was the aesthetic movement . . . popularized . . . by . . . Walter Pater" (Randall 1960, 2). Randall further claims that Walter Pater and the "art for art's sake" movement was one of the primary areas upon which Cather's value system rested. While Randall admits that the Aesthetic movement influenced Cather, he does not give much detail. His admission—and omission—begs for further investigation.

Cather's columns from the *Nebraska State Journal* and the Lincoln *Courier* from the 1890s show that she did, indeed, subscribe to Aestheticism at this time. In a September 23, 1894, column from the *Nebraska State Journal* entitled "Commitment," she states the gospel of the art for art's sake movement in her own words:

> In a work of art intrinsic beauty is the *raison d'être*. Any piece of art is its own excuse for being. Art, like wisdom, is born full-armed without the will or consent of man. He cannot say it yea or nay. . . . No man, or woman, is ever justified in making a book to preach a sermon. It is a degradation of art. . . . An artist should have no moral purpose in mind other than just his art. His mission is not to clean the Augean stables. . . . The mind that can follow a "mission" is not an artistic one. An artist can know no other purpose than his art. . . . An artist should not be vexed by human hobbies or human follies; he

should be able to lift himself up into the clear firmament of creation where the world is not. He should be among men but not one of them, in the world but not of the world. (Cather 1894/1966, 406-407)

Not only does Cather clearly state her allegiance to the art for art's sake movement in this column, but many of her other columns as reprinted in both *The Kingdom of Art* and *The World and the Parish* are punctuated with various names associated with the broader Aesthetic movement in France and England—not only Walter Pater and Oscar Wilde but also Théophile Gautier, Charles Baudelaire, Gustave Flaubert, Dante Gabriel Rossetti, Christina Rossetti, Charles Algernon Swinburne, William Morris, Sir Edward Burne-Jones, James A. McNeill Whistler, and Henry James.

Aestheticism was an important influence on Cather's own criticism as well as on her early fiction. In a column published in the Lincoln *Courier* on September 21, 1895, she writes about the art of acting in almost Paterian terms, comparing the methods of Sarah Bernhardt and Eleanora Duse who will soon "burn out" in the flame of her art:

Signora Duse has always played with the highest, noblest qualities of her soul, with what was best and liveliest in her, and that wears an artist out quickly. . . . Upon the stainless heights of art she has dreamed and created, the heights on which it is not given to a mortal to live long. Some women act with their senses, some with their soul. The soulful ones burn out the quickest. It is a bad thing for an actress to be too sensitive. Bernhardt's acting is a matter of physical excitement, Duse's of spiritual exaltation. . . . She takes her work too hard. Art is Bernhardt's dissipation, a sort of Bacchic orgy. It is Duse's consecration, her religion, her martyrdom. (1895a/1966, 119)

The connection between art and religion shown here is a motif that runs throughout Cather's writing, a motif that recalls Flaubert's reference to "the religion of beauty" (Abrams 1988, 3). On March 1, 1896, she stated that "In the kingdom of art there is no God, but one God, and his service is so exacting that there are few men born of woman who are strong enough to take the vows" (Cather 1896/1966, 417).

Cather's early acceptance of Aestheticism strongly influenced her to write, as she does in the short stories of *The Troll Garden*, about the plight of the true as well as the false artist. For example, "Paul's Case" is "a treatise on the excesses of the Aesthetic Movement," and Caroline Noble's brother in "The Garden Lodge" and Hugh Treffinger (based on Edward Burne-Jones) in "The Marriage of Phaedra" are both decadent aesthetes (Watson 1999, 15-29). In *Alexander's Bridge* Maurice Mainhall has qualities of the Aesthetic Movement (Quirk 2007, 208), and even Bartley Alexander is mildly reminiscent of Dorian Gray in his selfish obsession with youth and desire.[4]

Focusing on the beauty of art, *The Song of the Lark* moves to a higher level of Aestheticism. The words *beauty* and *beautiful*—especially in regard to art—occur numerous times in the novel, and Thea's declaration that her work—her art—has become her life (Cather 1915, 455) clearly supports the idea of art for art's sake over any moral nay-saying. Moreover, the famous passage about "the stream and the broken pottery" has Paterian echoes: "What was any art but an effort to make a sheath, a mould in which to imprison for a moment the shining, elusive element which is life itself,—life hurrying past us and running away, too strong to stop, to sweet to lose? The Indian women had held it in their jars. In the sculpture she had seen in the Art Institute, it had been caught in a flash of arrested motion" (304). Although Pater is describing the quality of human life in general and not the artist in particular, his belief that art proposes "to give nothing but the highest quality to your moments as they pass, and simply for those moments' sake" (1873/1986, 153) also encourages capturing the moment in the flux, or the "flash of arrested motion."

An aesthetic vision also lies at the heart of *A Lost Lady* (1923). Cather wrote a friend that in the novel she was trying to create "a portrait like a thin miniature painted on ivory," adding that when she was little she was interested only in the "lovely hair" and delightful laugh of Mrs. Lyra Garber, the prototype for Marian Forrester (Woodress 1987, 340). When Niel Herbert discovers Mrs. Forrester in bed with Frank Ellinger, he realizes it is not "a moral scruple she had outraged, but an aesthetic ideal" (Cather 1923/1997, 83). The continuing influence on Cather of the element of beauty in Aestheticism can also be seen from statements that she made later in her career. In her 1925 introduction to *The Best Stories of Sarah Orne Jewett*, Cather alludes to beauty in Paterian terms, declaring that, unlike Jewett's, most stories "are not very interesting to read and reread today; they have not the one thing that survives all arresting situations, all good writing and clever story-making—inherent, individual beauty; the kind of beauty we feel when a beautiful song is sung by a beautiful voice that is exactly suited to the song" (1925a/1988, 49). Cather follows this statement with a specific reference to Pater, declaring that just as "Pater said that every truly great drama must, in the end, linger in the reader's mind as a sort of ballad," so must a good story remain in one's memory (49–50).

However, in Cather's later fiction, the search for beauty that marks the "art for art's sake" phase of her early work began to wear thin, especially in the postwar world of the 1920s, which she describes as a time when "The world broke in two" (Cather 1936b/1988, v). Perhaps she even foresaw the decline of art that Theodor W. Adorno discusses in *Aesthetic Theory* (1970/1997).[5] Cather continued to be influenced by Aestheticism, but by a different type. As R. V. Johnson explains, the transformation "from aestheticism as a view of art to aestheticism as a view of life," as explained in Pater's concluding essay in *The Renaissance*, is to turn from beauty as an object to beauty as "dramatic spectacle" (1969, 18). It is exactly such a spectacle that Professor Godfrey St. Peter describes in *The Professor's House* (1925b)—a spectacle of the "gorgeous drama with God that once occurred in cathedrals on Easter Sundays." St. Peter's conclusion that "Art and religion (they are the same thing, in the end, of course) have given man the only happiness he has ever had" (68–69) is echoed by Cather's personal statement in her 1936 essay on "Escapism" that "Religion and art spring from the same root and are close kin" (1936a/1988, 27). Johnson's argument that the "aesthetic approach to life is . . . contemplative" (1969, 20) also places the characters of Jean Latour in *Death Comes for the Archbishop* (1927)—clearly both a religious man and a lover of beauty—and Jeanne Le Ber in *Shadows on the Rock* (1931) in the realm of Aestheticism.

Although, like Pater's, Cather's aestheticism grew and developed, becoming more closely connected to life and to religion, it remained a vital part of her literary creed. Thus, the connections between art and beauty, between aestheticism and life, persist throughout Cather's fiction. This book explores those connections.

OVERVIEW OF CHAPTERS

Willa Cather and Aestheticism is divided into four sections. Composed of five essays, Part I focuses on the Aesthetic movement itself as it related to Cather. Arranged chronologically based on the Cather works discussed, this section opens with Timothy W. Bintrim's "Exit Smiling: The Case for Paul's Dandyism." Bintrim effectively argues that "dandyism explains much of Paul's behavior, including his ennui, impertinence, and unnatural smile; his pleasure in dress; his diva worship; and even his choice of death." In their essay "Innocence and Experience, Good and Evil, and Doppelgangers: Decadent Aesthetics in Cather's 'Consequences,' James's 'The Jolly Corner,' and Wilde's *The Picture of Dorian Gray*," Sonja J. Lynch and Robert L. Lynch analyze the character of playboy Kier Cavanaugh, the protagonist in Cather's story "Consequences," by drawing fascinating parallels between him and the protagonists of the aforenamed stories by James and Wilde. Initially juxtaposing the drowning scene in which Bartley Alexander is dragged into the river by workers falling from his collapsing bridge with the Morlocks' attack of H. G. Wells's time traveler, Peter Betjemann argues convincingly for Wells's *Time Machine* as a source for *Alexander's Bridge*. At the heart of Betjemann's essay, "Willa Cather's Time Machine: *Alexander's Bridge*, H. G. Wells, and the Suspended Aesthetic," is an exploration of the relationships among art, purpose, and progress. In "Cather's Two Europes: Aestheticism and the Dispossessed,"

Nicholas Birns brings European Aestheticism to America through Cather's immigrant characters in *My Antonia, O Pioneers!, The Song of the Lark,* and other novels—characters who are not princes or elitists but who often accomplish great artistic goals. His central argument is that "Cather's aestheticism is not always true to our own stereotypes of aestheticism as being brittle and elitist. Rather, her aestheticism is one of high standards, yet popularly available," qualities also associated with Pater's essay "Prince of Court Painters." Through a comparison of Pater's Epicurean Aestheticism with Professor Godfrey St. Peter's personal Epicureanism in *The Professor's House,* Sarah Watson argues that Epicurean philosophy informs both Cather and Pater in "Willa Cather's Disenchanted Epicurean: Godfrey St. Peter in *The Professor's House.*" Watson effectively demonstrates that the Epicurean Aestheticism of Pater is not the decadent Aestheticism of Oscar Wilde and that Cather rejected Wilde's philosophy while accepting Pater's and reflecting it through the main character of *The Professor's House.*

Part II of this collection focuses on the visual arts. This section begins with Leona Sevick's argument in "The Arts and Crafts on Willa Cather's Frontier" that Cather's "keen aesthetic sensibility . . . guided her taste not only in poetry and writing but in clothing, furnishings, food, and in art." Cather's criticism of modern values in *O Pioneers!, The Song of the Lark, My Ántonia,* and *One of Ours,* Sevick concludes, is the common thread that ties her work to the Arts and Crafts movement. Moving to the visual arts, Joseph C. Murphy's essay "Cather's 'Twilight Stage': Aestheticism, Tonalism, and Modernist Sentiment" brings to our attention the influence of the Tonalist painters on Willa Cather's aesthetic. Murphy traces Cather's debt to the tonalists through her verbal application of their technique of reducing contrast and coating paintings with darkly shimmering light; indeed, he points out that "Through the dreamwork of twilight, Cather's characters construct futures around loss, absence, and memory." Mark Facknitz demonstrates in "Willa Cather, the Nabi of Red Cloud" that her painterly technique evolved from that of the Barbizon romantic realists to the "brighter swaths of color, the raised horizons, and the colors straight from the tube" that distinguish the postimpressionist Nabis, a group whose paintings she had ample opportunity to observe in her trips to France. The final two essays in this section take a feminist approach to Cather and the visual arts. Angela Conrad shows that Cather employs archetypes used by the Pre-Raphaelites—the Lost Lady, the muse or Blessed Damsel, and the Crushed Flower—to set up male-oriented plots in *A Lost Lady, My Ántonia,* and "Coming, Aphrodite!" but then gives her female subjects the power to create their own roles. In "Fernand Léger and Willa Cather's 'Coming, Aphrodite!'" Jacqueline H. Harris draws parallels between French painter and Aesthete Fernand Léger and Cather's protagonist Don Hedger, particularly between the studios and the skills of the two painters. Harris also compares details from Léger's paintings to the circus episode and other scenes in Cather's story, ultimately arguing that Eden Bower retains the power over herself and her art that Hedger wants to take from her.

Janis P. Stout's essay "'The Nude Had Descended the Staircase': Katherine Anne Porter Looks at Willa Cather Looking at Modern Art" provides an excellent transition to part III: Movement toward Modernism. Recognizing that Katherine Anne Porter employed Marcel Duchamp's painting *Nude Descending the Staircase, No. 2* as an "icon of modernism" in her essay "Reflections on Willa Cather," Stout not only argues that Porter purposefully denied Cather's modernist aesthetic but also explores in her journalism, essays, and letters "what we can know of Cather's interest in modern art, especially visual art." Stout demonstrates that Porter was wrong—that Cather was not only a practitioner of literary modernism but also open to modernism in music and painting. Olga Aksakalova's "Bridging Walter Pater's Aestheticism and Willa Cather's Modernism" connects back to part I while it also develops the modernist theme of this section. Establishing Pater as a necessary precursor to the Modernist aesthetic, Aksakalova connects Cather's minimalist view of art with Pater's similar view that great art avoids "uncharacteristic or tarnished or vulgar decoration." This section concludes with Jo Ann Middleton's essay "From British Aestheticism to American Modernism: Cather's Transforming Vision," which develops the thesis that Cather's "attention to the lessons of Henry James ultimately led her to an aesthetic of her own, an artistic sensibility which, in fact, germinated into something new, a very American form of modernism that not only shares . . . characteristics with what we now call high modernism, but is expansive enough to retain, renew, and incorporate the best of other literary traditions, such as classicism, realism, romanticism, and naturalism."

Part IV on Art and Religion is composed of a single essay by John J. Murphy. First presented as the Santa Fe 400th Anniversary Lecture at St. John's College on March 5, 2010, his essay "Willa Cather's Sheltering Art: Cather's Cathedral and the Adams Factor" demonstrates not only Cather's bracketing of art and religion but also the value of Henry Adams's *Mont Saint Michel and Chartres* for elucidating Cather's "Catholic novels." Both Cather and Adams sought retreat from the disillusionment and materialism of the present in the medieval cult of the Virgin; however, whereas Adams perceives "an empty church" and "a dead faith" in the modern age, the characters in *Death Comes for the Archbishop, Shadows on the Rock,* and her Avignon fragment "exist securely if not always comfortably" within the "sheltering space" of their cathedrals. Although Cather's preceding two novels *My Mortal Enemy* and *The Professor's House* do not fully confirm Adams's view, her "fictionalized Church . . . has, indeed, been vacated" in these novels. "We will never know what or how much Cather believed," Murphy concludes, although she used the Middle Ages as the basis for building a "sheltering art" that is certainly aesthetic and perhaps religious.

NOTES

1. In *Aestheticism*, R. V. Johnson proposes a rather strict definition of Aestheticism that would exclude Ruskin, implying that although he valued "the arts and the experience of beauty," he did not "give them a paramount and exclusive importance among human activities" (1969, 11).

2. Hilary Fraser provides an effective summary of critical interpretations that do and do not place Pater's "religious thought closer to a normative conception of Christianity" (213).

3. Quoted in Gordon Graham, *Philosophy of the Arts: In Introduction to Aesthetics*, 3rd ed. (2005, 222), from Suzanne K. Langer, *Feeling and Form* (1953, 53).

4. Cather's preface to the 1932 English reprinting of *The Song of the Lark* reveals a critical understanding—and even admiration—of Wilde's novel *The Picture of Dorian Gray*. Cather observes that the "chief fault" of *The Song of the Lark* is that it "describes a descending curve. . . . Success is never so interesting as struggle—not even to the successful, not even to the most mercenary forms of ambition." Cather further states that "[t]he life of nearly every artist who succeeds in the true sense (succeeds in delivering himself completely to his art) is more or less like Wilde's story *The Picture of Dorian Gray*. As Thea Kronborg is more and more released into the dramatic and musical possibilities of her profession, as her artistic life grows fuller and richer, it becomes more interesting to her than her own life" (xxxi–xxxii). Cather also shows Bartley Alexander's struggles with his new life to be more interesting to him that his real—and very successful—life.

5. Adorno—like Cather—is concerned with the negative impact of materialism and commercialism on art and aesthetics. He writes, for example, that "For a society in which art no longer has a place and which is pathological in all its reactions to it, art fragments on one hand into a reified, hardened cultural possession and on the other into a source of pleasure that the customer pockets and that for the most part has little to do with the object itself" (15).

WORKS CITED

Abrams, M. H. 1988. *A Glossary of Literary Terms*. 5th ed. New York: Holt, Rinehart and Winston.

Adams, Hazard, ed. 1992. *Critical Theory since Plato*. Rev. ed. Fort Worth: Harcourt, Brace, Jovanovich.

Adorno, Theodor W. 1970/1997. *Aesthetic Theory*, edited by Gretel Adorno and Rok Tiedemann. Translated and edited by Robert Hullot-Kentor. Minneapolis: University of Minnesota Press.

Cather, Willa. 1894/1966. "Commitment." In *The Kingdom of Art: Willa Cather's First Principles and Critical Statements, 1893–1896*, edited by Bernice Slote. Lincoln: University of Nebraska Press, 406–407.

——. 1895a/1966. "Signora Duse is Dying." In *The Kingdom of Art: Willa Cather's First Principles and Critical Statements, 1893–1896*, edited by Bernice Slote. Lincoln: University of Nebraska Press, 119.

——. 1895b/1970. "The Aesthetic Movement: "fatal and dangerous." In *The World and the Parish: Willa Cather's Articles and Reviews 1893–1902*, edited by William M. Curtin. Lincoln: University of Nebraska Press, 153–54.

——. 1896/1966. "A Mighty Craft." In *The Kingdom of Art: Willa Cather's First Principles and Critical Statements, 1893–1896*, edited by Bernice Slote. Lincoln: University of Nebraska Press, 415–17.

——. 1897/1970. "Philistines on the March." In *The World and the Parish: Willa Cather's Articles and Reviews 1893–1902*, edited by William M. Curtin. Lincoln: University of Nebraska Press, 514–517.

——. 1905/1983. *The Troll Garden*. Lincoln: University of Nebraska Press.

——. 1915. *The Song of the Lark*. Boston: Houghton Mifflin.

——. 1923/1997. *A Lost Lady*. Willa Cather Scholarly Edition. Edited by Charles W. Mignon and Frederick M. Link with Kari A. Ronning. Historical essay and explanatory notes by Susan J. Rosowski with Kari A. Ronning. Explanatory notes by Kari A. Ronning. Lincoln: University of Nebraska Press.

——. 1925a/1988. "The Best Stories of Sarah Orne Jewett. In *Willa Cather on Writing : Critical Studies on Writing as an Art*, 47–59. Lincoln: University of Nebraska Press.

——. 1925b/2002. *The Professor's House*, Willa Cather Scholarly Edition. Edited by Frederick M. Link. Historical essay by James Woodress. Explanatory notes by James Woodress with Kari A. Ronning. Lincoln: University of Nebraska Press.

——. 1927/1999. *Death Comes for the Archbishop*. Willa Cather Scholarly Edition. Edited by Charles W. Mignon with Frederick M. Link and Kari A. Ronning. Historical essay and explanatory notes by John J. Murphy. Lincoln: University of Nebraska Press.

——. 1931/2005. *Shadows on the Rock*. Willa Cather Scholarly Edition. Historical essay by John J. Murphy and David Stouck. Explanatory notes by John J. Murphy and David Stouck. Textual editing by Frederick M. Link. Lincoln: University of Nebraska Press.

——. 1932. "Preface." *The Song of the Lark*. Travellers' Library. No. 183. London: J. Cape.

——. 1936a/1988. "Escapism." In *Willa Cather on Writing: Critical Studies on Writing as an Art*, 18–29. Lincoln: University of Nebraska Press.

——. 1936b/1988. "Prefactory Note." In *Not Under Forty*, v. Lincoln: University of Nebraska Press.

——. 1949/1988. "The Novel Démeublé." In *Willa Cather on Writing: Critical Studies on Writing as an Art*, 35–43. Lincoln: University of Nebraska Press.

Crudden, J. A. 1977. *A Dictionary of Literary Terms*. Garden City, NY: Doubleday.

Curtin, William M., ed. 1970. *The World and the Parish: Willa Cather's Articles and Reviews 1893–1902*. Lincoln: University of Nebraska Press.

Fraser, Hilary. 1986. *Beauty and Belief: Aesthetics and Religion in Victorian Literature*. Cambridge: Cambridge University Press.

Freedman, Jonathan. 1990. *Professions of Taste: Henry James, British Aestheticism, and Commodity Culture*. Stanford: Stanford University Press.

Gaunt, William. 1945. *The Aesthetic Adventure*. New York: Harcourt, Brace.

Graham, Gordon. 2005. *Philosophy of the Arts: An Introduction to Aeshetics*. 3rd ed. London: Routledge.

Greenhalgh, Paul. 2000. "The Style and the Age." In *Art Nouveau 1890–1914*, edited by Paul Greenhalgh. London: V&A Publications.

Johnson, R. V. 1969. *Aestheticism: The Critical Idiom*. London: Methuen.

Keats, John. 1819/1962. "Ode on a Grecian Urn." In *Keats: Poems and Selected Letters*, edited by Carlos Baker. New York: Scribner's, 84–85.

Langer, Suzanne K. 1953. Feeling and Form: A Theory of Art. New York: Scribner.

Mendelssohn, Michèle. 2007. *Henry James, Oscar Wilde and Aesthetic Culture*. Edinburgh: Edinburgh University Press.

Naylor, Gillian.1971. *The Arts and Crafts Movement: A Study of Its Sources, Ideals and Influence on Design Theory*. Cambridge, MA: MIT Press.

Pater, Walter. 1873/1986. *The Renaissance: Studies in Art and Poetry*. Edited by Adam Phillips. Oxford: Oxford University Press.

———. 1885/1985. *Marius the Epicurean*. Edited by Michael Levey. New York: Viking Penguin.

Quirk, Tom. 2007. "Explanatory Notes." In *Alexander's Bridge* by Willa Cather. Scholarly Edition. Edited by Frederick M. Link. Lincoln: University of Nebraska Press.

Randall, John H., III. 1960. *The Landscape and the Looking Glass: Willa Cather's Search for Value*. Boston: Houghton Mifflin.

Slote, Bernice. 1966. "First Principles." In *The Kingdom of Art: Willa Cather's First Principles and Critical Statements, 1893–1896*, edited by Bernice Slote. Lincoln: University of Nebraska Press, 1–112.

Slote, Bernice, ed. 1966. *The Kingdom of Art: Willa Cather's First Principles and Critical Statements, 1893–1896*. Lincoln: University of Nebraska Press.

Waddell, Roberta. 1977. "Introduction." In *The Art Nouveau Style in Jewelry, Metalwork, Glass, Ceramics, Textiles, Architecture and Furniture*. New York: Dover.

Watson, Sarah Cheney. 1999. "Servant of Beauty: Willa Cather and the Aesthetic Movement." EdD Diss. Commerce: Texas A&M University.

Woodress, James. 1987. *Willa Cather: A Literary Life*. Lincoln: University of Nebraska Press.

Part I

THE AESTHETIC MOVEMENT

Chapter 1

Exit Smiling

The Case for Paul's Dandyism

Timothy W. Bintrim

Venting the collective frustration of the Pittsburgh high school faculty, Paul's drawing master admits "there was something about the boy which none of them understood" (Cather 1905, 224). Likewise, scholars have long struggled to explain Paul's behavior with theories ranging from Cather's conflicted feelings toward Oscar Wilde (Summers 1990, 103-119) to a diagnosis of narcissistic personality disorder (Saari 1997, 389–95). But one explanation raised by the story itself has not been satisfactorily considered: that Paul is a literary and cultural type—a fin de siècle dandy. Remarkably, the critical record contains no extended study of Paul's dandyism, although other, less likely characters in Cather's fiction have received such analysis. Most recently, Jessica Feldman devotes two chapters of her book, *Gender on the Divide: The Dandy in Modernist Literature*, to three Cather texts: "A Wagner Matinee," *The Professor's House*, and *My Ántonia* (1993). Her omission of Paul is nearly as surprising as her finding that Jim Burden and Ántonia herself (but not Ántonia's betrayer, Larry Donovan) are dandies (171–72). Feldman's analysis, heavily freighted with gender theory, concentrates on Cather's "major" fiction. For a more general background in dandyism, some may prefer Ellen Moers's landmark 1960 cultural history, *The Dandy: Brummell to Beerbohm*, which does not treat Cather directly but does examine some of her favorite dandy artists: Thackeray, Dickens, and Baudelaire. Or one may plunge right into the journalism and short stories of Cather's early career, which offer dandies aplenty, only under a variety of names.

Focusing on "Paul's Case," this essay seeks to contextualize Cather's understanding of the literary, philosophical, and theatrical manifestations of dandies and their first cousins: dudes, mashers, and chappies. Within these pages I will argue that dandyism explains much of Paul's behavior, including his ennui, impertinence, and unnatural smile; his pleasure in dress; his diva worship; even his manner of death.

Feldman observes that Cather's "dandies appear in other guises and under assumed names" (144). Cather does seem to favor the Americanism "dude" over the British-leaning "dandy," but "dandy" appears twice in her 1898 *Home Monthly* story, "The Way of the World," in which it is used synonymously with "dude," which occurs only once, but conspicuously at the story's climax. With their bachelors' paradise dissolving around them, the Speckleville town council ejects Mary Eliza and the offensive New Boy, howling, "We won't have that Chicago dude hanging around here any longer!" (Cather 1898, 395–404). The New Boy, John March and Kari Ronning found, was based upon Cather's childhood acquaintance Sidney Alden, the Red Cloud milliner's son.[1] The real Sidney Alden, a playmate of the Cather siblings, probably had no choice but to dress as a walking advertisement for his mama's store; the New Boy, by contrast, cultivates affectations. He "invariably wore shoes and stockings, a habit disgustingly effeminate to any true and loyal Specklevillian" (402); he laughed at the town currency of pins and insisted upon using real money; he wore a perfumed paper rose, smoked "cubeb cigarettes" rather than the approved corn silk; he even wrote upon monogrammed stationery (401).

Apparently, Cather "absorbed" a loathing for the ways of dudes and dandies, along with other material for her mature writing, even before she was fifteen, when she recorded in a friend's autograph album that the "trait [she most detest[ed]" in men was "dudishness" (Funda and Anderson 2004, 5, 8). Judging from references in her university journalism, she shared the newspaper humorists' opinion, oft recited, that the best antidote for dudishness was a manly thrashing. For example, her Lincoln *Journal* column of December 2, 1894, pronounced, "Athletics are the one resisting force that curbs the growing tendencies toward effeminacy so prevalent in the eastern colleges. Football is the deadliest foe that chappieism has. . . . It renders distasteful the maudlin, trivial dissipations that sap the energies of the youth of the wealthier classes. . . . It doesn't do Chollie or Fweddy any harm to have his collar bone smashed occasionally. He is better off than his soft-handed, soft-headed friend, who, for reasons not very creditable to himself, could not play on the eleven if he wanted to" (Cather 1894c/1966, 213). As a young journalist, she knew these stereotypes well enough to give the men-about-town "Chollie and Fweddy" the usual effeminate British accents. On the other hand, Cather also appreciated dandyism as a strategy of resistance to convention, or a "revolt against the homilies by which the world is run" (Cather 1905, 260). Having shorn her hair and donned a sharp suit and bowler hat during her "prep" days at the university, she knew the power of transgressive dress. Much later, of course, her attitudes toward dandies changed again as she came to know Stephen Tennant, described by his friends as a fastidious dresser and a great sissy.[2] We wouldn't expect Cather in her maturity to punch him in the shoulder and bellow, "Man-up, Stephen!"

Because a comprehensive definition of dandyism is elusive, an anatomy or historical typography may be more useful. The *Oxford English Diction-ary* (1993 edition) denotes the dandy as "One who studies ostentatiously to dress fashionably and elegantly; a fop, an exquisite"; but the same dictionary's definition of "dude," the American term favored by Cather, seems more apropos to Paul: "A name given in ridicule to a man affecting an exaggerated fastidiousness in dress, speech, and deportment, and very particular about what is aesthetically 'good form'; hence, extended to an exquisite, a dandy, 'a swell.'"

The period terms "chappie" and "exquisite," seldom heard today, also crop up within Cather's early fiction and journalism. For example, in a February 10, 1901, *Journal* column, she reported her surprise that natural-ist Ernest Thompson Seton (known at the time as Ernest Seton-Thomp-son), whom she met at a dinner party, "was something of an exquisite in regard to his clothes" (1901/1970, 822), utterly unlike her mental image of the grubby, distracted woodsmen Audubon and Burroughs.

Although the word "dandy" appears only once in "Paul's Case," it is placed strategically within her first description of Paul, separating his current reality from his first crude attempts to make himself over as the boy "he had always wanted to be": "Paul entered the faculty room suave and smiling. His clothes were a trifle outgrown and the tan velvet on the collar of his open overcoat was frayed and worn; but for all that there was *something of the dandy about him*, and he wore an opal pin in his neatly knotted black four-in-hand, and a red carnation in his button hole" (emphasis added) (1905, 243). While outwardly conforming to his father's ideals of thrift and modesty (wearing last year's street clothes topped by a distressed overcoat), Paul flaunts convention and academic censure by adorning himself with jaunty neckwear (his four-in-hand an update of the Regency dandy's cravat), a fancy opal pin, and, cheekiest of all, a "scandalous" red carnation. Inserted between his Cordelia Street togs and his aristocratic accessories, the provocative blossom and the mutable opal pin foretell his metamorphosis into a butterfly. After his theft, flight, and transformation, Paul quickly acquires the insignia of the dandy—buying at Tiffany's an expensive silver-mounted scarf pin, probably encrusted with diamonds—and replaces the carnation in his buttonhole with hothouse flowers ordered from the Waldorf's room service (254, 256). Although their costume was highly variable, most dandies favored showy jewelry, as often as not fake (*New York Times* 1889). Cather noted one such bogus accoutrement in her September 23, 1894, *Nebraska State Journal* caricature of a Lincoln "Bowery dude":

> He comes down to breakfast about 10 o'clock, attired in patent leather house slippers, checked trousers, a shirt with flowers embroidered on the front, a light blue tie, a watchchain disappearing in each of his trousers pockets, a light felt dressing gown hanging open, and a tall silk hat thrust on the back of his head. In this strange garb he comes down the street to the restaurant. He hangs up his hat and cane, settles the cluster of diamonds in his scarf and yawns wearily as he throws himself into a chair and taps for the waiter. He asks for the bill of fare and the wine list and sits stroking his smoothly shaven chin as he reads it over with an air of general ennui. At last he lays down the list and whipping out a white silk handkerchief scented with Eau de Espagne he orders a cup of coffee and five cents' worth of toast. (Cather 1894a, 13)

This "Bowery dude" shares with Paul certain typecast characteristics—indolence, perfumed hands, ennui, and a showy scarf pin. But the skimpy breakfast ordered by the Lincoln dude betrays that he, like Paul, is a two-bit pretender: his fashion is foppish, his leisure is laziness, his jewelry is disingenuous. Yet, a decade later, after Paul steals the means, he cuts no such ridiculous figure: "he wore his spoils with dignity and in no way made himself conspicuous" (1905, 257).

In Cather's day, as in our own, dandyism stood for a bewildering array of signifiers in dress, mannerisms, and enthusiasms. An 1898 *Atlantic Monthly* essay, "The Evolution of the Gentleman," gives a sense of the spectrum of display: "In each generation there have been men of fashion who have mistaken themselves for gentlemen. . . . Each generation imagines that it has discovered a new variety, and invents a name for it. The dude, the swell, the dandy, the fop, the spark, the macaroni, the blade, the popinjay, the coxcomb—these are butterflies of different summers" (Crothers 1898, 715).

Then, as now, dandies ranged from effeminate sissies (fops, coxcombs, macaronis, exquisites) to menacing metrosexuals (sparks, blades, ladykillers, and mashers). Although dandyism most often connotes ineffectualness and idleness, a few literary dandies, like the Baroness Orczy's Sir Percy Blakeney (hero of *The Scarlet Pimpernel*) and Ian Fleming's Agent 007 are men of deadly and decisive action.

Dandyism came to be identified with literary Aestheticism in France during the 1850s when novelist Theophile Gautier and the much younger poet and essayist Charles Baudelaire rallied their fellow Bohemians against France's philistine middle class under the banner "*L'Art pour l'Art*." As William Gaunt explains in his classic study, *The Aesthetic Adventure*, the movement took its particular course in France because that country's aristocratic and educated classes had been twice decimated by the Reign of Terror and the Napoleonic Wars, leaving the Third Estate commanded by a practical, unimaginative bourgeoisie who had little use for art or artists (1945, 3–4). During the 1890s, Cather found in Pittsburgh a similar social order: a few Bohemians besieged by the greater powers of "Presbyteria," whose foot soldiers Cather imagined as the burghers of Cordelia Street. Deprived of noble patronage, French artists in the 1850s had little status and few legal sources of income. According to Gaunt, "the Bohemian [necessarily became] a sort of anarchist" to survive (9). Identifying the smug bourgeois as the enemy, the Bohemians "lived careless of law and landlords, and began to adopt a defensive attitude of gay mockery" (9). To the aesthetes, Art became a religion and they its priests and protectors; they imagined themselves as a new kind of aristocracy of natural gentlemen. Paul re-enacts the evolution of French dandyism at the Waldorf as he suppresses his ties to Cordelia Street in order to fabricate his own personal history as an aristocrat: "Cordelia Street— Ah! that belonged to another time and country; had he not always been thus, had he not sat here night after night, from as far back as he could remember . . .? He rather thought he had" (1905, 257). Before creating Paul, Cather encountered the prototype of the dandy in the lives and writings of Gautier, Baudelaire, and Verlaine (Summers 1990, 80). She made Gautier a favorite of Harold Buchanan and Count de Koch in her early story "The Count of Crow's Nest" (1896, 449–72), but more significant is Eden Bower's affectionate memory for Gautier's scandalous 1835 novel *Mademoiselle de Maupin*, which "centers upon the amorous adventures of the bisexual heroine after which the work is titled" (Madigan 2009, 390). As if the Mademoiselle were not decadent enough, the novel's male hero, according to William Gaunt, "praised the vicious Caesars and irresponsible pleasure seekers of the ancient world. All ecstasies and all excesses were justified in the search for sensation and the delight in beauty which, the author implied, was a law unto itself" (1945, 8). Although Paul was no reader, he shared Gautier's basic world view that luxury "was what all the world was fighting for" (Cather 1905, 256). George Seibel recalled that he and his wife had read Baudelaire in the French with Cather, but he does not specify which works they read—probably not *Les Fleurs du Mal*, more likely Baudelaire's appreciation of Poe (Seibel 1949, 195–207). Possibly they also discovered within *The Painter of Modern Life* (1863)— Baudelaire's book-length study of his acquaintance, Constantin Guys—a brief but luminous chapter titled "The Dandy" (Moers 1960, 276–81). With its few pages, Baudelaire effectively redefined dandyism as a strategy of

modernist rebellion: "[Dandies] have no other status but that of cultivating the idea of beauty in their own persons, of satisfying their passions,
of feeling and thinking. . . . Contrary to what a lot of thoughtless people
seem to believe, dandyism is not even an excessive delight in clothes and
material elegance. . . . These things are no more than the symbol of the
aristocratic superiority of his mind. Thus, in [the dandy's] eyes, . . . perfection in dress consists in *absolute simplicity*, which is, indeed, the best way
of being distinguished" (Baudelaire 1883). Looking about for a paragon
of elegant simplicity, Baudelaire settled upon the singularly ineffective
British sire of dandyism, Beau Brummell (1778–1840), a onetime parlor
soldier and favorite of the Prince Regent. Though considered by some a
wit, Brummell's only real genius was as an arbiter of fashion. Within this
limited sphere, Brummell's smug individuality had a profound effect on
Western history. In an age defined by foppish excess, Brummell led the
British away from wigs and face powder and instituted hygienic reforms
such as a daily regimen of bathing, brushing the teeth, and shaving. Uni-
versally admired for his taste, Brummell convinced gentlemen to give up
knee-breeches for pantaloons, leading the way to modern trousers. But
his crowning achievement in sartorial reform was his championing of
simple, well cut, and immaculately brushed dark jackets, worn over white
shirts with cravats of subdued colors (Moers 1960, 276–81). With minor
variations, Brummell's model of the power suit would dominate male
formal-wear for the next two centuries (Kelly 2006, 1–2). In the 1870s,
when the French aesthetes adopted Brummell as an honorary father figure, Baudelaire himself favored a black coat, brown trousers, and black
tie. Spending much of his inheritance dressing and acting the dandy, the
poet preferred his garb to look slightly worn, in the manner of Paul's
street dress (Moers 1960, 272).

However, at the beginning of Cather's story, Paul takes his holidays
in a much dressier coat. One of the perks he enjoys at Carnegie Hall is
his usher's uniform, which he does not resent as a badge of servility, but
thinks "very becoming" and "one of the few that at all approached fitting"
(Cather 1905, 245)—body and soul. We are told that Paul is touchy about
his narrow chest, but a trim figure was always valued by the dandy, an
ideal reflected in Brummell's famous putdown of his former benefactor,
the Prince Regent. According to legend, Brummell accomplished the snub
by asking the Prince's current favorite, "Who's your fat friend?" (Moers
1960, 28). Dressed in this "tight, straight coat" that evokes the tailored
coats introduced by Brummell and anticipates the frock coat that will be
one of his own first purchases in New York, Paul can imagine that he is
the host, not a lackey, of the performance. Although the color of Paul's
jacket is not specified, it is worth noting that even after his theft, when he
has the means to spend extravagantly, Paul cultivates an elegant simplic-

ity. Like Brummell, whose toilet is said to have averaged three hours, Paul spends two hours "buying [dress clothes] with endless reconsidering and great care"; he makes additional stops "at a hatter's and a shoe house," at Tiffany's, "where he selected his silver and a new scarf-pin," and finally at a trunk shop (Cather 1905, 254). The two boy-thieves who provided Cather with the outline of her plot practiced no such restraint: they spent money like millionaires, booking rooms in a luxury hotel and buying flashy new clothes, watches, and diamond rings (Bintrim and Madigan 2007, 112). Their "hilarious conduct" was immediately noticed by the Chicago police, leading to their arrest and extradition to Pittsburgh. In marked contrast to the behavior of his prototypes, Paul derives "quiet pleasure" from his clothes. With the possible exceptions of his silk underwear and red robe (to be enjoyed in private), his purchases are sober and subdued. The "forced aggressiveness" that once made him conspicuous is abandoned when the cut of his coat marks him as a member of the aristocracy: "Nobody questioned the purple; he had only to wear it passively" (Cather 1905, 257). Paul is perfectly content to be idle, and Baudelaire insisted that idleness was the dandy's occupation (Baudelaire 1883).

Before he dons the cloak of invisibility at the Waldorf-Astoria, Paul displays the combination of disdain and ennui that is the dandy's characteristic pose. Toward the paragon of Cordelia Street or the Cumberland minister, Paul is alternately hostile or aloof. Baudelaire wrote, "all [dandies] share the same characteristic of opposition and revolt . . . to combat and destroy triviality. That is the source, in your dandy, of that haughty, patrician attitude, aggressive even in its coldness" (1883). Away from home, Paul's haughtiness is directed at his teachers, "prosy men who never wore frock coats, or violets in their buttonholes; the women with their dull gowns, shrill voices, and pitiful seriousness" (Cather 1905, 252), whose very existence, to Paul, defined triviality. His teachers, for their part, rankled under "the contempt which they all knew he felt for them, and which he seemingly made no effort to conceal" (243). Habitually Paul made a display of his ennui, adjusting his performance to the perceived weakness of the teacher: "In one class he habitually sat with his hand shading his eyes; in another he always looked out of the window during the recitation; in another he made a running commentary on the lecture, with humorous intention" (244). Like all dandies, Paul must be seen to be effective.

Acting just within bounds of accepted conduct, Paul adopts an exaggerated dance of dress and manners that his teachers, occupied by the practical difficulties of math and Latin, find annoying and unsettling. In the earliest and most familiar example, his teachers agree that the elaborate bow with which he leaves the suspension hearing is "but a repetition of the scandalous red carnation" (244), but they cannot fault his etiquette.

Staying within the lines of propriety, his ridiculous bow and flippant carnation are neither "polite [nor] impolite" (244) but are, as his teachers accurately perceive, ambivalent signifiers capering on the edge of open mockery.

But the most suggestive evidence that Cather knew Baudelaire's essay "The Dandy" is Paul's strange habit of smiling at the least opportune moments. Baudelaire defined dandyism as "the pleasure of causing surprise in others, and the proud satisfaction of never showing any [surprise] oneself. A dandy may be blasé, he may even suffer pain, but in the latter case *he will keep smiling*, like the Spartan under the bite of the fox" (1883, emphasis added). "The pleasure of causing surprise in others" motivates Paul's disruptions of his classes; he fabricates lies "to be noticed and admired, to assert his difference from the other Cordelia Street boys" (Cather 1905, 258); and he wishes, after his suspension hearing, that some of his teachers might be watching to "writhe under his lightheartedness" (245). Paul's fixed grin during his hearing at the Pittsburgh High School and at other moments of duress (even in the prelude to his suicide) seems to allude to the legend of the Spartan boy who smilingly protested his innocence even as the fox he had stolen and hidden under his cloak chewed open the boy's belly, bringing a swift but painful death. Cather knew this passage about Lycurgus in Plutarch's *Lives*, later applying it to Scott McGregor in *The Professor's House* (March 1993, 587). In its original context, the story of "the Spartan boy's fox" valorizes stoic self-denial and grim resolve. Metonymically, Paul's tortured smile connects him with Spartan youth who were trained as liars and thieves (skills useful to warriors) literally under the lash of the whip. During their training, Spartan boys were kept on short rations, then given a chance to steal food—if they dared face a phalanx of older boys bearing whips—an image reminiscent of Paul's "baptism of fire" as he defies the verbal lashing from his teachers, like "a miserable street cat set at bay by a ring of tormenters" (Cather 1905, 244).

As a dresser to Charley Edwards at the local stock company theater and an usher at Pittsburgh's Carnegie Hall, Paul would have had abundant opportunity to study the types of dandies endemic to the theater districts. Especially reviled by the press were the "mashers," young, working class dandies who harassed unescorted women with sexual remarks or unwelcome advances. Mashers caused such alarm and outrage during the early years of the last century that undercover police and vigilante societies were deployed against them in a "war against woman annoyers" stretching from Berlin to St. Louis to Minneapolis (*New York Times* 1883, 1903, 1908). The accepted punishment for a masher caught in the act of insulting a woman was horse-whipping, although some offenders were brought to trial (sometimes collared by the very women they assaulted) and sentenced to break stones in the workhouse (*New York Times* 1883, 1904, 1921). Paul's "impertinent remark" to his female English teacher that so offends the high school principal may place Paul in the cadre of mashers (Cather 1905, 244). Similarly, the "evil gesture" Paul makes at the Venus de Milo as he passes the cast room in the Carnegie Institute would be out of character for an aesthete but is perfectly in character for a masher (or any dandy for that matter) because dandies considered their own beauty superior to any external ideal. As he raises a finger to Aphrodite and grimaces at Caesar, Paul is making his way to the ushers' dressing room, where donning his uniform promises transformation and escape. Anticipating this pleasure, he fancies he has become the equal of a goddess or an emperor.

If some of Paul's behavior is misogynistic (as is the essay by Baudelaire), at other times Paul engages in diva worship, which some take as evidence of Paul's homosexuality (Summers 1990, 103–119). But Paul's adoration of the German soprano after her performance at Carnegie Hall also smacks of chappieism, another variety of dandyism described in Cather's journalism (Cather 1894b/1966, 134). "Chappie" was a long-lived but seldom defined slang term used on both sides of the Atlantic from the 1870s to the 1910s. An American slang dictionary published in 1890 defines "chappie" as "the latest variety of man about town; a term of intimacy" (Farmer 1890/1965). Eric Partridge notes that "as a Society term, ["chappie"] flourished in the [18]80s" (Partridge and Beale 1984). From sporadic references in the stage press and the historic *New York Times*, I gather that chappies were young, moneyed dandies who, like the working-class mashers, were special nuisances to stage actresses and divas. Still higher in status were "Stage Door Johnnies," older, moneyed men who traded upon their fortunes or titles to press matrimony on popular actresses such as the "Gaiety Girls" of London's Gaiety Theatre. Theatrical papers of the 1890s complained that the substandard acting and writing of burlesques catered to the limited intellects of chappies, Johnnies, and mashers ("Review of *Ariel*" 1883/2004, 271–72). Cather refers explicitly to chappies twice in *Nebraska State Journal* columns a week apart. The first, contrasting American and German tastes in operatic divas, seems to anticipate Paul's worship of the mature German soprano. Cather observes that German audiences will ignore a prima donna's age if she has voice. "But the Americans, like the French, prefer action to music"; that is, they require singers to be comely. In light opera, particularly, American audiences require a prima donna to be conventionally beautiful, "or like Marie Tempest she must . . . have such an elusive and fascinating sort of homeliness that she can make the public believe it is beauty. This is not a repetition of the adoration of the chappies; it is an indisputable fact, and perhaps it is not a fact to be proud of. No woman who did not possess unusual physical charms has ever succeeded in [American] light opera" (Cather 1894b/1966, 134). Curiously, although

Paul has only the tin ear of a chappie, he is not moved to the usual "adoration" of a singer's face or figure but instead shares the discrimination of German audiences (personified in the Pittsburgh symphony conductor) who see beyond surfaces. As Peter Sullivan has noted, Cather credited the Germans with much of the musical culture in Pittsburgh (1996, 26–30). During the years she was reviewing plays in Pittsburgh and became the backstage and dressing room acolyte of stock company favorite Lizzie Hudson Collier (Cather 1900/1970, 766), Cather would have had many additional opportunities to observe (and scorn) the chappies.

Finally, and perhaps most important, Paul's dandified tastes determine the course of his death. As I have discussed elsewhere, real railroad suicides are messy affairs, scarcely less gruesome than shooting oneself in the head (Bintrim and Madigan 2007, 120). Yet, improbably, Cather makes Paul's swan dive a work of art. As Paul's body is deflected by the locomotive's forward inertia, his corpse gains composure as it gains velocity: "his body was being thrown swiftly through the air, on and on, immeasurably far and fast, while his limbs were gently relaxed" (1905/1970, 261). Rather than passing under steel wheels or sticking to the boiler as we might expect, Paul's body drops intact "back into the immense design of things" (261). His death is exactly what a dandy, concerned with shocking others while remaining unruffled himself, would wish. Cather takes care to specify that at his last moment, Paul's "lips [are] drawn away from [his teeth] in a frightened smile" (260). Even in his last act, Paul awaits his cue, then makes his exit smiling.

NOTES

Acknowledgment: I am grateful to the School of Arts and Letters of Saint Francis University, whose Faculty Research Grant aided this study. I thank Andrew Jewell, Kari Ronning, and the other editors of the Cather Electronic Journalism Project at *The Willa Cather Archive* for making formerly obscure texts not only accessible but searchable.

1. John March (1993) and Kari A. Ronning, e-mail message to author, December 5, 2008. Ronning found that the *Red Cloud Republican* reported Mrs. G. S. Alden opening a millinery store on the Moon Block in 1889. In September of that year, Mrs. Alden advertised in the *Republican* that she had "spent a few weeks in the great western metropolis, Chicago, for the express purpose of studying the latest and most approved styles" and promised, "my patrons can depend on getting the best at the lowest price for stylish goods. A good assortment of Fancy Goods, Laces, Pocket Handkerchiefs and Drapes" (September 13, 1889).

2. Film director John Waters notes that Tennant's "eccentric vocation [was] doing nothing in life—but doing it with great originality and flamboyance" (1991).

WORKS CITED

Baudelaire, Charles. 1883. "The Dandy." In *The Painter of Modern Life*. Translated by P. E. Charvet. *Dandyism.net*. Edited by Christian Chensvold. n.d. http://www.dandyism.net/?page_id=178.

Bintrim, Timothy W., and Mark J. Madigan. 2007. "From Larceny to Suicide: The Denny Case and 'Paul's Case.'" In *Violence, The Arts, and Willa Cather*, edited by Joseph R. Urgo and Merrill Maguire Skaggs. Madison: Fairleigh Dickinson University Press, 109–123.

Cather, Willa. 1894a. "Utterly Irrelevant [On the Lincoln Bowery Dude]." *Nebraska State Journal* 13 (September 23). *The Willa Cather Archive*. University of Nebraska. http://cather.unl.edu/j00066.html.

———. 1894b/1966. "Kinds of Opera," November 25. In *The Kingdom of Art: Willa Cather's First Principles and Critical Statements 1893–1896*, edited by Bernice Slote. Lincoln: University of Nebraska Press, 134.

———. 1894c/1966. "[Apropos of football]," December 2. In *The Kingdom of Art: Willa Cather's First Principles and Critical Statements 1893–1896*, edited by Bernice Slote. Lincoln: University of Nebraska Press, 212–13.

———. 1896/1970. "The Count of Crow's Nest." In *Collected Short Fiction 1892–1912*, rev. ed., edited by Virginia Faulkner. Lincoln: University of Nebraska Press, 449–71.

———. 1898/1970. "The Way of the World." In *Collected Short Fiction 1892–1912*, rev. ed., edited by Virginia Faulkner. Lincoln: University of Nebraska Press, 395–404.

———. 1900/1970. "One of Our Conquerers," June 2. In *The World and the Parish: Willa Cather's Articles and Reviews, 1893–1902*, edited by William M. Curtin. Lincoln: University of Nebraska Press, 764–69.

———. 1901/1970. "Ernest Seton-Thompson," February 10. In *The World and the Parish: Willa Cather's Articles and Reviews, 1893–1902*, edited by William M. Curtin. Lincoln: University of Nebraska Press, 822–24.

———. 1905/1970. "Paul's Case." In *Collected Short Fiction 1892–1912*, rev. ed., edited by Virginia Faulkner. Lincoln: University of Nebraska Press, 243–61.

———. 1920/2009. *Youth and the Bright Medusa*. Willa Cather Scholarly Edition Series. Historical essay and explanatory notes by Mark J. Madigan; textual essay and editing by Frederick M. Link, Charles W. Mignon, Judith Boss, and Kari A. Ronning. Lincoln: University of Nebraska Press.

Crothers, S. M. 1898. "The Evolution of the Gentleman." *The Atlantic Monthly* 81, Issue 487 (May 1898): 709–717. The Making of America Collection, Cornell University, http://ebooks.library.cornell.edu/m/moa/.

Farmer, John S., ed. 1890/1965. *Slang and Its Analogues, Past and Present*. New York: Krause.

Feldman, Jessica R. 1993. *Gender on the Divide: The Dandy in Modernist Literature*. Ithaca, NY: Cornell University Press.

Funda, Evelyn I., and Susan Andersen. 2004. "Predicting Willa Cather," *Teaching Cather* 4 (Spring): 4–12.

Gaunt, William. 1945. *The Aesthetic Adventure*. New York: Harcourt.

Kelly, Ian. 2006. *Beau Brummell: The Ultimate Man of Style*. New York: Free Press, 1–2.

Madigan, Mark J..2009. Historical essay and explanatory notes. In *Youth and the Bright Medusa*, by Willa Cather. Lincoln: University of Nebraska Press, 390.

March, John. 1993. *A Reader's Companion to the Fiction of Willa Cather*. Edited by Marilyn Arnold with Debra Lynn Thornton. Westport: Greenwood.

Moers, Ellen. 1960. *The Dandy: Brummell to Beerbohm*. London: Secker and Warburg.

New York Times. 1883. "A Whip for Scoundrels' Backs: The St. Louis Fire Marshall Thrashes a 'Masher' And Is Rewarded." January 17. http://query.nytimes .com/mem/archive-free/pdf?res=F00A12FB395F15738DDDAE0994D9405B83 84F0D3.

New York Times. 1889. "British Sham Jewelry: American and Other Buyers in London—Rich Customers." December 8. http://query.nytimes.com/mem/ archive-free/pdf?res=F0061FF7355C10738DDDA10894DA415B8984F0D3.

New York Times. 1903. "To Protect Berlin Women: Police President Directed to Organize a Special 'Mashers' Squad." September 6. http://query.nytimes.com/mem/ archive-free/pdf?res=F20711FB355414728DDDAF0894D1405B838CF1D3.

New York Times. 1904. "Woman Lashes a 'Masher.'" January 25. http://query .nytimes.com/mem/archive-free/pdf?res=F60F11FC395C12738DDDAC0A94 D9405B848CF1D3.

New York Times. 1908. "Rock Pile for Mashers: Minneapolis Is Aroused Over the Prevalence of Its Women Annoyers." August 11. http://query.nytimes .com/mem/archive-free/pdf?res=FB0A11F6385512738DDDA80994D0405B88 8CF1D3.

New York Times. 1921. "Woman Has Scalps of Nine Mashers." August 14. http:// query.nytimes.com/mem/archive-free/pdf?res=F60F10FD3F5D14738DDDAD 0994D0405B818EF1D3.

Oxford English Dictionary, 1993 edition, s.v. "dandy" and "dude."

Partridge, Eric, and Paul Beale, eds. 1984. *A Dictionary of Slang and Unconventional English*, 8th ed. New York: MacMillan.

Review of *Ariel*. 1883. [Burlesque performed at the Gaiety Theatre, London, October 8, 1883.] *The Theatre*, November 1, 271–72. *Footlight Notes* no. 347, edited by John Culme. http://footlightnotes.tripod.com/20040515home.html.

Saari, Rob. 1997. "'Paul's Case': A Narcissistic Personality Disorder." *Studies in Short Fiction* 34 (Summer): 389–95.

Seibel, George. 1949. "Miss Willa Cather from Nebraska." *New Colophon* (September): 195–207.

Sullivan, Peter M. 1996. "Willa Cather's Pittsburgh German Friends and Literary Connections." *The Nassau Review* 7 (2): 19–33.

Summers, Claude J. 1990. "A Losing Game in the End: Aestheticism and Homosexuality in Cather's 'Paul's Case.'" *Modern Fiction Studies* 36: 103–119.

Waters, John. 1991. "The Man Who Stayed in Bed." Review of *Serious Pleasures: The Life of Stephen Tennant*," by Philip Hoare. *The New York Times*, February 3. http://www.nytimes.com/1991/02/03/books/the-man-who-stayed-in-bed .html?pagewanted=all&src=pm

Chapter 2

Innocence and Experience, Good and Evil, and Doppelgangers

Decadent Aesthetics in Cather's "Consequences," James's "The Jolly Corner," and Wilde's *The Picture of Dorian Gray*

Sonja Froiland Lynch and Robert Lee Lynch

Willa Cather's admiration for and indebtedness to Henry James, especially in terms of her early writing, are well documented. By contrast, her public sentiments about Oscar Wilde are not nearly as flattering. In an 1895 article for the *Nebraska State Journal* about Wilde, she describes aestheticism as "the most fatal and dangerous school of art that has ever voiced itself in the English tongue" (Cather 1894/1970, 153). Yet, Cather's short story "Consequences," which first appeared in the November 1915[1] issue of *McClure's* (Meyering 1994, 46), has been linked to both James's short story "The Jolly Corner" (1908) and Wilde's novel *The Picture of Dorian Gray* (1891). Marilyn Arnold, echoing Bernice Slote, points out that "'Consequences' is undeniably similar to James's 'The Jolly Corner,'" but points out some notable differences (1984, 100). Sheryl Meyering notes that "Cather has reverted here to her old habit of imitating Henry James" (1994, 46). And Arnold and James Woodress identify similarities between "Consequences" and *The Picture of Dorian Gray* (Arnold 1984, 100; Woodress 1987, 275). Woodress further explains that Wilde's novel was a piece "Cather knew and thought well of" (275), and biographer Hermione Lee notes that despite Cather's disapproval of Wilde's behavior, "she was enthusiastic for 1890s decadence" (Lee 1989, 11). In their explorations of innocence and experience, good and evil, and the divided self, "Consequences," "The Jolly Corner," and *The Picture of Dorian Gray* examine the notion of decadence and its negative implications for a worthwhile life.

All three stories focus on the contrast between youth and age, innocence and experience. In Cather's "Consequences," this contrast is shown in the three-tiered character of Kier Cavenaugh. Youth is embodied in his twin brother, Brian, who died when they were sixteen. An enlarged photo of him high jumping hangs on Cavenaugh's wall; in its perpetual motion, the face is somewhat blurred, which might indicate a blurring of these two characters. Capturing the boy's athleticism, the "Kodak" underscores the vibrancy and promise of youth, and, like Dorian Gray's youthful visage, the photo never ages.

Cavenaugh's present self is a playboy whose family came into petroleum money shortly before his father died, and who came "to New York to burn some of the oil" (Cather 1915/1973, 71). At the time of the story, he is thirty-two and still going strong. The narrative hints at his decadent life: "His motor hit the Park every morning as if it were the first time ever. He took people out to supper every night. He went from restaurant to restaurant, sometimes to half-a-dozen in an evening. The head waiters were his hosts and their cordiality made him happy. They made a life-line for him up Broadway and down Fifth Avenue" (71).

Age is reflected in the old man who "haunts" Cavenaugh, "a most unattractive old gentleman," who wears "shabby evening clothes and a top hat, and . . . white gloves" (78). While he most frequently appears when Cavenaugh is alone or in a crowd on the street, he is more corporeal than a ghost: the narrator Eastman sees him; he even picks up one of his gloves from the floor of Cavenaugh's apartment after the old man has exited out the window. This character clearly is the image of Cavenaugh in his old age, an embodiment of his conscience. The young man comments that the elder knows "everything I've ever done or thought" and is frustrated that "when he recalls them, he throws a bad light on them, somehow" (81). The old man possesses a key to Cavenaugh's apartment, and he knows the names and intimate details of Cavenaugh's friends, even so far as to reveal what happens to them in the future.

In addition to the contrasts among the three personae of Cavenaugh, the contrast between innocence and experience is also explored in the interplay between Cavenaugh and Eastman, the lawyer who narrates Cather's tale. Eastman is forty, a few years older than Cavenaugh. He likes the younger man, in part because he is still so vibrant, and his fast-paced lifestyle, filled with people all around New York, has not yet taken a toll on his appearance. However, Eastman does not desire to lead such a life himself. In fact, the contrast between these two is somewhat ironic. While Eastman has been a New York lawyer for twelve years and is aware of many disagreeable or sordid events, even some that involved friends and acquaintances, his own behavior suggests that he has done more observing of life than involving himself in it. He routinely forgoes going out in the evening in order to accomplish more work at his desk. Thus, while he presents himself as the more knowledgeable of the two men, and he readily gives Cavenaugh advice about how he should live, it appears that the younger man has more experience in the "muck" of life, as it were, than the older one does, thus blurring the distinction between innocence and experience. What is not blurred, however, is that Eastman's behavior is upright while Cavenaugh's is decadent.

In a somewhat different manner, James's "The Jolly Corner" examines the contrast between innocence and experience in the character of Spencer Brydon. Initially, the subject is broached when Brydon explains his past decadence to Alice Staverton: "I believe I'm thought in a hundred quarters to have been barely decent. I've followed strange paths and worshiped strange gods; it must have come to you again and again—in fact you've admitted to me as much—that I was leading, at any time these thirty years, a selfish frivolous scandalous life" (James, 350). Brydon is no longer the innocent young man he was when he left New York for Europe. However, the tale pursues this notion even more fully in the character of his alter ego, the figure of himself as he might have been had he stayed in America and not gone to live abroad. Having discovered late in life that he has an aptitude for business and construction, he can envision a life that would have made him wealthy beyond his dreams had he stayed in America and discovered his talents early. In fact, he romanticizes his alter ego because he thinks he would be an attractive, accomplished figure, someone Brydon would like to have been.

However, the spectral vision of the alternate Brydon reveals what his imagination has not taken into account: that even though the end result may be wealth, the road to that wealth may be quite difficult indeed. In Brydon's final vision, when he sees the visage of his alter ego, he realizes that the alternate path was significantly harder than the one he ultimately chose. His alter ego sports a hand missing two fingers, and his face is "the face of a stranger . . . evil, odious, blatant, vulgar." He senses "the roused passion of a life larger than his own." This is not an attractive image; Brydon does not want to own this version of his life. What he perceives his alter ego to have experienced is undesirable. The narrative elucidates: "He had been 'sold,' he inwardly moaned, stalking such game as this: the presence before him was a presence, the horror within him a horror, but the waste of his nights had been only grotesque and the success of his adventure an irony. Such an identity fitted his at *no* point, made its alternative monstrous" (365).

Thus, while Brydon initially romanticizes what his alter ego would be like, he comes to abhor him, a feeling that Cavenaugh maintains toward his "haunt" from the beginning. Cavenaugh has no inclination to romanticize about his future self because the figure is odious to him from their initial meeting. Nothing about the man is attractive. Moreover, the comments that the old man makes encouraging Cavenaugh to be cautious about the future are also disagreeable to the young man. He doesn't want to change his ways; he is still youthful enough to dismiss being implicated in the downfall of others.

Wilde's *The Picture of Dorian Gray* also examines the line between innocence and experience in its titular character, who, at the outset of the novel, is notably young and innocent. When Lord Henry Wotton first meets Dorian Gray, the older man notes, "There was something in his face that made one trust him at once. All the candor of youth was there, as well as all youth's passionate purity. One felt that he had kept himself unspotted from the world" (Wilde 1891, 17). Basil Hallward is concerned about the effect that Wotton will have on Dorian Gray and implores him not to "spoil" the young man, but Dorian Gray's progress from innocence into decadence is the focal point of the novel, and the portrait that reveals in physical terms the changes wrought in Gray's soul underscores his decline and the severity of his experiences.

Unlike Cavenaugh and Brydon, Dorian Gray revels for a time in the contrast between his youthful visage and the ever-changing portrait. In one significant scene, he notes the differences between the painting and his face in the mirror, ignoring the moral implications of the changes he sees: "He grew more and more enamored of his own beauty, more and more interested in the corruption of his own soul. He would examine with minute care, and sometimes with a monstrous and terrible delight, the hideous lines that seared the wrinkling forehead or crawled around the heavy, sensual mouth, wondering sometimes which were the more horrible, the signs of sin or the signs of age" (106). Like Cavenaugh's immature response to his "haunt," Dorian Gray shrugs off the warnings and refuses to take any blame for the consequences of his actions. He repeatedly places the blame on others for their downfall, denying his own involvement in their circumstances. We see this early on, in one of his early responses to Sybil Vane's suicide: "She had no right to kill herself," he says. "It was selfish of her" (84). And later, when he is much more mired in debauchery and Basil Hallward confronts him about his actions, he similarly deflects the accusations, saying, "In this country it is enough for a man to have distinction and brains for every common tongue to wag against him" (127). This, too, is an immature response. Because Dorian Gray has found a way to conceal the evidence of his increasingly immoral and decadent experiences from his face, he doesn't have to "grow up" and take responsibility for his actions.

The relationship between each protagonist and his alter ego in these three stories is marked, initially, at least, by a secretive nature, which reflects the presence of good and evil in each tale. Cavenaugh has been "haunted" by the old gentleman for quite some time before he reveals his presence to Eastman, and when the lawyer nearly encounters him for the first time in Cavenaugh's apartment, he is immediately on guard about the nature of the visitor. The narrative reveals that Eastman "had got a whiff of something unwholesome about the fellow—bad nerves, bad company, something on hand that he was ashamed of" (Cather 1915/1973, 72). For Eastman, this is very off-putting, and he limits his dealings with Cavenaugh as a result.

As the story develops, however, we discover that the old gentleman is not as evil as Eastman first supposed he might be. In fact, as Cavenaugh reveals more about his alter ego to Eastman, he implicates himself and his actions more than he implicates the older man. The old man's comments to Cavenaugh imply his involvement in unpleasant experiences or unfortunate circumstances for his friends. In an indictment of decadence, he cautions the young man to save some money for the future, and he upbraids him about his all-consuming lifestyle, saying, "Ah, you young fellows are greedy. You drink it all up. You drink it all up, all up—up!" (79). When the old man tells Cavenaugh about Kate, a young woman who will become a dope addict, Cavenaugh dismisses this as "nonsense, of course" (79), refusing to see the possibility of his involvement in her downfall.

While Cavenaugh is open with Eastman about his encounters with his "haunt," he clearly understands that some might question the validity of such an experience. As they discuss the nature of suicide, Cavenaugh opines that sometimes people might have secrets that would help explain to others their suicidal behavior. To this, Eastman replies, "There is no such thing as a secret. To make any move at all one has to employ human agencies, employ at least one human agent. Even when the pirates killed the men who buried their gold for them, the bones told the story." Such a comment calms Cavenaugh, who says, "I like that idea. It's reassuring. If we can have no secrets, it means that we can't, after all, go so far afield as we might" (79).

Cavenaugh's comment implies that he might be contemplating actions that would go "far afield," a notion that Cather likely keeps deliberately obscure. He seems to seek reassurance that he would be kept morally clean, knowing that he wouldn't be able to keep his questionable actions—whatever they may be—secret long. Eastman thinks that personal integrity is a necessary and ongoing human project, but here, again, Cavenaugh searches for another source to blame. Rather than acknowledge the need for personal ethical vigilance, he states, "people can be chilled by a draft from outside, somewhere" (78). Blaming immoralities on a secret ghost is apparently easier than bearing the difficulties of living an upright life.

Secrets enhance Dorian Gray's descent into hedonism; his actions become easier when he discovers that he can keep them covert by secluding his portrait from others' eyes. In living purely for sensations, and being spared the physical repercussions of his actions, evil simply becomes another avenue to be explored: "a mode through which he could realize his conception of the beautiful" (Wilde, 123). However, in a conversation with Basil Hallward, in which the painter confronts Dorian with questions about his actions and encourages him to maintain his integrity and thus his good name, the painter makes a comment about secrets that parallels the above conversation between Eastman and Cavenaugh. Hallward says, "Sin is a thing that writes itself across a man's face. It cannot be concealed. People talk sometimes of secret vices. There are no such things. If a wretched man has a vice, it shows itself in the lines of his mouth, the droop of his eyelids, the molding of his hands even" (Wilde, 126). Dorian Gray capitalizes on this notion. He relishes the secret life he lives, comforted that his visage will not reveal his sins while his portrait, locked away, reveals them all.

Yet, as he descends further into decadence and immorality, Gray discovers that his actions do, in fact, have repercussions. Stalked by James Vane, who seeks revenge for the suicide of his sister, and fearful of being discovered as the killer of Basil Hallward, Dorian panics. His imagination terrifies him: "What sort of life would his be if, day and night, shadows of his crime were to peer at him from silent corners, to mock him from secret places, to whisper in his ear as he sat at the feast, to wake him with icy fingers as he lay asleep! As the thought crept through his brain, he grew pale with terror, and the air seemed to him to have become suddenly colder. . . . He saw it all again. Each hideous detail came back to him with added horror" (166). He tells Lord Henry, "I want to escape, to go away, to forget" (169). Gaining a momentary reprieve upon discovering James Vane dead, Dorian briefly appears to repent and change his ways. He breaks up with a young country girl he has been seeing rather than run away with her, leaving her "as flower-like as [he] had found her" (173). He even reflects negatively on his decadent life: "He knew that he had tarnished himself, filled his mind with corruption, and given horror to his fancy; that he had been an evil influence to others, and had experienced a terrible joy in being so; and that of the lives that had crossed his own it had been the fairest and the most full of promise that he had brought to shame" (181).

However, despite acknowledging his descent into evil and professing a desire to become good again, his impulses are more ruled by self-preservation than driven by morality. He can't bring himself to confess to the murder of the painter, and in examining the effect of his "good" actions on his portrait's visage, he realizes that he has been driven by vanity and hypocrisy: "There had been nothing more. Through vanity he had spared her. In hypocrisy he had worn the mask of goodness. For curiosity's sake he had tried the denial of self" (183). Eventually, however, the psychological repercussions of evil cannot be denied, and Dorian Gray comes to loathe the painting for its reminders of his transgressions, as Cavenaugh comes to loathe visits of the old man and his continual insinuations of the young man's blame.

Similarly, James's "The Jolly Corner" also entertains the notion of "good" and "evil," cloaking evil in secrecy at first, as well. Mrs. Muldoon, the woman Spencer Brydon has employed to clean his house on the "jolly corner," does not wish to come into the house after dark; she fears what she *might* see, "craping up to thim top storeys in the ayvil hours" (James, 346). Brydon, at this point, doesn't comment on Mrs. Muldoon's notion. The narrative notes, "The question of the 'evil' hours in his old home had already become too grave for him. He had begun some time since to 'crape'" (346).

Brydon is morbidly obsessed with how he might have turned out had he not gone to Europe as he did but had instead stayed in America. His alter ego's presence is cloaked in language that reflects dark, sinister implications. Alice Staverton suggests it would be "quite huge and monstrous," and Brydon responds, "Monstrous above all! . . . quite hideous and offensive" (349). His active searching for a visual representation of this image occurs after dark, in secret, when he can be alone, wandering through his house. When he does encounter his vision after a night of intense pursuit, it is indeed monstrous: "the bared identity was too hideous as *his* . . . evil, odious, blatant, vulgar" (364–65). In this description, Spencer Brydon's alter ego is clearly evil; pitted against his present form, it serves to put the protagonist's life in a better light, so that he can more fully appreciate what he has, instead of pining for a life he might have lived had he chosen differently as a youth.

All three of these stories also explore the notion of the divided self. This is not unusual for Cather; she often employs divided characters. Kier Cavenaugh is physically divided into three parts: his past, represented by his deceased 16-year-old twin, captured in a photograph hanging on his wall; his present, the 32-year-old playboy; and his future, the unattractive older gentleman who haunts him as his conscience. James's Spencer Brydon is divided into his present form and the vision of what he might have been, his life's "alternate ending," as it were. And Wilde's Dorian Gray is divided between his outward appearance and his inner soul, made visually apparent through the painting. Because of the nature of these doppelgangers—which are so intimately connected to the souls of these men, their secret actions and desires—the decadent nature of their lives is heightened.

Cavenaugh's old gentleman haunts him in darkness for the most part. When Eastman catches glimpses of him, he is shrouded in shadow, and it is only Cavenaugh who sees his face clearly. That he acts as the young man's conscience is clear. He knows everything about his actions and thoughts, "but when he recalls them, he throws a bad light on them, somehow. Things that weren't much off color look rotten. He doesn't leave one shred of self-respect, he really doesn't," notes Cavenaugh (Cather 1915/1973, 81–82). Thus, though he puts a positive light on his activities when he talks of them to Eastman, the presence of this older gentleman and his constant pestering of the young man raises questions about the nature of his actions. His desire to live in the present, enjoying the pleasures of the moment without consideration of their consequences, in combination with the old man's presence, establishes the decadent slant of this story and further justifies its juxtaposition with "The Jolly Corner" and *The Picture of Dorian Gray*.

"The Jolly Corner," while very much in keeping with James's proclivity for psychological realism, employs many details that play with the notion of decadence, seen in the other tales. While the decadent nature of Brydon's life in Europe has been noted above, his hunt for his alter ego also bears elements of decadence, as he enjoys it for the sensations he gets from it, even though they may be intense and frightful: "It had been the theory of many superficially-judging persons, he knew, that he was wasting that life in a surrender to sensations, but he had tasted of no pleasure so fine as his actual tension, had been introduced to no sport that demanded at once the patience and the nerve of this stalking of a creature more subtle, yet at bay perhaps more formidable, than any beast of the forest" (364). Decadence is underscored here in the degree to which these sensations are deemed pleasurable and the way Brydon characterizes his actions as desirable, in contrast with how others would view them. That he enjoys the tension he puts himself through presents the vice in the form of a virtue, a notably decadent reversal.[2]

At the height of the hunt, when he senses a "turn" on the part of his alter ego, it is noteworthy that Brydon experiences a "duplication of consciousness" (356). Thus, in the midst of the decadent, we are reminded that what he battles is a doppelganger, his double. His is a worthy opponent for the very reason that it is a form of himself. And this is a key to the death of the alter ego, as well. At bottom, only one version of Brydon's life can survive. He may wonder about how his life would have been lived and what kind of man he would have become had he made different choices when he was young, and he may be able to, albeit briefly, sustain a vision of such a man, but such a vision cannot hold forever. Only one outcome can live. Thus, when he collapses and is revived by Alice Staverton, he is even more alive in the present; he is no longer divided.

By facing his alter -ego, Brydon perceives that his life—indeed, his very being—would be quite different if he had stayed in America, and he doesn't like what he perceives he would have been: "a black stranger" (368). He comes to the conclusion that what he has is better than what he would have had, even if it had been billions of dollars, and he no longer needs to obsess over the path his life has taken. His vision of his other self is enough to show him the toll such a success story would have taken on him. In the end, "The Jolly Corner" is a redemptive piece. Spencer Brydon, staring into his alter ego's visage and realizing his revulsion, collapses—only to be revived by Alice, with her uplifting love, support, and belief in him. The description is of death and resurrection: "He made it out as she held him. 'Yes—I can only have died. You brought me literally to life'" (366). Brydon is "resurrected" by Alice, in an ironic play on Sleeping Beauty's kiss. The resultant realization that his present is the best option and that her love will sustain him gives him the courage to live, and perhaps improve, his life.

The close connection between the protagonists and their doubles in "Consequences" and *The Picture of Dorian Gray* also plays significantly into the protagonists' deaths. In both stories, the men are pushed so far that they seek to eliminate the being that stands for their pestering conscience. In Cavenaugh's situation, it is the old gentleman; in Dorian Gray's, it is his portrait. On the surface, Cather's ending seems diametrically opposed to James's, but it, too, depending on how one reads the details, may be redemptive. At one point, Cavenaugh exclaims, "Why can't they let me alone, damn it! I'd never hurt anybody, except, perhaps—" (Cather 1915/1973, 82), and Eastman finishes his sentence with, "Except your old gentleman, eh?" The old gentleman forces Cavenaugh to understand that he *is* in fact hurting others—if not directly, then indirectly. His actions and his failure to act are implicated in the old gentleman's comments. Although we aren't shown their interaction on Cavenaugh's final night, one can assume that it was similar to previous visits, and it may have played out in one of two ways. One possibility is that the old man made Cavenaugh so distraught, convincing him of his role in the downfall of his friends—Eastman wonders at the end, "had the old man been more convincing than usual?" (84)—that he takes his own life, which ironically redeems him, removing him from the destructive cycle claimed by the alter ego. A second, more likely, possibility is that in his distress with the older gentleman, Cavenaugh fulfills Eastman's foreshadowing comment and shoots the old man. However, by doing so, he eliminates his own future and thus takes his own life. Cavenaugh's comment that "people never really change" (82) holds true. He acts without considering the consequences his actions may bring, thereby killing himself.

In similar fashion, Dorian Gray's eventual hatred for the portrait and its reminder of his atrocious deeds drives him to see it as the "one bit of evidence against him" (Wilde 1891/2007, 183). Rather than confess his actions, he decides to destroy it in order to rid himself of the burden of conscience and his fear that others might discover it: "It had kept him awake at night. When he had been away, he had been filled with terror lest other eyes should look upon it. It had brought melancholy across his passions. Its mere memory had marred many moments of joy. It had been like conscience to him. Yes, it had been conscience. He would destroy it" (183). As he picks up the knife with which he killed Basil Hallward, he thinks, "As it had killed the painter, so it would kill the painter's work, and all that that meant. It would kill the past, and when that was dead he would be free. It would kill this monstrous soul-life, and without its hideous warnings he would be at peace" (183). Dorian's desire to destroy the painting is a desire to destroy his past and its attendant memories, but what he fails to take into account is that he cannot live without a past, just as a man cannot survive without his soul. So by destroying his double, he destroys himself, and ironically sets all to right again, the painting returning to its original form and his physical body taking on the aspects of his age and degradation, a final indictment of decadence.

All three of these pieces acknowledge the temptations of decadence, but they also recognize that the rewards of a decadent life are fleeting and illusory. By contrasting innocence and experience, good and evil, and the internal conflicts within one's self, the stories suggest that if one fails to confront or acknowledge one's transgressions, if one merely wishes to dismiss or forget them rather than effect a positive change in one's life, the consequences can be dire, indeed. While readers of Cather's "Consequences" find it reminiscent of James and Wilde,[3] what this piece ultimately reveals about Cather is her creative, lively mind. She teases a tale from the tradition of the ghost story and explores the negative ramifications of decadence in telling the bewildering and cautionary story of a playboy's life and death. Woodress notes that "under her calm, well-organized exterior there were doubts and uncertainties" (Woodress 1987, 275), acknowledging Cather's own divided self. Although she is most remembered for her fictions that celebrate the lives of hard-working, determined people who possess a pioneering spirit and an eye for the timelessness of art and culture, she didn't shy away from telling disturbing tales of violence, murder, and distress in the course of her longer works. The character of Wick Cutter, the legend of the death of the wedding party, and Mr. Shimerda's suicide in *My Ántonia*, alone, along with the purposeful poisoning of the town water supply through the suicide of the tramp in *The Song of the Lark*, remind us that she knew that humanity's ugly, cruel face can and does insert itself alongside and within the tales that inspire and affirm mankind's potential for good and the life-giving power of art.

NOTES

1. Interestingly, Cather composed "Consequences" shortly after formally resigning from *McClure's* magazine, and it is the penultimate story she wrote for that publication (Meyering 1994, 45). Taken in that context, one might also see in her tale recognition of the difficulties inherent in making significant changes as one matures and the unquestionable need to do so if one wishes to thrive.

2. Matei Călinescu discusses this idea more fully in his chapter on "Decadence" in *Five Faces of Modernity: Modernism, Avant-Garde, Decadence, Kitsch, Post-Modernism*. See especially the summary of Nietzsche's understanding of decadence in the nineteenth century on page 180.

3. Others have also noted similarities between Cather's "Consequences" and Poe's "William Wilson" (Arnold 1984, 100; Woodress 1987, 275; Meyering 1994, 45). We are indebted to editors Ann Moseley and Sarah Watson for suggesting parallels with Robert Louis Stevenson's *Dr. Jekyll and Mr. Hyde*, and Hans Christian Andersen's story "The Shadow," as well. Each of these pieces also features a double character split along lines of good and evil, and ends in the death of one of the "halves."

WORKS CITED

Arnold, Marilyn. 1984. *Willa Cather's Short Fiction*. Athens, OH: Ohio University Press.

Cather, Willa. 1894/1970. "The Aesthetic Movement: 'fatal and dangerous.'" In *The World and the Parish, Vol. 1: Willa Cather's Articles and Reviews, 1893–1902*. Edited by William M. Curtin, 153–54. Lincoln: University of Nebraska Press.

———. 1915/1973. "Consequences." In *Uncle Valentine and Other Stories: Willa Cather's Uncollected Short Fiction, 1915–1929*. Edited by Bernice Slote, 65–84. Lincoln: University of Nebraska Press.

Călinescu, Matei. 2003. *Five Faces of Modernity: Modernism, Avant-Garde, Decadence, Kitsch, Post-Modernism*. Durham, NC: Duke University Press.

James, Henry. 1908/2003. "The Jolly Corner." In *Tales of Henry James*. 2nd ed. Edited by Christof Webelin and Henry B. Wonham, 341–69. New York: Norton.

Lee, Hermione. 1989. *Willa Cather: Double Lives*. New York: Vintage.

Meyering, Sheryl L. 1994. *A Reader's Guide to the Short Stories of Willa Cather*, 45–48. New York: G. K. Hall.

Wilde, Oscar. 1891/2007. *The Picture of Dorian Gray*. Norton Critical Edition, 2nd ed. Edited by Michael Patrick Gillespie. New York: Norton.

Woodress, James. 1987. *Willa Cather: A Literary Life*. Lincoln: University of Nebraska Press.

Chapter 3

Willa Cather's Time Machine

Alexander's Bridge, H. G. Wells, and Aesthetic Temporality

Peter Betjemann

Bartley Alexander, the wealthy engineer who is the protagonist of Cather's first novel, dies in a river of struggling bodies. The laborers building his "Moorlock" bridge grasp at Bartley as the bridge collapses: "A gang of French Canadians fell almost on top of him. He thought he had cleared them, but they began coming up all around him, clutching at him and at each other. . . . Alexander tried to beat them off, but there were too many of them. One caught him about the neck, another gripped him about the middle, and they went down together" (Cather 1912/1977, 126). What happens at Moorlock, in *Alexander's Bridge* (1912), mirrors what happens in the nocturnal world of the Morlocks, in H. G. Wells's *The Time Machine* (1895). The Morlocks, a future race of laborers who live underground and operate machinery that supports an overcivilized aboveground race called the Eloi, attack the time traveler: "The Morlocks had their hands upon me. Flinging off their clutching fingers . . . I was caught by the neck, by the hair, by the arms, and pulled down. It was indescribably horrible in the darkness to feel all these soft creatures heaped upon me. I felt as if I were in a monstrous spider's web. I was overpowered, and went down" (Wells 1895/1987, 79).

The vertical hierarchies of both passages are clear. Both time travelers—Wells's protagonist, launching himself into the future, and Bartley, turning back time to conduct an adulterous affair with a lover from his youth—enjoy material comfort and creative freedom. Both are pulled downwards by the workers who haunt the novels. The Morlocks periodically emerge

41

from a subterranean world "full of the throb and hum of machinery" (Wells 1895/1987, 65); the laboring class in *Alexander's Bridge* also appears "like . . . some vast underground machinery" (Cather 1912/1977, 94) and sporadically becomes visible through Cather's references to the "strikes and delays" that hold up progress on Bartley's bridges (37).

Wells's description of, and appellation for, a largely invisible laboring underclass would have been known to Cather. *The Time Machine* was widely read, and Wells's weekly column for Samuel McClure, Cather's employer before the publication of *Alexander's Bridge* turned her energies to novel writing, had been one of the mainstays of McClure's early ventures in syndication. Cather met Wells on a trip to London for *McClure's* magazine in 1909, around the time Wells publically broke with the Fabian Socialists over what he described in an open letter as their "sterile and uninspiring" refusal to engage in political agitation (Wells 1909). The importance of the Wellsian source for what one character in *Alexander's Bridge* acknowledges as the "queer name" of the Moorlock Bridge thus lies most simply in its reminder that we cannot wholly accept Cather's assertions, in her own 1936 public letter "Escapism," that politics and "industrial conditions" are not the concern of fiction (1949/1953, 43). But the haunting of Cather's novel by a Morlockian underclass, I will posit, also shapes her inquiry into the traditions of fin-de-siècle Aestheticism: this essay argues in particular that *Alexander's Bridge* draws on *The Time Machine* to raise aesthetically coded questions about the relationship of insouciance (Bartley's and the Eloi's, to take the obvious but not the only cases) to the purposeful application made visible, for Wells and Cather alike, by manual labor. To put the same theme the other way around, the working class in these texts exemplifies persistent or goal-directed activity and therefore focuses the engagement of both novels with the interplay, central to Aestheticism and signified as such in the two texts, of idleness and intention, the pleasures of chance and the clarity of ends. Work itself, I should say, is barely depicted as such in these novels. But its subliminal presence is exactly my point. The Morlockian realm epitomizes the stakes of the shared novelistic project—assessing the relationship of art, purpose, and progress—that is the subject of this essay.

The aesthetic textures of *The Time Machine* are well established, particularly in the stereotyped decadence of the Eloi. Androgynous and childlike, possessing "bright red, rather thin lips" and a "Dresden-china type of prettiness" (Wells 1895/1987, 45), the fragile Eloi have "decayed to a mere beautiful futility" (68). Noting the "purposeless energy" of beings who use their pockets only to carry flowers (51), the time traveler (named only as such) offers an etiology of Aestheticism early in the novel: "this has ever been the fate of energy in security," he explains; "it takes to art and to eroticism, and then come languor and decay" (52). What interests me in this much-quoted passage is that the time traveler is wrong, not about what he sees but about its source. For the Eloi do not possess security, as the time traveler will discover when he descends into the labyrinthine world of the Morlocks. There, he sees not just the machinery that seems to maintain the Eloi "in their habitual needs" (68) but also the evidence that the Morlocks, on the dark nights of the new moon, prey on the Eloi for their own nourishment.

The time traveler's initial misreading reveals an attitude that the novel continually emphasizes: the projection of the beautiful as, we might say, sui generis, predicated on "security" and insulation from the competitive forces of history. The dynamics of this projection indeed frame the entire story of the future. Prior to launching himself into the eight-hundredth millennium and beyond, the time traveler displays his invention to a group of dinner guests that includes a doctor, a psychologist, and the narrator. Bernard Bergonzi has pointed out that this opening recalls the framing of some of Kipling's stories, presenting the "most ordinary and pedestrian" atmosphere of conversation among "club-men" (Bergonzi 1961, 43). But Wells's version of that scene also accrues a substantial charge of aesthetic energy as the time traveler explains the "recondite matter" of his research. Settled in chairs that "embraced and caressed us rather than submitted to be sat upon," the guests "lazily admired . . . [the] fecundity" of the time traveler's exposition of his "new paradox"; the "luxurious after-dinner atmosphere" sets a Wildean spectacle "when thought runs gracefully free of the trammels of precision" and the "lights in the lilies of silver caught the bubbles that flashed and passed in our glasses" (31). The ambiance created by this first paragraph of *The Time Machine* matters most particularly at the other end of the novel, when the time traveler returns with his story of civilization's ultimate reversion to a reptilian order—and with the wry acknowledgement that his auditors, again assembled for dinner, are likely to take his story as "a mere stroke of art" (87). To take the story as art (as they do, with the exception of the narrator), and to allow that the time traveler "was one of those men who are too clever to be believed" (a description clearly invoking Wilde), situates the narrative's meaning in the fantastical Aesthetic realm of the novel's opening rather than in the admonitory historical vision of a polarized class system (37). By fictionalizing the time traveler's report as "art"—that is, his auditors mirror both the Eloi, who suppress all sense of futurity by living blithely and spontaneously between new moons, and the time traveler himself prior to his discovery of the Morlocks—the time traveler's erroneous reading of art *as* security is recapitulated by the diners who, taking the story as a "'gaudy lie'" (89), place the narrative within the fortified aesthetic atmosphere they inhabit.

The novel, then, does not only satirize the outward codes of fin-de-siècle style, as represented by the Eloi and the atmosphere of the dinner table. More pointedly—and, I think, more importantly for Cather—*The Time Machine* interrogates the apparent insularity of art, dramatizing through time travel the cultural, historical, and sociopolitical sequences that lie outside the moment-oriented aestheticism of both the 1890s and the 800700s. The time traveler's major realization, while in the future, indeed ties his emerging, time-oriented diachronic vision of western civilization's progress to the productive and teleological processes of manual labor by which culture is sustained; gazing on the fine dress of the Eloi, their "pleasant fabrics" and "complex specimens of metal-work," he recognizes that "somehow such things must be made." Having theorized an "automatic civilization" and a "decadent humanity" whose beauty perpetuates itself—a hyperbolic instance of *l'art pour l'art*—the time traveler now realizes "how things were kept going" (57). In this phrase as in the novel more broadly, historical consciousness develops as the recollection of labor's instrumentality in the progression of culture from the late nineteenth century to the dismantled condition of the future.

The novel's dramatization of various false *projections* of a correlation between art and security strikes the keynote of what the Morlocks signify: the impossibility of an autonomous aesthetic realm. Their horrifying attacks on the Eloi and on the time traveler serve as grotesque reminders that cultures sustain themselves diachronically, dependent on the industry and productivity of the laboring classes; Aestheticism's indulgence in the present moment looks like a dangerous game where Morlocks lurk. *The Time Machine* as a whole, one might say, makes the case for an awareness of time itself. Depicting the violent uprising of a race of workers whose activities drive time, rather than suspend it, the tale resists the aestheticized realm of after-dinner languor and contradicts the time traveler's initial presumption that he has arrived in an art-centered world in which no one has to work purposefully. Cather, I have already suggested, clearly invokes *The Time Machine* by naming Alexander's bridge after the Morlocks (a neologism of Wells's) and by featuring the Moorlock span as the place where laborers overwhelm Bartley Alexander, himself a rebel against time. But if the end of Cather's novel makes the Wellsian connection most explicit, the relations of purpose, presentism, and Aestheticism in fact drive the novel from the very first paragraphs. Those paragraphs focus on the point of view of Bartley's former professor Lucius Wilson.

Wilson is usually described as a refugee from the Jamesian novel, a detached observer in the tradition of Winterbourne in *Daisy Miller* or Ralph Touchett in *The Portrait of a Lady*. But Lucius Wilson also has qualities of the aesthete that are presented very much in terms of his relation to time. The novel opens with Wilson standing "at the head of Chestnut Street," reliving his days as a student in Boston and "looking about him with the pleased air of a man of taste" (Cather 1912/1977, 1). Moving into Brimmer Street, he "fixed his sharp eye upon the house which he reasoned should be his objective point" (2–3). Wilson's vision, in these excerpts, defines his appreciation either of the Boston of his youth or his movement toward Bartley's house, where he is arriving after a long rail trip. But the long perspective of both of these instances—looking down a street toward his own past or toward the end of his current travels—fails in the second paragraph, "when he noticed a woman approaching rapidly from the opposite direction." Not yet knowing Bartley's wife, Winifred, Wilson "slackened his pace," developing a "blurred impression" of the woman's dress and bending his "appreciative glance" as she vanishes into the realm of the "costly privileges and fine spaces" that must define her existence (3). Cather goes on to describe the reorientation of Wilson's vision, from the long perspective that "should" define his "objective point" to the circumstantial impressions and inferences of the moment, in terms that echo the famous conclusion of Walter Pater's *The Renaissance* (1873). The "quickened, multiplied consciousness" of aesthetic experience for Pater operates speculatively, oriented as it is to circumstantial impressions created by the brief "concurrence . . . of forces parting sooner or later on their ways" (Pater 1873/1986, 150). The famous final line of Pater's text, praising beauty that offers "the highest quality to your moments as they pass . . . simply for those moments' sake" (153), describes a mode of appreciation predicated on perceptions in "perpetual flight" (151). Cather's language mirrors Pater's as she generalizes what Wilson's glimpse of Winifred signifies: his ability "to enjoy lovely things as they passed him on the wing as completely and as deliberately as if they had been dug-up marvels, long anticipated, and definitely fixed at the end of a railway journey" (Cather 1912/1977, 3).

That Wilson is precisely situated at the end of a railway journey, and that the first instances of his gaze *do* involve a prospect "long anticipated," dramatize the two kinds of appreciation introduced through the "man of taste." The anticipated and the circumstantial appear from the outset of *Alexander's Bridge* as modes of visual appreciation that operate in two different temporal frames. Shortly after the encounter described above, Wilson enters the home, meets Winifred, and again casts his eye towards the horizon of the past; "what you want," he says in response to her queries about Bartley's youth, "is a picture of him, standing back there at the other end of twenty years. You want to look down through my memory" (8). To "look down through" recapitulates the long perspective of Chestnut or Brimmer Streets, but what makes the episode significant is that Cather again shatters the diachronic view. Bartley's immediate entrance, looking not like the university student of twenty years prior but as a successful "tamer of rivers ought to look," prompts Winifred's explication of the precise experience that she herself, outside the house, had occasioned for Wilson: "Away with perspective! No past, no future for Bartley; just the fiery moment. The only moment that ever was or will be in the world!" (8)

In the context of the opening chapter's ruminations on aesthetic perspective, the "fiery moment" of Bartley's existence recalls Wilson's experience on the street and the notoriously "flame-like" nature of Pater's presentism—a "flickering" of momentary impressions (Pater 1873/ 1986,150). But all of these outlets for the instantaneity of impression and the security of the aesthetic against time, including Pater's, are also juxtaposed with their obverse: the longer time frame that makes the present significant in the first place. Cather's novel opens with a Manichean struggle between two temporal perspectives, alternately focusing on the experience of an instant and the distant horizons of the past or the future. This struggle characterizes Aestheticism, for its advocates were hardly blind to the temporal consequences of indulging in the subjective experiences of the moment. Pater's flame may be "eager," but it is also "devouring"; under the action of aesthetic impressionability, experience inevitably "dwindles down" and proves "limited by time" (150–51). As Carolyn Williams has demonstrated, the notorious "ecstasy" Pater associates with experience as it "melts under our feet" (152) paradoxically serves Pater's historicism by reactivating the past, directing the viewer's attention back to the original source of the impression (Williams 2001, 77–99 passim). Marion Thain describes the "temporal paradox" of the Aesthetic movement, its desire to "still the moment in its perfection" and the necessary predication of that very desire on an acute awareness of the "flux and variety" of history (Thain 2007, 16, 41). This tension is most famously exemplified by Oscar Wilde's *The Picture of Dorian Gray*, in which the obverse of Dorian's eternal youth is the registration of time by the painting in the attic.

The inexorably aging image of Dorian has something of the force of the Morlocks in *The Time Machine*; Wilde and Wells both offer terrifying reminders of the historical forces lying in wait behind the face of aesthetic insouciance. Diachronicity is marked for Wilde by aging and for Wells by the purposeful activities of the repressed working class. Cather's novel is also structured by constant undercurrents that disrupt aesthetic experiences of the moment. *Alexander's Bridge*, I will suggest in the remainder of this essay, depends throughout its pages on the double view of time characteristic of aestheticism and ultimately, as the novel moves to its tragic denouement, echoes *The Time Machine* by associating history's forward movement with the activities of Morlockian (or rather, Moorlockian) laborers.

The most obvious example of the split temporal frame of the novel is of course Bartley's affair with Hilda Burgoyne, for that affair is more properly "with someone vastly dearer to [Bartley] than she had ever been—his own young self" (Cather 1912/1977, 40). If in London it "seemed as if all the clocks in the world had stopped" (58), in North America the clock in Bartley's library "tick[s] through the minutes" of his maturity (63). The interest of this fissure in time is that the double self living like Dorian Gray—in one reality that shields him from time and another that keeps it—is explicitly anticipated as an *aesthetic* problem, a matter of taste and appreciation, by the Paterian doubleness of Wilson's visual perspective in the opening chapter.

The dialectical tension of sequential time and the "fiery moment" subsequently develops across the novel through other aesthetic conventions. Arriving in London on the visit that will rekindle his romance with Hilda, Bartley is immediately snapped up for the evening by Maurice Mainhall, a stereotype of Wildean mannerisms who assails Bartley with literary gossip, aphorizes his "preconceived ideas about everything," and wears the "rapt expression of a very emotional man listening to music" when he himself "was talking well" (21).[1] But from the point of view of the novel's relation to aesthetic temporality, the fact that Mainhall has published a "study of 'The Poetry of Ernest Dowson'" matters more than his behavioral typecasting (21). For no aesthetic poet was more associated than Dowson with the dialectical weaving of the ecstasy of youth and the inexorability of time. As Murray G. H. Pittock observes, Dowson's early essay "The Cult of the Child" anticipates his "lifelong pursuit of little girls" as poetic subjects whose beauty Dowson, a consumptive who died at thirty-three, opposes to the proximity of death he feels in adult sexual consummation; mature love, in Dowson's belief, seems to intimate joys that grow "less and less," revealing "the burden of the days that are to be" (Dowson 1922, 9; Pittock 1993, 137). Describing Hilda's theatrical triumphs to Bartley, Mainhall echoes Dowson's fetish of youth while mirroring Bartley's addiction to his own past through the girlish figure of "little Hilda" (Cather 1912/1977, 30): "there's everything," Mainhall says, "in seeing Hilda while she's fresh in a part. She's apt to grow a bit stale after a time. The ones who have any imagination do" (22).

As the novel develops, we learn that Bartley also acknowledges the specter of decay clinging to and, according to Mainhall, defining Hilda's youth, imagination, and intoxicating freshness. Bartley's memory of their visits to the mummy room at the British Museum involves the erotic frisson of experiencing "dead things . . . to make one's hour of youth more precious"; Bartley feels the "flaming liquor" of today by way of a contrast with the "awful brevity" suggested by the British Museum as a "repository of mortality" (33). That Bartley's perception of Hilda should be anticipated by Mainhall's assessment of her artistic career suggests the undercurrent of Aesthetic philosophy in *Alexander's Bridge*—an undercurrent defined less by the fetish of youth per se than by the artistically, visually, and erotically charged relations of the diachronic and the synchronic, the long "perspective" and the "fiery moment."

The novel presents other, simpler associations between London and aestheticism. Hilda's dress and home, for instance, are insistently characterized by the color associated with illicit desire in the "yellow 90s." If Gaston Deschamps, writing in the *New York Times* about his 1901 tour of the United States, found yellow "barred from the parlor table" as "décadente" for its associations with yellow-wrapped French novels and *The Yellow Book* (23), the surfaces of Hilda's rooms support yellow irises and "yellow Rhone wine," the "yellow light" of her candles setting off her yellow gown and canary-yellow slippers (Cather 1912/1977, 49–54). But these codes are not incidental markers of Bartley's London indulgences. Rather, they appear in the context of the novel's ruminations on the aesthetic relations of time and taste, time and desire. Signifying escape or indulgence as functions of the inexorabilities of history, aestheticism thus informs the central portrayal in *Alexander's Bridge* of a man who feels at once the "energy of youth" (115) and the simultaneous, correlative sense of himself "fading and dying" as he becomes a "mechanism useful to society" (39).

It is in this context that the novel's reminders of who builds Bartley's bridges become legible. Bartley's aesthetically coded dalliance with Hilda is also aesthetically coded by the threat of change that stalks it—a threat Bartley experiences, like Dowson, as his fading *into* time and that he compares to becoming like a machine. The laborers haunting the novel, referenced in a sentence here and there, represent what Bartley fears, for they are never anything *but* faded as a result of the anonymity of their historical roles; and they appear as symbols of a mechanized, industrial economy. Working people in London come "hungrily," Morlock-like, into the dusk; the crowd of indistinct people they form pulsates with the "deep vibration" of the "vast underground machinery" that clearly suggests *The Time Machine* (Cather 1912/1977, 93–94). When Bartley goes to New York near the end of the novel, the *Times* publishes a note saying that the engineer "was in town" (an announcement that, bringing Hilda to his rooms, causes him to miss the telegram detailing the dangerous strain on the Moorlock span) *and* that a steel strike is blocking progress on a bridge he has designed in New Jersey (104). Such subtle intimations of "general industrial unrest" in *Alexander's Bridge* (37) are scaled quite differently than the novel's familiar themes. The text has been discussed as a study of a heroic type (the virile engineer), an anticipation of Cather's later and better novels (rehearsing the process of returning to one's youth that would produce *O Pioneers!*), and a story about a psychological schism.[2] The collapse of the Moorlock bridge has appeared particularly relevant to this latter theme as an allegory for the "spiritual state of the person it represents" (Tichi 1987, 173). To Tichi, "[Bartley] drowns in the clutches of panicked workmen, but we are meant to understand that the collapse of the bridge symbolizes the destruction of a man unable to reconcile two antagonistic parts of his psyche" (177).

Tichi is right, in my opinion, precisely because she emphasizes the fading of the workers into the background of what "we are meant" to understand as the novel's major theme. But *Alexander's Bridge* is also a text whose shadowy margins, its "unlovely" working-class people (Cather 1912/1977, 119), connect to its center; the novel's meditations on time, taste, progress, and—cohering all these—aestheticism build to the dramatic collapse of the Moorlock Bridge, when Bartley is dragged down by the unlovely, machine-like avatars of the novel's undercurrent of diachronicity. For Wells, that Morlockian undercurrent satirizes the foolishness of parceling off, as art for art's sake, the "security" of the aesthetic. For Cather, the Moorlockian undercurrent is more complicatedly engaged with the temporal dualities of aestheticism itself, as described by Pater, Wilde, and Dowson and as represented by both Bartley and Lucius Wilson.

But for both authors, labor (and, more particularly, the sense of historical embedding it suggests) operates as aestheticism's specter: the working class, alternately appearing and disappearing from view, haunts the attempt to live in the moment. Cather may have been drawn to this theme—and to *The Time Machine*—by the political questions about the visibility, and the rights, of the working classes that characterized the Progressive era. Consider a story Cather composed while revising *Alexander's Bridge* in the fall of 1911 (Woodress 1987, 216). In "Behind the Singer Tower," she rewrote the tragedy of the Triangle Factory Fire of 1911, in which 146 textile workers perished. However, Cather changed the facts, describing instead a conflagration that kills the wealthiest citizens at the top of an upscale hotel. On the one hand, as Robert K. Miller has pointed out, Cather's reimagining of the Triangle Fire collapses the security of the distinction between upper- and lower-class space; the penthouse suite proves as vulnerable as the sweatshop (2000, 75–89 passim). On the other hand, however, resituating the Triangle Fire in the Mont Blanc hotel affords Cather the ability to present industrial labor *as* an echo, an image intimated by the generic similarity between the two blazes. The story as a whole locates manual labor at the mere threshold of recognizability. The setting—the night after the Mont Blanc fire, as six professional men reflect on the tragedy from a boat in New York harbor—occasions the main character's reminiscences of his own labors as a young engineer on the hotel's foundation. Tragedy, we learn, haunts that space: Hallet describes the death of an Italian worker that the chief engineer covered up. Recalling his descent into the subterranean "hole" on which the Mont Blanc would be built, Hallet describes "crumpled, broken little men" working in extreme heat with "terrifying, complicated machinery" (Cather 1912/1970, 48–49). The workers, "bending over [and] huddled together" (51) like "swarms of eager, panting animals" (48), call to mind nothing so much as the "stooping," "indistinct," and "obscene" creatures who operate the underground machinery in Wells's unseen world and who swarm the time traveler as he, like Hallet, descends the narrow access shafts (Wells 1895/1987, 65–66).

"Behind the Singer Tower" thus helps elucidate the ending of *Alexander's Bridge*, not just as a psychological drama but as the revelation of Morlockian laborers otherwise present only as the specters on the edges of the novel. The curious title of the story establishes the theme that Cather also pursues in the longer work, for the Singer Tower (a separate building from the Mont Blanc) has almost nothing to do with the narrative. Instead, the title operates as a reminiscence, hinting at the textile workers killed in the Triangle fire and recalling a massive strike at the Singer Company in the spring of 1911. Most important, it establishes a vantage point (from the men's boat south of Manhattan with the city and the hotel appearing "behind the Singer Tower") that emphasizes the kinds of looking—around, behind, and beneath—that Cather insisted upon in the work of 1912. The haunting of the story by spectral figures of history, laboring figures as well as wealthy engineers, may explain one of the most grotesque images in Cather's fictional corpus, a severed hand witnessed by the narrator in the aftermath of the blaze, and that "kept recurring to me" (45).[3] The hand, a sign of what cannot be repressed and of the productive forces of history that haunt aesthetic temporality, also keeps reverberating through Cather's early career: for Bartley Alexander, for the reader of *Alexander's Bridge*, and for the author herself.

NOTES

1. Quirk (2007) describes Maurice Mainhall as "representative of the aesthetic movement," suggesting that Cather may have based his character on Arthur Symons, author of "an edition of Ernest Dowson's poetry in 1909" (208).

2. On Bartley and the Victorian culture of masculine force, see Ammons (1986) and O'Brien (1987). On the novel as marking Cather's recovery of her own youth, see Wasserman (1999) and Rosowski (1986). On the psychological dimensions of the novel, see Skaggs (1982), Oehlschlaeger (1986), and Tichi (1987).

3. That the hand is not a laboring hand, but one belonging to an opera singer, reinforces rather than contradicts the point, for it draws out the associative processes in the story's presentation of work. The image of Graziani's severed hand uncannily echoes the other Italian hands—those belonging to the laborers in the

hole—that are variously pictured as "smashed up" (51), "trembling" when they do dangerous work, or "holding [the] hand" of an injured workman (49).

WORKS CITED

Ammons, Elizabeth. 1986. "The Engineer as Cultural Hero and Willa Cather's First Novel, *Alexander's Bridge*," *American Quarterly* 38 (5): 746–60.

Bergonzi, Bernard. 1961. *The Early H. G. Wells.* Manchester: Manchester University Press.

Cather, Willa. 1912/1970. "Behind the Singer Tower." In *Collected Short Fiction, 1892–1912.* Edited by Virginia Faulkner, 43–54. Lincoln: University of Nebraska Press.

———. 1912/1977. *Alexander's Bridge.* Lincoln: University of Nebraska Press.

———. 1949/1953. "Escapism: A Letter to *The Commonweal*." In *On Writing: Critical Studies on Writing as an Art.* New York: Knopf.

Deschamps, Gaston. 1901. "The French Critic's Impressions of America: The Pernicious 'Yellow Book'," *New York Times*, April 6.

Dowson, Ernest. 1922. "My Lady April." In *The Poems of Ernest Dowson*, 9. New York: Dodd, Mead.

Miller, Robert K. 2000. "'Behind the Singer Tower': A Transatlantic Tale." In *Willa Cather's New York*, ed. Merrill Maguire Skaggs, 75–89. Madison: Farleigh Dickinson University Press.

New York Times. 1901. "Gaston Deschamps: The French Critic's Impressions of America." 6 April, 243.

O'Brien, Sharon. 1987. *Willa Cather: The Emerging Voice.* Cambridge: Harvard University Press.

Oehlschlaeger, Fritz. 1986. "Willa Cather's 'Consequences' and *Alexander's Bridge*: An Approach through R. D. Laing and Ernest Becker." *Modern Fiction Studies* 32 (2): 191–202.

Pater, Walter. 1873/1986. *The Renaissance.* Oxford: Oxford University Press.

Pittock, Murray G. H. 1993. *Spectrum of Decadence.* London: Routledge.

Quirk, Tom. 2007. "Explanatory Notes." In *Alexander's Bridge* by Willa Cather. Scholarly Edition. Edited by Frederick M. Link, 199–241. Lincoln: University of Nebraska Press.

Rosowski, Susan. 1986. *The Voyage Perilous: Willa Cather's Romanticism.* Lincoln: University of Nebraska Press.

Skaggs, Merrill Maguire. 1982. "Poe's Shadow on *Alexander's Bridge*," *Mississippi Quarterly* 35 (4): 365–74.

Thain, Marion. 2007. *"Michael Field": Poetry, Aestheticism, and the Fin-de-Siècle.* Cambridge: Cambridge University Press.

Tichi, Cecilia. 1987. *Shifting Gears: Technology, Literature, and Culture in Modernist America.* Chapel Hill: University of North Carolina Press.

Wasserman, Loretta. 1999. *"Alexander's Bridge*: The 'Other' First Novel." In *Willa Cather's Canadian and Old World Connections*, edited by Robert Thacker and Michael Peterman, 294–306. *Cather Studies*, volume 4. Lincoln: University of Nebraska Press.

Wells, H. G. 1909. "Why I Joined the National Committee." Letter to the Editor, *Christian Commonwealth,* July 1909. Quoted in *The New Age* 7 (10): 236.

———. 1895/1987. *The Definitive Time Machine: A Critical Edition of H. G. Wells's Scientific Romance with Introduction and Notes by Harry M. Geduld.* Edited by Harry M. Geduld. Bloomington: Indiana University Press.

Williams, Carolyn. 2001. "Walter Pater's Impressionism and the Form of Historical Revival." In *Knowing the Past: Victorian Literature and Culture,* edited by Suzy Anger, 77–99. Ithaca: Cornell University Press.

Woodress, James. 1987. *Willa Cather: A Literary Life.* Lincoln: University of Nebraska Press.

Chapter 4

Aestheticism and the Dispossessed

Cather's Dual Europe in America

Nicholas Birns

RISE OF THE BEAUX-ARTS

An interest in European high culture stands at the heart of Willa Cather's relation to Aestheticism. Indeed, in her day there could be no other plausible route to Aestheticism than through Europe. Yet the European in Cather's work is also the migrant, the dispossessed. In *O Pioneers!*, Bohemians and French mingle as Americans, playing baseball together, formulating a scratch-as-scratch can prairie multiculturalism that is American, for America is the place where Europe can recombine, making a kind of "European Union" before Europe was able in any way to unite. Yet the Europe these people flee is also the Europe that Aunt Georgiana seeks to access on her train trip to Boston to see her Wagner matinée, the Europe that Mr. Shimerda so poignantly misses amid the vacancy of a prairie where he cannot flourish. As Philip Rahv put it in 1947, the year of Cather's death, "What is Europe to the immigrant population of this country? It is the realm of ignorance, poverty, and political oppression. But as a cultural entity Europe has also stood for spontaneity, sensibility, poetry, intellectual freedom, moral idealism" (Rahv 1947, 5). One Europe is the harmonious cultural diversity Cather found on the Plains; the other is the cresting wave of high culture she went back East to New York to catch.

Cather's era was the last great period of the European *beaux-arts*—the symphony, the museum, the opera house. These institutions, as Walter Pater demonstrates in his portrait of Watteau in "A Prince of Court Painters" (1887/1997, 21–44), represent the role of the arts in the waning of aristocracy and the rise of the bourgeoisie. Opera singers emerge (such as *My Ántonia*'s fictive "Vasakova"), conductors and painters become modern-day cynosures, and royal authority is replaced by cultural stardom[1] And this Europe is tempting, but not sufficient for Cather; Aunt Georgiana in "A Wagner Matinée" (1904) goes to Boston to hear music, for she cannot get culture in Nebraska. Yet, as Emil's discussion of Norse mythology in his early courtship with Marie Shabata in *O Pioneers!* indicates, the legends from which Wagner's work arose might have been better understood on the multicultural prairie than in the big cities of the East (Cather 1913/1992, 138). Archbishop Vaillant in *Death Comes for the Archbishop* frets about salad oil even as he ministers to the unconverted and relapsed on the mesas (1927/1999, 38). And, in *Shadows on the Rock*, Euclide Auclair's disciplined apothecary's willingness to use his theoretical wisdom to a practical purpose does not totally fit frontier Québec (1931/2005, 29). In Cather's fiction there is a Europe of high culture and the metropolis, which is seamlessly redeployed to the New World, and a Europe of struggle and aspiration, which is transplanted to the frontier with both exhilaration and trauma. European culture migrates to New York, but people speaking European languages migrate to Nebraska, Québec, New Mexico. As Jim Burden and the aunt find out, in America one can have one or the other of these two Europes—but in Cather's time, seldom both at once.

Like the European culture she portrays in her fiction, Cather's aestheticism is not always true to our own stereotypes of Aestheticism as being brittle and elitist. Rather, her aestheticism is one of high standards, yet popularly available. It is analogous, in the late nineteenth century, to the operas of Wagner, Verdi, and Puccini; to the orchestral music of Franck, Saint-Saëns, and Grieg; to the soaring, decorative utilitarianism of the Galleria in Milan; to the nuanced, poised realism of a painter Cather much admired like Bastien-Lepage; or to the mannered yet pungent classicism of Puvis de Chavannes. Cather took this accessible aestheticism and then pruned it, trimmed it back from a purely popular taste, made it more designed, and more implicitly lent it what the narrator of Pater's "Prince of Court Painters" called "a marvelous tact of omission" (1887/1997, 21).

Pater's text serves almost as an anticipatory gloss on Cather's aestheticism. His portrait—as reflected through the prism of an admiring female narrator—of Antoine Watteau (called "Antony" in the text) embodies both the artistic confidence and the practical democracy that Cather's depiction of the imaginative life also suggests. The very phrase "Prince of Court Painters" used by the nameless female narrator—itself a very Catherian device—means the end of absolute monarchy; even if the terms of that monarchy are used as a vehicle of superlative praise, Watteau arose during the *declining* years of Louis XIV. Indeed, Watteau's art, described as "a new manner of painting" (14), did not observe the strict neoclassical

Figure 4.1. Antoine Watteau. *An Embarrassing Proposal,* **1715–1716. Oil on canvas. 65 × 84.5 cm. The State Hermitage Museum, St. Petersburg. Photograph © The State Hermitage Museum. Photo by Vladimir Terebenin, Leonard Kheifets, Yuri Molodkovets.**

canons associated with thinkers such as René Rapin and Nicolas Boileau-Déspreaux, who were patronized by that monarch. Living among "the wealthy and refined" (17), Watteau still found that social life "somewhat of a burden" (19) and directs his art to pursuit of a "moral purity" (23). Watteau's art, as airy and frivolous as it seems, points the way to a new era of "fraternity, liberty, humanity" (35).

Watteau heralds the robust, vigorous, yet subtle and self-aware aestheticism that in Cather's time had surged to the forefront in architecture, opera, and painting. Once a court painter could be called a prince, painting became sufficiently important to emerge from the shadow of the court into what eventually became the bourgeois marketplace. The artist was the new prince; a celebrity culture open to merit and achievement had replaced, or seemed on the verge of replacing, the old court culture with its dependence on inheritance and privilege. If Pater idealized the artist, other writers of the era did not. One of these was Alphonse Daudet, who often portrayed artists in his fiction as rascals who were abusive toward women and obsessed with their own financial prosperity.[2] Cather's own sense of the breed was somewhere between the two. But Cather, Daudet, and Pater all concur in seeing the artist as the cavalier of the day.

It is well known that Cather preferred Pater to the more public and demonstrative Wilde among British aesthetes. Indeed, Cather's denunciation of Wilde is so severe that it might at first have seemed a misconception when W. J. Simon in 1936 in the *San Francisco Chronicle* called Cather (alluding to the title of Thomas Beer's 1920s history of the 1890s) "the foremost representative in American letters of the mauve decade" (O'Connor 2001, 489). If Cather's mauveness, as it were, comes through very strongly, it is through her interest in opera, in the visual arts, and in Pater. Pater, on the other hand, saw himself as a European; his family name was of Flemish origin, and part of the nuance in "A Prince of Court Painters" is that Watteau's chief pupil was actually named "Pater" and that both Watteau and Pater were as much Flemish as French, provincial "ethnics" gravitating to the art and culture of the metropolis. Pater's art is one not only of refinement but also of migration. For all its frivolity, Watteau, as limned by Pater's words, has a decidedly populist streak. Pater boldly links Watteau and revolution where few might see the relation of one to the other. Cather preferred Pater to Wilde not only because he did not act out but also because Pater had a palpable sense of the historical that allowed for historical change without being teleological or privileging modernity, what Carolyn Williams has influentially, in the title of her 1989 book, called an "aesthetic historicism." Pater's influence, as Anne K. Wilson (1997) and Deborah Lindsay Williams (1998) have demonstrated, was overtly registered in Cather's own intermingling of fiction and reality, art and event.

Pater was Cather's favorite English writer because, as Robert Nelson (1988) points out, she favored France far more than England and was more interested in the Continent in general as a cultural fount. It is no accident that Claude Wheeler, in *One of Ours* (1922/1991), along with most of Americans who fought morally or literally in his war, went to save France, not England.[3] This tendency towards the Continent, though it is different from standard-issue snobbery or pretension, did not involve glazing oneself in a veneer of sophistication. Cather's interest in continental art and music tended to be in recent and somewhat "popular" work, and she was overtly admiring of painters who, even in their day, seemed, notwithstanding their undeniable greatness, more crowd-pleasing than experimental, such as Bastien-Lepage and Puvis de Chavannes. But her taste was broader and less severe in music and art than in literature.

It may be that Cather was simply more *interested* in continental European art and music than in continental European fiction. Though she admired French writers such as Flaubert, she would never sit down and write a near-textbook American *Madame Bovary* as Kate Chopin did in

The Awakening. Cather's novels were not imitations of European genres or specific works of European fiction. They were far more likely to be suggested by certain emphases or perspectives in works—of all media—she had appreciated and then adapted to both a setting and viewpoint that was indubitably her own. Cather was passionately committed both to democracy and to high standards of artistic achievement and personal conduct.[4] The art Cather celebrates is similar in both its social and artistic values. Indeed, Cather's references to opera and painting raise the question voiced by the female narrator of "A Prince of Court Painters" when she says of Watteau, "tis a pity to incorporate so much of his work, of himself, with objects of use, which must perish by work, or disappear" (Pater 1887/1997, 31). This potential commercialization and ephemerality is the necessary underside of a democratic art, and this is the perennial divide that Cather's references to the arts continually canvass. Cather's Europe is different from Cather's America not—as Henry James would have it, in his essay on Hawthorne—that America lacked Europe's infrastructure of custom and high society (1879/1986, 109) but that Europe did not permit the democratic possibilities for the full expression of that art that only the United States could manifest.

Cather's interest in European aestheticism involved a refracted emulation, not a direct transposition of it to American shores. Cather's high society is an American, "Park Avenue" high society; there are very few European aristocrats in her work. To find Cather's Europe in America, as opposed to the Europe in Europe that she admired for its aesthetic achievements, we must go far inland and regard a different tableau entirely.

GOING INLAND

In *O Pioneers!*, Cather does move inland to Nebraska, and we shift from aesthetics to kinesthetics to look at the other side of Cather's dual Europe. When first- and second-generation Swedish and French-Canadian immigrants have time for recreation, they are not wearing opera glasses but are pioneers disporting themselves in their "white baseball suits" having "just come up from a Sunday practice game down in the ballgrounds" (1913/1992, 159). Later, Emil Bergson and Carl Linstrum, Alexandra Bergson's brother and love interest respectively, come to watch their friend Amedée pitch his "lightning balls" in preparation for a game against a team from the much larger town of Hastings. This seemingly American-as-apple-pie moment is quintessentially part of Cather's other European aspect—the Europe of the dispossessed. When I taught American literature 1865–1914 in the fall of 2008, on a reading list featuring such macho, outdoors-minded authors as Frank Norris, Jack London, and Mark

Twain, the two books to feature baseball were *O Pioneers!* and *Mrs. Spring Fragrance,* by Sui Sin Far, a female writer of Anglo-Chinese background. In the first story of Sui Sin Far's book, Kai Tzu is described as "one of the finest pitchers on the Coast" (1912/1995, 17). This could be an instance of marking by authors who were either immigrants themselves or writing about immigrants, using the incipient national game to make the idea of America visible. The macho writers no more needed to mention baseball than, to use Jorge Luis Borges's example, the Qu'ran needed to mention camels; for the Argentine writer, the fact that there were no camels mentioned in the Muslim holy book was indubitable proof of its authenticity (1962, 181).

But there is something else afoot here: the white male writers do not mention baseball because in their frontier America, where the struggle for survival and prosperity is still raw, organized sport is a luxury that even virile men cannot spend much time pursuing. Cather and Sui Sin Far—one woman who made her reputation writing about immigrants and the other who was an immigrant herself—are writing in the wake of the hybridization and population flows that made possible the twentieth-century America in which organized sport fully took hold of the country. That playing baseball is foregrounded in immigrant novels is because it is a part, a product, of their America. In other words, the baseball playing operates in three ways. It is an index of Americanization: Amedée would not have been playing baseball had he stayed in France; rather, art would have more likely been his pastime, though given his presumed class circumstances he would have had to move to the city where art was far more accessible to all. It is an index of proletarianization: It is a working-class, male activity, precisely the sort of thing Paul, in "Paul's Case," fled Pittsburgh for New York to escape. It is, finally, an index of consumerism: Baseball, like the arts, is a form of *play,* and it is a slight step towards the "shift from producer to consumer orientation" that Jackson Lears discusses in his influential study of American culture at the turn of the century (1981, 22).

Just as baseball can be a hybridizing agent, giving Swedish and French young men a sport they never would have had in common had either remained in their home countries, so poetry and music can serve not as highbrow markers of exclusion but as inclusive forms connecting personal destinies and cultural trajectories. Cather's Europe in America also focuses on poetry and music. Aesthetic appreciation is something one can grow into; it has a necessary discontinuity with personal experience, but it also depends on experience. This can be seen in the final section of *My Ántonia,* "Cuzak's Boys." Cuzak, Ántonia's husband, returns from Denver to find Jim Burden, his wife's childhood friend whom he has never met, in the house, spreading largesse to his children and enjoying his family's musical heritage.

After making pleasantries with Jim, Cuzak speaks animatedly to his wife in their shared native language about "Vasakova," which Jim eventually realizes refers to (the fictional) Maria Vasak, "the singer" (Cather 1918/1994,189), whose hijinks are being chronicled in the gossip pages of the Bohemian illustrated newspapers. Cuzak asks "incredulously" if Burden has heard of Vasak. The incredulity has to do with Cuzak thinking that Vasak is an "ethnic" or "national" figure, whereas to Burden she is quite the opposite, an international star. He has heard of Vasak less because he was friendly with Bohemians in his youth on the prairies than because being a cosmopolitan New York sophisticate entailed seeing Vasak sing. Indeed, so international is Burden that he has been back to the old country much more recently than Cuzak, who is tied to the land by his lack of funds and by his obligation to work the farm.

It is Cuzak who asks Jim about "the Ringstrasse and the theatres" (193), whereas twenty years earlier it would have been the reverse. In effect, Burden and Cuzak have changed places: Burden was once the American farm boy looking wide-eyed at the panoply of immigrants on the prairies, but now Cuzak, a somewhat displaced "city man," is working the fields which Burden has left for success and world travel.[5] That Burden finds his position in life hollow and unsatisfying—a "burden," as many have pointed out—and Cuzak seems to enjoy a rich and happy life, even if he finds himself slightly puzzled by it, is part of the pathos of the situation. The reference to "Vasak"—bracketing the entire issue of Jim's previous relationship with Ántonia—is what keeps the social situation from being tragic. The two men have their admiration for opera in common; the triumph of music means they can look each other in the eye despite their different lots in life. European high culture becomes something Jim and Cuzak can share, something which binds them, something which makes them both "Americans." It is important that Vasak appears in the same book that has earlier featured Blind D'Arnault, the African American pianist; the latter's music could not have come in Europe, nor could Jim and Cuzak's sharing of music as equals have occurred on the Continent. D'Arnault's presence expresses the motif of music as both emerging from suffering and helping transcend that suffering, which pertains to the life stories of Jim, Ántonia, and Cuzak as well. Jim's redemptive reunion with the Cuzak family is, in a sense, vouchsafed by what Toni Morrison would call D'Arnault's "Africanist presence" (1992, 7).

THE MEETING OF THE EUROPES

Cuzak's Nebraska farm is one of the few places in the United States Jim could have the conversation that he does with Cuzak. He might be able to talk about Vasak in New York in the affected tones of music aficionados insecure in their knowledge—as one imagines Mrs. Burden's protégés to be—but only in Nebraska can he talk about Vasak the celebrity with a European who understands the populist aspects of her art. The Midwest is more European than the East; in the East the imperatives of role and finance cause assimilation, for European and Midwesterner alike, into a kind of pseudo-Englishness. However, the very struggle of the Cuzaks' daily grind means they are under no pressure to give up their cultural heritage. The dispossessed have become the ones who can manifest continuity. It is the poor people like the Cuzaks who remember the past, who cherish it as a part of their future. The need to divest themselves of the past, to make a clean break, that historically accompanied much of the rhetoric of Americanism is not only unnecessary but would in fact add a further cultural impoverishment to the financial impoverishment the Cuzaks are already facing. The European legacy is their cultural nest egg, a reserve that stays them through economic bad times.

So it would be an oversimplification to say that Cather's two Europes never meet, for they obviously do in *O Pioneers!* and *My Ántonia*. However, the novel where they converge the most is what is now Cather's most neglected major novel, *The Song of the Lark*. Having provoked a slight sense of discomfort to some readers, *The Song of the Lark* is often treated as a bulky detour that, despite being of considerable interest, was a massive working-out of artistic problems that were later smoothed out in novels deemed more central to their author's canon. (Edith Wharton's *The Fruit of the Tree* is also discussed in very similar terms). But Cather successfully links her "growing up on the prairie" theme with "excelling in European beaux-arts" theme in *The Song of the Lark* (1915); indeed, if one considers that this novel contains Cather's first engagement with the American Southwest, one can see the novel as encyclopedic of Cather's main thematic concerns. The Arizona scene in the novel shows not just that there is a difference between the American and European landscapes, but that the American landscape is "lacking" so much in terms of European notions of sublimity that new aesthetics must be devised to measure its beauty. It is not so much that America is a new world free from Europe, but America is a place where the democratic aesthetic can unfurl itself without being retarded by residual hierarchies of sublimity and decorum.

Everybody knows that the novel is about an opera singer, but what is less often appreciated is that the title of *The Song of the Lark* is given by a Jules Breton painting. If, in Paterian terms, all art constantly aspires to the condition of music (1877/1986, 156), Cather has nonetheless framed her musical tale in a visual tableau. This is not just an encounter of spatial and temporal modes of perception but an alignment of what the two media meant, temperamentally, to Cather. Like painting, opera is not just a matter of virtuosic training or inborn talent but a participation in the life of the arts, in an artistic way of knowing. And this thorough immersion in "the arts" may be why Cather's one dedicated *Künstlerroman,* her one book given over to a sustained biographical treatment of an artist, is also her most social novel, the novel that gives the fullest and most detailed rendition of American life.

Cather's vision of American life is a very European one, not only because of characters like Wunsch and Harsanyi who have so much of Europe literally in them, but also by people like Dr. Archie, the physician, who clearly have an interest in the arts and the artistic temperament and a sense of the democratic possibilities of culture, even if they do not themselves practice the arts in the way that Thea Kronborg does. As Celia Harris said in her contemporary review of *O Pioneers!* for the *Lincoln Sunday State Journal,* "Cather's Swedes and Czechs, for all their Americanism, sent one across the sea to their melancholy or complacent or passionate brothers in European literature" (O'Connor 2001, 52). This is not to say that European origin and artistic inclinations are automatically concomitant; far from it. Some of the characters are too dispossessed, materially or culturally, to be interested in aesthetics. And it may be in America alone that these people could come into contact with their counterparts more drawn to the Muses.

In *My Ántonia,* neither Jim nor the Cuzaks end the novel without losing something: Jim's ties with Nebraska can only be resumed temporarily. Cuzak has left the old country for good, although he can still follow its gossip. In *O Pioneers!* the weathered, reunited couple, Carl and Alexandra, are on the divide, with the fertility of the land before them. But the possibility of resuming ties to Europe is as unlikely as their ability to physically reproduce themselves; their fate will be determined as Americans. In *The Song of the Lark,* though, there is a bridge between America and Europe, and it is through opera and the severe aesthetic standards that Thea—and Cather—survive and triumph themselves. Thea's "intellectual and spiritual development" (1915/1987, 699) reaches out to European succor, but its reverberation brings her home town of Moonstone, Colorado, "real refreshment" (706). The conceited simile Cather uses, of the sandbars in Venice being renewed by "fresh brine" (706), is on its face about only Europe; but when applied to Moonstone it is about how Europe can nurture America—returning, in a sense, the gift America has given Europe by presenting it to Thea [AU: Edit okay?] who is the crowning result of European hopes for art, fully manifest in America. Marilee Lindemann, in another context, cites Thea as subverting the game "by mastering it through sheer force of will" (1999, 7); this could well express how Kronberg accepts Europe but is unmastered by it, remaining her own unique amalgam. *The Song of the Lark*—a book about opera named after a painting —is the novel where Cather's dual Europes most converge into one America, the one that can still keep Europe in the minds of its characters and readers.

An art that has had to struggle for its spirit in more problematic circumstances adds layers of nuance to a land that has known peace and prosperity more than great art. This is the odd interdependence between the frontier and the beaux-arts. In *The Cowboy and the Dandy*, Meisel (1998) argues that these antithetical cultural archetypes become, in the late nineteenth century, interdependent and mutually nourishing. In this vision, America becomes a kind of outer forum of Europe where fates can be not so much transformed as realized. When Cather visited Europe in 1902, she saw "children who clambered out of the gutters" to see Lord Kitchener's imperial triumph (1931/1988, 159) and "miserable, shivering Latins" (93) in France, her very citadel of civilization. Europe cannot realize its own hope; America can. In Europe, the residuum of the aristocracy for whom Pater's Watteau had to "go to Paris" to work is still holding onto some aspects of power, but in America, art, celebrity, and commerce have no rival from courts or titled aristocracies. This does not mean that there is neither hierarchy nor economic polarities in the United States; the prairie men in their white baseball suits have little chance to meet Jim Burden's wife and her salons for second-rate artists or hear Thea Kronborg sing in Carnegie Hall. To traverse these two worlds at all is an achievement. But there is a movement underway—a movement not finalized in Cather's works, nor perhaps ever fully finalizable, but nonetheless as steadily and unobtrusively persistent as "the easy-blowing morning wind" (1913/1992, 15).

For Willa Cather, the people who epitomized European values became not the courtier or the potentate but the opera singer and the painter, and these were eminencies that did not build armies or national identities, and from whom people did not have to flee in coming to America. Indeed, these immigrant Americans could retain and even amplify the possibility of making their talents matter in art and in life. Cather's sense of this possibility was both indelibly European and inescapably American.

NOTES

1. Richard Giannone (2001) and Wendy Perriman (2009) provide specific treatments of music and dance in Cather; Jonathan Goldberg (2001), though ranging more widely in theoretical terms, is of equivalent usefulness in terms of opera. Surprisingly, there has been no single book-length study of Cather and the visual arts, though Jean Schwind's work (1993) is a good start.

2. Sherard refers to Daudet's depiction of "semi-artists . . . distinguished by the uncleanliness of their appearance" (1894, 220).

3. As seen in Margaret O'Connor's volume of contemporary reviews (2001), the London reviews of Cather's books were not outstandingly complimentary or comprehending (the reviewer of *The Professor's House* placed most of the action in Kansas, and that of *One of Ours* stated Claude owned land in South America, rather than, just once, threatening to go there).

4. In her 1933 NBC radio speech, Cather referred to the novel as "the child of democracy and the coming years." In her prefatory discussion of Sarah Orne Jewett's *Country of the Pointed Firs* (1925), Cather praised Jewett for "inherent, individual beauty; the kind of beauty we feel when a beautiful song is sung by a beautiful voice that is exactly suited to the song." (1925/1988, 49).

5. And Ántonia has not married a man like her cultured, sensitive father; Burden is more like Mr. Shimerda than Cuzak is.

WORKS CITED

Beer, Thomas. 1926. *The Mauve Decade: American Life at the End of the Nineteenth Century.* New York: Garden City Press.

Borges, Jorge Luis. 1962. *Labyrinths.* New York: New Directions.

Cather, Willa. 1902/1988. *Willa Cather in Europe: Her Own Story of the First Journey.* Edited by George N. Kates. Lincoln: University of Nebraska Press.

———. 1904/2000. "A Wagner Matinée." In *The Troll Garden and Other Stories,* 94–102. Lincoln: University of Nebraska Press.

———. 1913/1992. *O Pioneers!* Lincoln: University of Nebraska Press.

———. 1915/1987. *The Song of the Lark.* In *Willa Cather: Early Novels and Stories.* Edited by Sharon O'Brien. New York: Library of America.

———. 1918/1994. *My Ántonia.* New York: Vintage.

———. 1922/1991. *One of Ours.* New York: Vintage.

———. 1925/1988. "The Best Stories of Sarah Orne Jewett." In *Willa Cather on Writing.* Lincoln: University of Nebraska Press.

———. 1927/1999. *Death Comes for the Archbishop.* Lincoln: University of Nebraska Press.

———. 1931/1988. "My First Novels [There Were Two]. In *Willa Cather on Writing: Critical Studies on Writing as an Art.* Lincoln: University of Nebraska Press.

———. 1931/2005. *Shadows on the Rock.* Lincoln: University of Nebraska Press.

———. 1933/1986. "On the Novel," Speech given at the Pulitzer Prize awards and broadcast by NBC Radio. In *Willa Cather in Person: Interviews, Speeches, and Letters.* Edited by L. Brent Bohlke. Lincoln: University of Nebraska Press, 168–70.

Giannone, Richard. 2001. *Music in Willa Cather's Fiction.* Lincoln: University of Nebraska Press.

Goldberg, Jonathan. 2001. *Willa Cather and Others.* Durham, NC: Duke University Press.

James, Henry. 1879/1986. "From 'Hawthorne' (1879)." In *Henry James on the Art and Theory of Criticism.* Edited by William R. Veeder and Susan M. Griffin, 101–31. Chicago: University of Chicago Press.

Lears, T. J. Jackson. 1981. *No Place of Grace: Antimodernism and the Transformation of American Culture.* Chicago: University of Chicago Press.

Lindemann, Marilee. 1999. *Willa Cather: Queering America.* New York: Columbia University Press.

Meisel, Perry. 1998. *The Cowboy and the Dandy.* New York: Oxford University Press.

Morrison, Toni. 1992. *Playing in the Dark: Whiteness and the American Literary Imagination.* Cambridge: Harvard University Press.

Nelson, Robert. 1988. *Willa Cather and France: In Search of the Lost Language.* Urbana: University of Illinois Press.

O'Connor, Margaret Anne, ed. 2001. *Willa Cather: The Contemporary Reviews.* Cambridge: Cambridge University Press.

Pater, Walter. 1877/1986. *The Renaissance: Studies in the History of the Renaissance.* In *Three Major Texts.* Edited by William Buckler, 4–173. New York: New York University Press.

———. 1887/1997. "A Prince of Court Painters." In *Imaginary Portraits,* 21–44. New York: Allworth.

Perriman, Wendy K. 2009. *Willa Cather and the Dance: "A Most Satisfying Elegance."* Madison, NJ: Fairleigh Dickinson University Press.

Rahv, Philip, ed. 1947. *Discovery of Europe.* New York: Houghton Mifflin.

Schwind, Jean. 1993. "This Is a Frame-Up: Mother Eve in *The Professor's House.*" In *Cather Studies,* volume 2. Edited by Susan Rosowski, 72–91. Lincoln: University of Nebraska Press.

Sherard, Robert Harbrough.1894. *Alphonse Daudet: Biographical and Critical Study.* London: Edward Arnold.

Sui Sin Far. 1912/1995. *Mrs. Spring Fragrance and Other Writings.* Edited by Annette White-Parks. Urbana: University of Illinois Press.

Williams, Carolyn. 1989. *Transfigured World: Walter Pater's Aesthetic Historicism.* Ithaca, NY: Cornell University Press.

Williams, Deborah Lindsay. 1998. "Cather, Woolf, and the Two Mrs. Ramsays." *College English* 61 (1): 29–40.

Wilson, Anne Krichels. 1997. "Revising the Lighthouse: Interrogations of Christian Narrative Models in the Literature of the Transition." PhD diss., New York University, Graduate School of Arts and Sciences.

Chapter 5

Willa Cather's Disenchanted Epicurean

Godfrey St. Peter in *The Professor's House*

Sarah Cheney Watson

To Cather, the choice of art over relationship is an identifying trait of the Aesthete, a type about which she had written in "Paul's Case" and other stories in *The Troll Garden* (1905). According to John H. Randall, Cather sees little hope for the character type since the

> Aesthete, in his single-minded search for beauty, cuts himself off from all human relationships; a conflict develops between him and the people around him, and since he has broken the moral code by placing beauty above goodness and thus denying his kinships with mankind, he must pay the penalty. (1960, 275)

As Cather matured, gathering experiences and encountering her own crisis of soul, her characters also confront challenges associated with middle age. While Godfrey St. Peter in *The Professor's House* may have once leaned in the direction of a self-indulgent aestheticism like Paul's, by the time the novel is set he is more truly an Epicurean as Walter Pater understood the term. Although later critics have identified Pater's writings with the Aesthetic movement, Pater, himself, apparently never embraced the term "Aestheticism." Rather, he preferred the term "Epicurean," as seen in the title of his 1885 novel *Marius the Epicurean*, in which the main character holds many of the attributes set forth by Epicurus in *Vatican Sayings*, a philosophy described by William Harmon as:

> similar to that of the Greek Epicurus, who saw philosophy as the art of making life happy, with pleasure the highest goal, and pain and emotional

disturbance the greatest evils. But *Epicurus was not a simple hedonist . . . ; for him pleasure came not primarily from sensual delights but from serenity. . . .* The Epicurean, therefore, seeks not wine, women, and song, but serenity of spirit. The term "Epicurean" is often but erroneously considered synonymous with hedonistic. (2012, 177; emphasis mine)

Marius is Pater's Aesthetic hero, his Epicurean martyr. Indeed, in his note to the "Conclusion" in the 1893 edition of *The Renaissance,* Pater says as much:

This brief 'Conclusion' was omitted in the second edition of this book as I conceived it might possibly mislead some of those young men into whose hands it might fall. On the whole, I have thought it best to reprint it here, with some slight changes which bring it closer to my original meaning. I have dealt more fully in *Marius the Epicurean* with the thoughts suggested by it. (1873/1986, 150)

Cather's near-martyr, Godfrey St. Peter in *The Professor's House,* shows the clear influence of Pater's Epicurean Aestheticism.

SERENITY

For the most part, Cather's truest, most effective artist-aesthete is characterized by an Epicurean "serenity of spirit," following Pater's example of Marius who possesses "natural Epicureanism . . . prompting him to conceive of himself as but the passive spectator of the world around him" (1885/1985, 107). While Professor St. Peter is, in a general sense, one of Cather's Aesthetic heroes, she had little use for the life of the Victorian-era aesthetes, particularly Oscar Wilde, who described Pater's *Renaissance* as "the very flower of decadence"[1] and called it "that book which has had such strange influence over my life" (1905/1913). Indeed, Wilde was in all probability one of the "young men" who mistakenly, according to Pater, followed his call to "burn always with [a] hard gem-like flame" with little if any sense of the restraint found in Pater's hero. St. Peter is hardly one of those "young men"; he is in reality a Paterian "Epicurean" rather than a Wildean "aesthete." Like those of Marius the Epicurean, St. Peter's life and philosophy are infused with *ascêsis,* Pater's term for "self-restraint, a skilful economy of means" (1888/1974, 110) or "the austere and serious girding of the loins in youth" (1873/1986, xxxii).

From the beginning, Cather's St. Peter is described as an Epicurean, a self-controlled Epicurean. His one reason for living is pleasure—not for a hedonistic sating of the physical senses, but for a subtle self-centered desire to experience the personal joy that accompanies artistic success.

While St. Peter's old house is admittedly ugly, he has created a beautiful French "walled garden" to which he retreats regularly (Cather 1925, 14–15). And the attic-office is the place where he undertook the greatest pleasure of his life, the writing of his series of books. Moreover, it looks out on Lake Michigan, "the inland sea of his childhood," where he often spent the day in release from his labors (29). Although the house needs many repairs, including replacement of the old unreliable gas stove in his office, St. Peter is "by no means an ascetic. He . . . was terribly selfish about personal pleasures, fought for them. If a thing gave him delight, he got it, if he sold his shirt for it" (26–27).

In addition to requiring beautiful surroundings, St. Peter is rather vain about his own appearance. After a description of him as a very handsome, middle-aged man in the first chapter, Chapter Two opens with a discussion between St. Peter and his wife about the new house. She mentions that having a room of his own is more dignified at his age, and he replies: "'It's convenient, certainly, though I hope I'm not so old as to be personally repulsive?' He glanced into the mirror and straightened his shoulders as if he were trying on a coat" (34). In this passage, St. Peter realizes that his good looks will wane as the years go by, one of many disappointments—large and small, personal and professional—that make up St. Peter's larger crisis. If Epicureans value serenity as the "ultimate purpose" and define it as "the physical and mental welfare or pleasure of the individual" (Turner 1947, 353), St. Peter's mental state is now far from serene. In a person who delights in beauty as St. Peter does, learning "to live without delight" (282) will be very hard, almost impossible.

While St. Peter's aesthetic sense is repulsed by ugliness, he is more importantly disgusted in an Epicurean sense by the degree of acquisitiveness he sees growing in the hearts of his wife and daughters. For the Epicureans, "the quiet pleasures of moderation produce the finest life" (Soccio 1995, 28), but St. Peter's family have become conspicuous in their consumption of material goods. Nevertheless, his own feelings about material possessions are ambiguous. While he rejects Rosamond's offer to "settle an income" on him, he realizes that much of his happiness with his wife Lillian has been due to the small income she inherited from her father that "had made all the difference in the world" (Cather 1925, 257). When St. Peter travels with his wife and the Marselluses to Chicago to give a series of lectures, he cancels his original reservation at a less expensive residence when he discovers that his son-in-law has rented rooms for them at the luxurious Blackstone Hotel. By accepting Marsellus's provision of more comfortable quarters, St. Peter is caught in an awkward situation. He must accept the subsequent entertainment and conspicuous, almost hedonistic, dining that becomes part of the package—all the while deploring the "public magnificence" (96) in which his son-in-law indulges. Conflicted over his son-in-law's vulgar materialism, he later regrets accepting Louis's hospitality, saying, "When I consented to occupy an apartment I couldn't afford, I let myself in for whatever might follow" (96). And the final insult is, of course, the Marselluses' decision to name their new monstrosity of a house after Tom Outland, whose death provided their fortune.

Indeed, behind St. Peter's hesitation to accept money that he has not earned lies the crass materialism that has overtaken his family, his university, and his friends. During the year that elapses in the telling of the story, St. Peter's family moves into a new house, his daughters (already married) become an affliction rather than a blessing, and one of his friends turns against him in an effort to acquire some of the money from their mutual friend's—Tom Outland's—invention. These exterior pressures give St. Peter a great deal to come to terms with, yet—more important—he still has his own internal, spiritual/aesthetic journey to complete.

Over that same period, St. Peter and his family move apart emotionally. His older daughter Rosamond, who has inherited Tom Outland's fortune, and her husband Louis are furnishing their newly built home and, in the process, spending a great deal of money. Rosamond has become so self-centered that she is unwilling to relinquish any of her worldly goods to help others, not even their childhood seamstress Augusta, and St. Peter realizes that his other daughter Kathleen, having abandoned her artistic promise, is now deeply jealous of her sister. He withdraws from his sons-in-law, who, while attractive, are lacking in some way; most likely, they are not Tom Outland, the son he never had. Furthermore, he no longer sees his wife Lillian, once the great love of his life, as a kindred spirit; rather, he now considers her to be a philistine.

Equally disturbing is the fact that his friend and colleague, Crane, who once fought along with St. Peter against the university's desire to become more profitable, should demand compensation for his part in Tom Outland's invention. While pondering Crane's betrayal, St. Peter "brought himself back [to the present] with a jerk. Ah, yes, Crane; that was the trouble. If Outland were here to-night, he might say with Mark Antony, *My fortunes have corrupted honest men*" (150). His long friendship with Crane is being destroyed by a disagreement over money. Here is, along with that of his family, another sacrifice for St. Peter at the altar of materialism.

ART, BEAUTY, AND EPICUREANISM

As his family travels to Europe in the summer of Part III, St. Peter works in his garden and plans to prepare Tom Outland's diary for publication.

He ponders the loss of Outland and remembers the summer after Tom graduated from the university. At this point, Tom Outland's story—his discovery of the extinct civilization of the Blue Mesa, his disappointment with an unsympathetic bureaucracy, and his arrival in Hamilton and subsequent invention of the profitable Outland vacuum—is inserted into the larger narrative of *The Professor's House.* This idealized period of close friendship, youth, kindred spirits, and discovery contrasts deeply with St. Peter's present circumstances. Set against the past, the professor's life in Hamilton pales in comparison with Outland's life on the Blue Mesa. And set beside the spiritualized cliff dwellings of Blue Mesa, the ostentatious house being constructed by Rosamond and Louis Marsellus near Lake Michigan becomes a mockery rather than a tribute to Tom Outland. Through Tom's eyes, St. Peter had seen the beauty of the cliff dwellings, and after they visited Blue Mesa together he came to love the place as well as Tom did. Because of their mutual understanding and appreciation of the simple, understated beauty of the Anasazi architecture and the artifacts discovered on the Blue Mesa and in Cliff City, St. Peter "couldn't see Tom building 'Outland'" (260). It was at its heart simply in bad taste.

This story also illustrates the understanding the professor has developed about the relationship between art and religion. Just as the German speculator Fechtig took over Blue Mesa, raiding it of its artifacts, Professor St. Peter suspects that modern science is depriving people of the things that matter—art, religion, beauty—and replacing them with the cold certitude of industry, which "[gives] us a lot of ingenious toys [that] take our attention away from the real problems" (68). Because of his Epicureanism, he feels that these toys are a very poor substitute for pondering the "old riddles" that "make life more interesting" (68). At this point in the novel—several years after his trip with Tom to Cliff City—he believes that religion is best understood in terms of art and that only the resulting conflation of art with religion can satisfy the human need for happiness and serenity. To a question from one of his students about the place of science in the modern world, St. Peter replies:

> But the fact is the human mind, the individual mind, has always been made more interesting by dwelling on the old riddles, even if it makes nothing of them. . . . As long as every man and woman who crowded into the cathedrals on Easter Sunday was a principal in a gorgeous drama with God, glittering angels on one side and the shadows of evil coming and going on the other, life was a rich thing. . . . And that's what makes men happy, believing in the mystery and importance of their own little individual lives. It makes us happy to surround our creature needs and bodily instincts with as much pomp and circumstance as possible. Art and religion (they are the same thing, in the end, of course) have given man the only happiness he has ever had. . . . They might, without sacrilege, have changed the prayer a little and

said, *Thy will be done in art, as it is in heaven.* How can it be done anywhere else *as* it is in heaven? (68–69)

This passage clearly asserts that for St. Peter, happiness is the goal of humankind, and it can be achieved only through art and religion "(and they are the same thing in the end, of course) [which] have given man the only happiness he has ever had" (69). Of course, this statement assumes, as do the Epicureans, that the goal of every person is to achieve happiness; in fact, according to Turner, "Epicurus' interest was in happiness, which he unwisely termed pleasure, to be obtained by removing the reasons for unhappiness" (1947, 351).

So does art/religion remove the reasons for unhappiness? For Cather's St. Peter, the connection is promised but not easily achieved. But if we trace Cather's ideas back to Walter Pater's "Preface" to *The Renaissance* we find that he proposes a specific role for art in achieving human pleasure/happiness. One reason for St. Peter's nostalgic longing for Cliff City and the cathedrals of the Middle Ages and for his disaffection with "Outland" can be seen in the aesthetic notion of "renaissance" as developed by Walter Pater. He explains that art or "the fairer forms of nature and human life [must be regarded as] forces producing pleasurable sensations, each of a more or less peculiar or unique kind" (1873/1986, xxx). And Pater claims that a capital "R" Renaissance is a time when the "fairer forms" of many disciplines worked together to bring about an era "of more favourable conditions, in which the thoughts of men draw nearer together than is their wont, and the many interests of the intellectual world combine in one complete type of general culture" (xxxiii). However, smaller renaissances can be recognized in the history of the world. And "renaissance" can occur at any time in any place, for:

In all ages there have been some excellent workmen, and some excellent work done. The question . . . is always:—In whom did the stir, the genius, the sentiment of the period find itself? Where was the receptacle of its refinement, its elevation, its taste? "The ages are all equal," says William Blake, "but genius is always above its age." (xxxi)

Pater admits that he is "giving [the term 'renaissance'] a much wider scope than was intended by those who originally used it to denote that revival of classical antiquity in the fifteenth century" (xxxi). Any "outbreak of the human spirit," according to Pater, may be entitled a "renaissance" (xxxii). Such a renaissance is described in Cather's inserted story about Tom Outland's discovery of Cliff City. After a visit to the site, Father Duchesne tells Tom:

I am inclined to think that your tribe were a superior people. Perhaps they were not so when they first came upon this mesa, but in an orderly and secure life they developed considerably the arts of peace. There is evidence on every hand that they lived for something more than food and shelter. . . . There is unquestionably a distinct feeling for design in what you call the Cliff City. Buildings are not grouped like that by pure accident. (1925, 219)

This place has the "grave dignity and influence" (Pater 1873/1986, xxxiii) that makes it recognizable to succeeding generations as a place of renaissance. Cliff City's organic form is:

beautifully proportioned . . . . But the really splendid thing about our city, the thing that made it delightful to work there, and must have made it delightful to live there, was the setting. The town hung like a bird's nest in the cliff, looking off into the box canyon below, and beyond into the wide valley we called Cow Canyon, facing an ocean of clear air. (213)

Tom's description of the serenity of Cliff City clearly connects with Pater's notion of *ascêsis*, "self-restraint [and the] skilful economy of means" (1888/1974, 110), which echoes the Epicurean teaching that "the quiet pleasures of moderation produce the finest life" (Soccio 1995, 228). Moreover, Tom's reaction to the beautiful, serene Cliff City borders on the

Figure 5.1. *Mesa Verde's Cliff Palace*, 2010, National Park Service. 7 × 5.25 inches. **Photo credit: Martha Smith.**

religious: "Such silence and stillness and repose—immortal repose. That village sat looking down into the canyon with the calmness of eternity" (Cather 1925, 201). Here, in Outland's attempt to describe his first discovery of Cliff City, is one of those moments for which Pater urges us to live, a moment in which "some form grows perfect . . . ; some tone on the hills or the sea is choicer than the rest" (1888/1974, 152). The moment, described in painterly, artistic terms, is clearly a religious experience, and Tom even wonders if it is a place too sacred to share with his friend, Roddy: "As I stood looking up at it, I wondered whether I ought to tell even Blake about it; whether I ought not to go back across the river and keep that secret as the mesa had kept it" (Cather 1925, 202).

For Tom, and ultimately for St. Peter, Cliff City becomes the ideal form for beautiful dwellings; they feel that this organic architecture, in which the buildings seem to grow out of the earth, signifies a high civilization, "a fine people" (213), a "renaissance." And in this moment, art and religion become "the same thing, in the end."

EPICUREAN FRIENDSHIP

The two plots in *The Professor's House*—Tom Outland's story and the main narrative of St. Peter—are not only connected by the contrast between Cliff City and "Outland" that illustrates the aesthetic combination of art and religion, but also by the friendship between Tom Outland and St. Peter. Epicurean philosophy describes and may perhaps inform their relationship, which is portrayed as a sort of completion each of the other:

> Just when the morning brightness of the world was wearing off for him, along came Outland and brought him a kind of second youth. Through Outland's studies, long after they had ceased to be pupil and master, he had been able to experience afresh things that had grown dull with use. (258)

And through Tom's fresh eyes, St. Peter is able to re-envision his magnum opus to its great benefit:

> If the last four volumes of "The Spanish Adventurers" were more simple and inevitable than those that went before, it was largely because of Outland. When St. Peter first began his work, he realized that his great drawback was the lack of early association, the fact that he had not spent his youth in the . . . South-west country. . . . [Then] into his house walked a boy who had grown up there . . . who had in his pocket the secrets which old trail and stone and water-courses tell only to adolescence. (258–59)

After Outland graduated from the university, they retraced the journey of St. Peter's source, a Spanish diarist; on this trip St. Peter visited Cliff City.

The two friends also went to Mexico together and planned a trip to Paris, but the war intervened, and Outland enlisted only to die soon afterward. Over the intervening years, St. Peter's grief had been tempered by the belief that Outland "had escaped all [the disillusionment that followed the war]. He had made something new in the world—and the rewards, the meaningless conventional gestures, he had left to others" (261). Their friendship has been so close that St. Peter knows and speaks for Outland throughout the book. In Epicurean terms, St. Peter "sees almost another self in the friend" (Soccio 1995, 230).

As friends, the two spent a great deal of time in each other's company, sharing food and philosophy. Their evenings together recall gatherings in Epicurus's Garden, his school, which "was as well known for good living and pleasant socializing as it was for its philosophy" (221). During the summer after Outland's graduation—when St. Peter is alone in the house and is very happy—he and Outland share many fine evenings:

> When he [St. Peter] cooked a fine leg of lamb, *saignant*, well rubbed with garlic before it went into the pan, then he asked Outland to dinner. Over a dish of steaming asparagus, swathed in a napkin to keep it hot, and a bottle of sparkling Asti, they talked and watched night fall in the garden. If the evening happened to be rainy or chilly, they sat inside and read Lucretius. (Cather 1925, 176)

Significantly, Lucretius (c. 99–55 BCE) is the Roman poet whose only surviving work is *De Rerum Natura*, a poetical rendering of the philosophy of Epicurus. In the above-cited scene from *The Professor's House*, Cather portrays St. Peter and Outland's friendship in terms of Epicurean pleasure or happiness. Not only did Epicurus consider serenity to be more important for pleasure than "sensual delight," but he also believed that "intellectual processes [are] superior to bodily pleasures" (Harmon 2012, 177). Admittedly, the bodily pleasures are important to the Epicurean, but they are heightened when experienced in conjunction with intellectual processes. So in this scene, we find Tom Outland and St. Peter indulging in both culinary pleasure—delicious food, fine wine—and intellectual pleasure—a great book and philosophical discussion.

ART AS REVELATION

Like Tom Outland who desires to sleep without wakening in reaction to Roddy's materialism (Cather 1925, 248), St. Peter seeks death once he realizes that his whole family has embraced the same sort of materialism so that even love no longer exists for him: "He thought of eternal solitude with gratefulness; as a release from every obligation, every form of effort.

It was the Truth" (272). While death becomes welcome to him, St. Peter wonders if taking his own life would be moral. A few days later, alone in his study, St. Peter is meditating upon his misfortunes. He falls asleep, and his unpredictable little gas stove blows out in the wind that closes the only window to the room:

> When St. Peter at last awoke, the room was pitch black and full of gas. He was cold and numb, felt sick and rather dazed. The storm had blown the stove out and the window shut. The thing to do was to get up and open the window. But suppose he did not get up ——? How far was a man required to exert himself against accident? How would such a case be decided under English law? He hadn't lifted his hand against himself—was he required to lift it for himself? (276)

He does, however, try to get out of the room once he is nearly overtaken, and Augusta, dropping by to get the house keys to prepare for his family's arrival, hears and rescues him.

By the end of *The Professor's House*, Cather can no longer hold to the idea that "Art and religion . . . are the same thing, in the end, of course" (69). Had St. Peter died in his attic office, we could have said that he, too, is a martyr to beauty as is Marius at the end of *Marius the Epicurean*. However, he doesn't die. Although the symbolic savior, the Christian Cornelius, fails to return in time to save Marius' life, the devout Catholic Augusta does succeed in saving St. Peter:

> At midnight St. Peter was lying in his study, on his box-couch, covered up with blankets, a hot water bottle at his feet; he knew it was midnight, for the clock of Augusta's church across the park was ringing the hour. Augusta herself was there in the room, sitting in her old sewing-chair by the kerosene lamp, wrapped up in a shawl. She was reading a little much-worn religious book that she always carried in her handbag. . . .
> "When did you happen in?"
> "Not any too soon, sir," she said gravely, with a touch of reproof. "You never would take my cautions about that old stove, and it very nearly asphyxiated you. I was barely in time to pull you out." (277)

That the one avowedly Christian character in the novel is the person who discovers and rescues St. Peter marks a change in his life and may also be significant to Cather's life, since she had just recently joined the Episcopal Church (Woodress 1987, 337).

Before her crisis—whatever it was—in the early 1920s, Cather believed that art and religion are the same thing. In 1896, Cather had written a letter (paraphrased by Bohlke) to Mariel Gere in which "she had decided that there was no god but one God and that she believed Art was his revealer. . . . It was all she wanted from life, and she felt she could get as much good from it as other folk did from their religions" (Bohlke 1982, 66). For the Paterian aesthete or Epicurean, art provides some mystical ecstasy, a gem-like flame, a pulsation—again, words that connote a religious experience centered in the senses. If a person can no longer experience this pleasure in art, and if that person believes that art and religion are the same thing in the end, what is left for her? Simply, as St. Peter says, one must learn to live without delight: "Theoretically he knew that life is possible, may be even pleasant without joy, without passionate griefs. But it had never occurred to him that he might have to live like that" (282).

Returning to life after his near suicide, St. Peter lies on his couch contemplating Augusta's presence as she reads in the "little much-worn religious book that she always carried in her handbag" (277). He begins to think about his future:

> If he had thought of Augusta sooner, he would have got up from the couch sooner. Her image would have at once suggested the proper action. . . .
> Augusta, he reflected, had always been a corrective, a remedial influence.
> . . . [She] was like the taste of bitter herbs; she was the bloomless side of life that he had always run away from,—yet when he had to face it, he found that it wasn't altogether repugnant. (279–80).

Augusta's presence at this crisis of St. Peter's life indicates that he may now be willing to look more closely at religion as a basis for living.

We are informed throughout the novel that St. Peter is not terribly interested in things Christian or religious. His name, for example, is an early clue—God-free St. Peter. He is named for the disciple who denied Christ three times at the time of his crucifixion, but who, after being forgiven, became the leader of the Apostles, recognized as the first pope, and who ultimately died a true martyr's death. Certainly Cather intends this name to bring the first St. Peter to mind, yet her St. Peter is curiously unlike that St. Peter. He is not a Christian; indeed, he is "God-free." As a child, he had apparently received little or no religious training; his mother "was a Methodist, there was no Catholic church in our town in Kansas, and I guess my father forgot his religion" (99). He denies even this sketchy religious heritage throughout most of the book, but in the end he begins to see its value. To see his near-death experience as a conversion may be something of a stretch; however, the experience has made it possible for St. Peter to continue living.

In *The Professor's House*, Cather portrays an intellectual man coming to terms with a swiftly changing world—one that to him seems to be changing for the worse. Through Godfrey St. Peter, Cather reconciles us to living in a world without delight. Coming to terms with such a world means trading Epicureanism—serenity of spirit through contemplation of beauty resulting in pleasure—for something less satisfying but as yet unnamed. Cather leaves the professor with the option of choosing a religious way of looking at life: he is friends with Augusta; he still respects her; and he may follow her one day into the Roman Catholic Church. On the other hand, he may choose not to follow that path; indeed he may have given up delight for absolutely nothing and may become embittered as a result. Such was the ambiguity that many of the aesthetically alert no doubt experienced in Cather's time, an ambiguity that gives her work much of its richness and, yes, beauty.

NOTE

1. Yeats quotes Oscar Wilde in his memoir *Four Years* (1921) from a conversation he remembers having at the regular Sunday Evenings presided over by W. E. Henley. Yeats was astonished by Wilde's command of language and conversation as much as he was taken with Wilde's admiration of Pater.

WORKS CITED

Bible. New International Version.

Bloom, Harold. 1974. "Introduction." *Selected Writings of Walter Pater*. Edited by Harold Bloom. New York: Columbia University Press.

Book of Common Prayer and Administration of the Sacraments and Other Rites and Ceremonies of the Church Together with the Psalter or Psalms of David According to the Use of the Episcopal Church. 1988. New York: Oxford University Press.

Bohlke, Landall Brent. 1982. "Seeking is Finding: Willa Cather and Religion." PhD diss., University of Nebraska, Lincoln, 1982. ProQuest (AAT 8318649).

Cather, Willa. 1925. *The Professor's House*. New York: Grosset.

Harmon, William. 2012. *A Handbook to Literature*. 12th ed. New York: Longman.

Pater, Walter. 1873/1986. *The Renaissance: Studies in Art and Poetry*. Edited by Adam Phillips. Oxford: Oxford University Press.

———. 1885/1985. *Marius the Epicurean*. Edited by Michael Levey. New York: Viking Penguin.

———. 1888/1974. "Style." *Appreciations*. In *Selected Writings of Walter Pater*. Edited by Harold Bloom. New York: Columbia University Press.

Randall, John H. III. 1960. *The Landscape and the Looking Glass: Willa Cather's Search for Value*. Boston: Houghton Mifflin.

Soccio, Douglas J. 1995. *Archetypes of Wisdom*. 2nd ed. Belmont, CA: Wadsworth.

Turner, J. Hilton. 1947. "Epicurus and Friendship." *The Classical Journal* 42 (6): 351–55.

Wilde, Oscar. 1905/1913. *De Profundis*. London: Methuen. From Gutenberg eBook #921, 2007.

Woodress, James. 1987. *Willa Cather: A Literary Life*. Lincoln: University of Nebraska Press.

Yeats, William Butler. 1921/2004. *Four Years 1887–1891*. Oxford MS: Gutenberg eBook #6865.

Part II

The Visual Arts

Chapter 6

The Arts and Crafts on Willa Cather's Frontier

Leona Sevick

Willa Cather, whose reputation as a "prairie" writer once denied her a place among other twentieth-century modern writers, possessed a divided nature as both a writer concerned with aesthetic issues and as an active businesswoman interested in marketing her writing.[1] Cather rejected the crudest emblems of modernity—conspicuous, gaudy markers of consumption that seemed to disregard the importance and persistence of good taste, tradition, and history. She had a keen aesthetic sensibility that guided her taste not only in poetry and writing but in clothing, furnishings, food, and art. She abandoned the boys' clothes in which, as a young girl, she was most comfortable and chose clothes that were attractive and well made, like the furniture with which she and Edith Lewis decorated their Bank Street apartment (Stout 2002, #97).[2] Cather's personal taste and writing philosophy were guided by her interest in quality materials and the value of simplicity, and so she dedicated a good deal of time to corresponding with publishers about paper quality, jacket and page design, and the placement and size of illustrations in her books. She was as interested in the production quality of her books as she was in the quality of her subjects and the language she used to render them. Indeed, Cather's writing concerns reflected contiguity with the aesthetic ideals of the Arts and Crafts, a movement that profoundly affected American society during its transition into the modern age. Cather outlined her own aesthetic interests in her 1922 essay "The Novel Démeublé": "The novel manufactured to entertain great multitudes of people must be considered exactly like a cheap soap or a cheap perfume, or cheap furniture. Fine quality is a distinct disadvantage in articles made for great numbers of people who do not want quality but quantity, who do not want a thing that 'wears,' but who want change, —a succession of new things that are quickly threadbare and can be lightly thrown away" (Cather 1936a/1988, 44).

While there is little evidence in her correspondence or other essays to suggest that Cather was directly influenced by a particular aesthetic ideology, her personal and professional interests seem to be very much in line with the ideals of this extraordinary movement. These ideals are made manifest in her depictions of characters in three of her most admired novels, *O Pioneers!*, *The Song of the Lark*, and *My Ántonia*. Cather, who declared in 1936 in her letter in *Commonweal*, "Escapism," that "Economics and art are strangers," insisted on distancing her artistic interests from the business of money-making (Cather 1936b/1988, 27). However, like promoters of the Arts and Crafts movement (and later Art Nouveau) who built fortunes on the rhetoric of aesthetic integrity, Cather's characters benefit financially from their simple tastes and lifestyles. While her admiration for the Arts and Crafts and its traditional underpinnings is evident in these novels, Cather also acknowledges that modern skills and forward-thinking attitudes help to create successful, vital people in twentieth-century America. Tradition, simplicity, and quality—hallmarks of the Arts and Crafts movement—also serve the modern drive for success and advancement in Cather's prairie novels.

The focus of this essay is the relationship between Cather and the Arts and Crafts movement, which began in England in the late nineteenth century and made its mark in America at the turn of the century under the direction of Oxford art historian John Ruskin and socialist writer and poet William Morris (Kaplan 1987). In 1896 Cather wrote that she admired Ruskin's belief "[t]hat beauty alone is truth, and truth is only beauty; that art is supreme" (Cather 1896/1966, 402). The most visible promoters of the Arts and Crafts movement in America were the furniture makers Elbert Hubbard and Gustav Stickley. Hubbard's New York craft community of furniture makers, called the Roycrofters, was, like other nineteenth-century experimental socialist communities, committed to self-support and a pleasing work environment for its inhabitants. Both Hubbard and Stickley began their own presses and modeled them after Morris's Kelmscott Press to promote the Arts and Crafts ideal in America. Their widely circulated publications, *The Philistine* (1895–1915) and *The Craftsman* (1901–1916), respectively, enjoyed faithful readerships for over a decade and inspired a number of similar publications and Arts and Crafts advertisements in America. *McClure's* magazine carried advertisements similar to the ones that appear in magazines like *The Philistine* and *The Craftsman*. Ads for Roycrofters' furniture, special book editions,

Figure 6.1. "Beauty for the Boudoir," Libbey Glass advertisement from *McClure's* Magazine, October 1904. Digital image credit: Willa Cather Pioneer Memorial Collection, Nebraska State Historical Society.

decorative glassware, and Pears' Soap, to name a few, appear in *McClure's* during the time of Cather's editorship. Here, advertisers appeal to the public's interest in "simplicity" and "quality," catchphrases used by Arts and Crafts advocates.

Still, most historians agree that Arts and Crafts in America strayed from the stricter socialist ideals that characterized the movement in England; and in spite of the spirit of labor reform and aesthetic design that Hubbard and Stickley espoused in their lectures and publications, the partners were thoroughgoing businessmen concerned with the sale of their products. According to one cultural historian, "Although Stickley and Hubbard might make favorable employers by offering cleaner, quieter, more desirable workplaces than the completely automated factory and by upholding the value of an individual's workmanship, their views on labor were far from the socialist ideal. . . . At best, Hubbard's press [as well as Stickley's] subtly blended socialism and capitalism using the rhetoric of the former to endorse the practice of the latter" (Willburn 1994, 56–57).

Although the movement's ideologues and critics in America resided in cities where industry and the arts flourished—Chicago, London, Paris— Cather's fiction shows us how the Arts and Crafts philosophy made its way into the small western towns of her prairie novels. In Cather's work, we see that these movements were deeply paradoxical: they offered their adherents a return to simpler ways of approaching their domestic affairs and their labor, and at the same time they helped to underscore the practices of a consumer culture. T. J. Jackson Lears argues that in the late nineteenth century, white, middle-class Americans experienced a renewed engagement in a preindustrial work culture that accepted the tenets and philosophies of the American Arts and Crafts movement. Through an interest in the Arts and Crafts, along with other "premodern" interests like militarism and spirituality, Americans waged an "antimodern protest" against capitalism and consumerism (Lears 1981, 58). While Cather's response to the Arts and Crafts seems to support Lears's theories, the antimodern protest and accommodation model is complicated in Cather's fiction by a variety of class, gender, ethnic, and environmental circumstances not taken into account in Lears's historical analysis. This variety, represented in Cather's fictional world by the immigrant, poor, female, queer, or otherwise misfit characters that appear in her fiction, portrays another face of antimodern protest, one in which the struggle for efficacy and power is more trenchantly felt than the need for spiritual regeneration. Cather's brand of antimodernism is more democratic and representative in its scope. By tracking the development—and decline— of the Arts and Crafts movement through characters and events in *O Pioneers!*, *The Song of the Lark*, and finally *My Ántonia*, we see how frontier Americans coped with the rapid social and economic changes that were moving at them from both shores. As this essay will show, these movements provided Cather's characters with a means of successfully connecting to a fully modernized twentieth century while maintaining a sort of homegrown integrity that seemed practical, pure, and honest.

O Pioneers! offers readers the inspirational figure of Alexandra Bergson, a woman whose respect for tradition and her own Swedish heritage, as well as her engaging simplicity, not only ally her with the values of the Arts and Crafts movement but also work in her favor as she acquires land and builds a solid financial empire. Alexandra embodies a commitment to both tradition and modernity, thus showing these categories to be overlapping. As Alexandra and Carl Linstrum ride home from Hanover at the beginning of the novel, she exhibits her commitment to the future as well as her abiding respect for the traditions that are part of her Swedish past. She respects the old Swedish ways and traditions in her home, a place where Mrs. Lee, her neighbor, can come and "do all the old things in the old way" (Cather 1913/1992, 91). Alexandra "liked plain things herself" (92), much like the objects in Ivar's humble, natural sod dwelling where he lives because he dislikes human habitations (84). The sitting room is where "Alexandra [had] brought together the old homely furniture that the Bergsons used in their first log house, the family portraits, and the few things her mother brought from Sweden" (80). What makes the room and its furnishings pleasant are their sincerity, practicality, and the folk tradition that define the Arts and Crafts movement and that are accurate characterizations of Alexandra herself. The comfortable, aesthetically pleasing home is also central to the Arts and Crafts ideology, and its advocates regarded the home and its decoration as the site of powerful moral influence in the community. In an interview in a 1905 issue of the *Artsman*, Mrs. Herbert Nelson, a home decorator, underscores the monumental importance of home decoration when she writes, "Inartistic homes ruin our manners and morals and wreck our nervous systems" (Boris 1905/1987, 220). Alexandra hires Swedish girls to maintain her household in familiar, simple, Swedish fashion, and she rejects poor quality items the Hanover furniture dealer has pawned off on her to satisfy the less discerning tastes of her family, whose own homes must have boasted what one advertisement for Arts and Crafts furniture condemns as "the depressing atmosphere of over-decorated & over-finished stuff" (*The Philistine* 1904). Even as Arts and Crafts ideology began to give way to more complex Art Nouveau styles, many interior designers leaned toward simplicity.

In Alexandra we find the finest qualities of the past and hope in the future, a combination that both aligns her with the spirit of the Arts and Crafts and identifies her as modern. Just as Alexandra seems to have an uncanny ability to recognize what the future of the farm will bring, she also recognizes that it is men like Emil—"more Swedish than any of

[them]" (Cather 1913/1992, 108)—who represent the future. Her successful farm ventures have been in service to Emil's education, both at the
university and later during his trip to Mexico, where he goes to have a
look around before he begins to study law in one of the big cities. Emil,
Alexandra believes, is part of the next generation that need not make its
fortune from backbreaking work in the soil. Although many Arts and
Crafts advocates idealized rural, agrarian life, imagining a kind of cooperative farm life and pure living, it is clear in this novel that Alexandra
sees her farm work as a business meant to cultivate a new kind of man
meant for a modern world.

While Emil represents in Alexandra's life the kind of balanced nature
that joins the past with modern sensibilities, other characters in the novel
do not adjust well to modernity. Carl Linstrum aligns himself with the
Arts and Crafts—he is passionate about wood engraving and decries
"cheap metal work" (113)—but he does not adjust well to modern life.
When he returns to Alexandra as an adult, he is broken and sad (107).
Alexandra's brothers Lou and Oscar represent the stagnation that attends
the failure to adjust to modernity along with its speculative business
practices. When poor farming yields discourage the brothers, it is Alexandra who takes correct stock of the land and convinces the brothers to
buy more and to experiment with new farming and planting techniques.
Experimental farming, developed in response to modernity's demands
for more quickly produced yields, was of great interest to Arts and Crafts
advocates like Mary Ware Dennett of the Society of Arts and Crafts in
Boston, and she wrote about such techniques in the April 1903 issue of
Handicraft, a popular Arts and Crafts magazine (noted in Boris 1905/1987,
212). Other "university ideas" about farming, like the growing of alfalfa
(Cather 1913/1992, 154), make their way into the daily operation of the
Bergson farm under Alexandra's management. Like the bankers and
businessmen in town who buy when others sell, Alexandra has the cool
head and confidence of a successful investor, and she understands the
workings of the market. This novel, which some have read as an idyllic
tale about the fruits of the land and its hardworking people, is also the
story of sound financial investment.[3]

Although the very best sentiments of the Arts and Crafts movement in
this novel may seem undermined by the enormity of Alexandra's success
and the affinities that help to shape that success, they are not. The Arts
and Crafts movement in America was very much in line with the spirit
of capitalist progress that marks the modern era. The Bergson farm is no
socialist experiment in subsistence farming or shared profits. Like the
successful turn-of-the-century furniture manufacturing business of Stickley, the farm is a money-making venture. It is a lucrative enterprise that
remains secure. In spite of Alexandra's generosity toward her neighbors

and perhaps *because of* her attractive appreciation for the simple things in the rural good life, Alexandra has managed to create a successful business. While her unshaken connection to the land expresses the benign, philanthropic spirit of the Arts and Crafts movement, Alexandra's final words in the novel are important: "We come and go, but the land is always here. And the people who love it and understand it are the people who own it—for a little while" (272–73). Clearly tied to Alexandra's belief that one only comes to "love" and "understand" through enterprise is her commentary on the transitory and speculative nature of ownership. The Arts and Crafts movement, whatever lofty aims its aesthetic rhetoric promoted, also helped to open the door to commercial success, a point that Cather explores in *O Pioneers!*

The Song of the Lark, Cather's most fully realized alignment with the Arts and Crafts philosophy, held that folk art forms, traditional values, and primitivism—when properly cultivated or "worked"—could help to thin the divide between worthwhile craft and fine art. In cultivating her singing career, Thea Kronborg draws on her knowledge of folk art forms and the traditional forms and values that she finds in Moonstone. One example of her early appreciation of folk art is her admiration of the Kohler's "piece-picture." The picture, woven by Fritz Kohler as his apprentice thesis, represents Napoleon's retreat from Moscow in beautifully shaded wool. Thea "was never tired of examining this work, of hearing how long it had taken Fritz to make it" (Cather 1915/1988, 26). Like her training to become a singer, the effort, time, and skill that went into the piece lent inspiration and individuality to the art. Thea's apprenticeship, unlike Fritz's, teaches her to make her way in a modern world that depends on commercial success and on the power of capital; and as the novel progresses, Thea becomes a successful entrepreneur—one who markets her own skills for profit in a way that is even more spectacular than in Cather's previous novel. In this way, tradition and progress are yoked together in Cather's modern consciousness.

While extolling the virtues of Thea's "natural" gifts, Andor Harsanyi, her voice teacher, compares her voice to something most *unnatural*: "Everything about her indicated it—the big mouth, the wide jaw and chin, the strong white teeth, the deep laugh. The machine was so simple and strong, seemed to be so easily operated" (171). Here, Harsanyi reconciles the natural, raw quality of Thea's voice with its machine-like reliability and ease of motion, a point that would appeal to those who believed that under the artist's direction the machine could produce unparalleled and nearly effortless beauty. Although Ruskin had openly condemned the use of machines because of their stultifying effect on the worker as well as the poor quality of goods he believed they produced, Frank Lloyd Wright believed that machines were useful to workers and beneficial to the overall aesthetic principles that the Arts and Crafts espoused. The out-spoken Wright, who once declared that "my god is machinery" (quoted in Kaplan 1987, 59), managed to convince many others, like professor of English at the University of Chicago and founder of the Chicago Arts and Crafts Society Oscar Lovell Triggs, that machines could produce beauti-ful, functional objects when they were correctly managed by skilled art-ists. Most important, Wright believed that machines freed human work-ers from many mundane, mind-dulling, and body-wasting tasks. Both Wright and Triggs committed themselves to the technological advances of modernity, which they believed did not compromise their Arts and Crafts aesthetic and labor ideology.

The trip Thea takes to Fred Ottenburg's Cliff-Dweller ruins in Panther Canyon becomes a turning point in her life. She admires the old, fine ma-sonry of the houses, the natural landscape of cedars and cottonwoods that frame their beauty, and she takes over one of the dwellings, fitting it with Navajo blankets and making it as thoroughly comfortable and simple as her tiny bedroom at home. Absent here are the clumsy furnishings and ugly additions that she found in the Moonstone parlors and the boarding houses of Chicago. Like Arts and Crafts advocates eager to development a "new" aesthetic based on the solid construction and simple design of past forms, Thea indulges in the simple tastes of the ancient Sinagua in her adopted living space (Moseley, 2003, 219-20).

Numerous *Craftsman* and *Artsman* articles lauded the benefits of a primitive retreat for those engaged in the workaday world of business; journalist Sylvester Baxter, writing about Arts and Crafts philosophy in 1903, argued, "we can in great measure bring into play the primitive springs of thought, impulse, and action that exist in every human be-ing and so put ourselves *en rapport* with the primitive state of mind and primitive view of things" (quoted in Lears 1981, 92). The observation speaks to Thea's sympathetic relation to these primitive inspirations and how she puts them to good use. When Fred joins her in the canyon, he recognizes the ways in which Thea naturally exploits her environment, telling her that "you ride and fence and walk and climb, but I know that all the while you're getting somewhere in your mind. All these things are instruments; and I, too, am an instrument" (Cather 1915/1988, 283). Cather's keen interest in physical health here was also in keeping with the importance that Arts and Crafts advocates placed on the integrity and upkeep of raw materials.

From Moonstone and, even more significantly, from her sojourn in Walnut Canyon, Thea is better prepared to face the challenges that await her in Chicago and beyond. She remembers Ray Kennedy's feelings about cliff dwellings and how "all these things made one feel that one ought to do one's best" (275). In these natural spaces, edifying effects combine with Thea's ambition to become successful beyond the hopes of provincials like her parents. Her enterprising business sense helps to form a corporation out of her artistic talents, one in which a number of unwitting investors—the Kohlers, Spanish Johnny, Ray Kennedy, and the Cliff-Dwellers—all have their share. That not all of these investors reap the rewards of their rightful portion is of no consequence; Thea spends her own share wisely. She is, as the epilogue declares, a perfect example of "Moonstone enterprise" (417), proving herself a successful modern through her ties to premodern culture.

Work is a central theme in Cather's 1918 novel *My Ántonia* about the brutal realities of farm life and the disappointed idealisms of youth. Like Thea, Jim Burden leaves Black Hawk for good, but he doesn't carry with him the primitive, folk inspiration that in the *Song of the Lark* transforms itself into the means of driving a successful career. Jim's memories of Ántonia and of his small town are romantic and, we suspect as readers, unreliable. In *My Ántonia*, there is a marked shift from the optimism of Alexandra's agrarian life outside of Hanover (in spite of the tragedy of Marie and Emil, who, after all, violate the rule of moderation) to the horrors that Jim communicates to readers early in this novel—a shift that may have been influenced by the atrocities of modern warfare and the subsequent decline of the Arts and Crafts.

Interiors in the novel recreate the beautiful, natural surroundings that Jim comes to love in his leisurely jaunts about the prairie. The Burdens' civilized home is juxtaposed to the dirty, gloomy mud dugout of the Shimerdas, who must depend on the kindness of their neighbors to survive their first months on the prairie. Mr. Shimerda was, like Fritz Kohler, a skilled tapestry and upholstery weaver, but like so many immigrants who made their way to America, he left his handicraft skills behind to discover himself thrust into the unfamiliar and brutal world of farming, the kind of work that his clever hands are ill suited for (Cather 1918/1994, 19–20). Unlike *O Pioneers!*, where the reader is not witness to the harsh farming realities of the Bergson's earliest endeavors, this novel traces the lives of immigrant farmers from their very first arrival. For the Bohemians, farming is again no idealized agricultural experience; it is a brutal means of survival.

After Mr. Shimerda shoots himself, and Jim's grandparents go to the family, Jim settles himself comfortably at home, where "it flashed upon [him] that if Mr. Shimerda's soul were lingering about in this world at all, it would be here, in our house, which had been more to his liking than any other in the neighborhood. . . . If he could have lived with us, this terrible thing would never have happened" (97). For Jim, the comforts of a clean and well-furnished home should be enough to save a man from the desperate act of suicide. Even Otto Fuch's coffin-making takes on an Arts and Crafts feel and significance: the "panting wheeze of the saw or the pleasing purring of the plane . . . were such cheerful noises" (105), and Jim admires how Otto "handled the tools as if he liked the feel of them; and when he planed, his hands went back and forth over the boards in an eager, beneficent way as if he were blessing them" (106). The beauty and the sheer craftsman's joy that goes into this woodworking, along with Jim's contented inspiration that Mr. Shimerda's spirit is lurking about the warmth of the Burdens' simple and practical home, offers readers a comforting response to the horror of a man's suicide, in itself a desperate answer to the brutalities and realities of farm labor and frontier life. Jim's response to this event, which suggests that a comfortable home will serve as a panacea to bloody death, is a hollow one. Perhaps in the aftermath of World War I, a wholesale belief in the civilizing and moral effects of a practical home seemed a hollow preoccupation. When the Burdens relocate to the town of Black Hawk in Book II, Jim becomes more and more restless and critical of the little town that he once cherished. He looks derisively on "The Black Hawk boys" who "looked forward to marrying Black Hawk girls, and living in a brand-new little house with best chairs that must not be sat upon, and hand-painted china that must not be used" (195), and he despises the "white-handed, high-collared clerks and bookkeepers" (198). Like many Arts and Crafts proponents, Jim detests non-utilitarian poseurs and effeminate, office-bound paper-pushers. But for all of his alignment with the philosophies of the movement, Jim himself is guilty of empty boasting, and in a test of his physical strength, he shows himself to be vulnerable and weak. His boyhood battle with a giant rattler, which earned him Ántonia's enduring respect and admiration, was, Jim admits, nothing more than a boy's adventure, and Wick Cutter's attack is emasculating. He is, perhaps, overcivilized, and in spite of his admiration for physical heartiness and strength, he hasn't the fortitude and savvy of an Alexandra or a Thea, or even a Lena Lingard. His success in a modern world—material, emotional, and psychological—is jeopardized by his failure to successfully adapt to his environment.

While Jim's Lincoln days, in which he unconvincingly and ineffectually pursues Lena, do not present him as a "greedy businessman," he does eventually become a successful lawyer for the largest kind of capitalist venture—the railroad; and unlike Lena he drifts away from any supportive community that could offer him comfort and grounding (Tisdale 1997, 177). Although Lena, through her work in dress design and tailoring, seems to be pursuing a craftsman lifestyle that Arts and Crafts advocates would have lauded, she nonetheless exists on the periphery of the story, a point that is underscored by her eventual move to the far western city of San Francisco. Her new life in the west is told second-hand, and while hers is a subtle move away from the heart of enterprise and advancement, Jim's move to New York City drops him into the very center of capitalist America. The good, fulfilling handwork that Lena does is eclipsed by the kinds of big business ventures that Jim must be engaged in—ventures that lead up to the beginning of World War I. And Cather's narrative witnesses not only the end of the Arts and Crafts period but the beginning of a new period of national inspiration—a deadly one in which technology will play a larger, less artistic, and less benevolent role.

By 1918, World War I and the Arts and Crafts movement were over. And through *My Ántonia* and her later, more modern novels Cather recognized that the beliefs propounded in *O Pioneers!* (and to some degree in *The Song of the Lark*)—that machines produced beauty, that handiwork and agriculture assured cooperative and fair business dealings, and that well-crafted, practical home interiors promised moral behavior—were impossibly naïve. While Alexandra Bergson and Thea Kronborg both become successful businesswomen, in part because of their effective alignment with Arts and Crafts ideals, the hopeful nostalgia of the Arts and Crafts philosophy in *My Ántonia* is undercut by Jim's narrow and often immature narrative perspective as well as his unmitigated involvement in modernity's big business world.

Cather would continue her criticism of modern values in *One of Ours*, when Claude Wheeler, whose brother's collection of useless gadgets "would have put a boy through college decently" (Cather 1922/2006, 19), discovers that machines "could not make pleasure, whatever else they could do. They could not make agreeable people, either" (38). And in her homage to a lost frontier, *A Lost Lady*, the narrative gives an accurate account of Cather's own desire for simplicity and quality when it describes the Forresters' home: "encircled by porches, too narrow for modern notions of comfort, supported by the fussy, fragile pillars of that time, when every honest stick of timber was tortured by the turning-lathe into something hideous" (Cather 1923/1997, 8). In *The Professor's House* (1925) Godfrey St. Peter has difficulty abandoning the inconvenient beauty of his old home, and his nostalgic values are continuously juxtaposed with Louie Marcellus's progressive ones. What begins in Cather's prairie novels as a growing distaste for ugly, shabby goods, conspicuous consumption, and useless technological complexity becomes, in her next three novels, a profound comment on the rapid decline of American labor and aesthetics. Although national interest in the Arts and Crafts movement was relatively short lived, Cather spent a lifetime dedicating herself and her work to the aesthetic ideals that aligned her with this movement and that were reflected in her very best writing.

NOTES

1. For more information on Cather's relationship to her publishers and on the reasons for her move from Houghton Mifflin to Alfred A. Knopf, see historical essays by Susan Rosowski (1997) in *A Lost Lady* and by Richard Harris (2006) in *One of Ours*. David Porter (2008) discusses Cather's divided aesthetic and material nature at length in his book *On the Divide: The Many Lives of Willa Cather*.

2. In her letter Cather makes reference to choosing furnishings with her parents (Stout 2002, #97), selecting the color of jackets and weight of paper for her books.

3. According to Alan Trachtenberg (1982, 52), mechanical advances in farming as well as new kinds of crops contributed to an unparalleled growth in the agricultural market and in productivity, and so the "total agricultural output [in America] tripl[ed] between 1870 and 1900," the time period during which the novel is set. The Bergson farm is only one example of how this "native industrialization" came about.

WORKS CITED

Boris, Eileen. 1905/1987. "Dream of Brotherhood and Beauty: The Social Ideas of the Arts and Crafts Movement." In *"The Art That Is Life": The Arts and Crafts Movement in America, 1875–1920*. Edited by Wendy Kaplan, 208–222. Boston: Little, Brown.

Cather, Willa. 1896/1966. "Ruskin." In *The Kingdom of Art: Willa Cather's First Principles and Critical Statements, 1893–1896*. Edited by Bernice Slote. Lincoln: University of Nebraska Press.

———. 1913/1992. *O Pioneers!* Willa Cather Scholarly Edition. Edited by Susan J. Rosowski and Charles W. Mignon with Kathleen Danker. Historical essay and explanatory notes by David Stouck. Lincoln: University of Nebraska Press.

———. 1915/1988. *The Song of the Lark*. Boston: Houghton Mifflin.

———. 1918/1994. *My Ántonia*. Willa Cather Scholarly Edition. Edited by Charles W. Mignon with Kari A. Ronning. Historical essay by James Woodress. Explanatory notes by James Woodress with Kari Ronning, Kathleen Danker, and Emily Levine. Lincoln: University of Nebraska Press.

———. 1922/2006. *One of Ours*. Willa Cather Scholarly Edition. Edited by Frederick M. Link with Kari A. Ronning. Historical essay and explanatory notes by Richard C. Harris. Lincoln: University of Nebraska Press.

———. 1923/1997. *A Lost Lady*. Willa Cather Scholarly Edition. Edited by Charles W. Mignon and Frederick M. Link with Kari A. Ronning. Historical essay and explanatory notes by Susan J. Rosowski with Kari A. Ronning. Explanatory notes by Kari A. Ronning. Lincoln: University of Nebraska Press.

———. 1936a/1988. "The Novel Démeublé." In *Not under Forty*, 43–51. Lincoln: University of Nebraska Press.

———. 1936b/1988. "Escapism." In *Willa Cather on Writing: Critical Studies on Writing as an Art*, 18–29. Lincoln: University of Nebraska Press.

———. 1966. *The Kingdom of Art: Willa Cather's First Principles and Critical Statements, 1893–1896*. Edited by Bernice Slote. Lincoln: University of Nebraska Press.

Harris, Richard. 2006. "Historical Essay." In *One of Ours*, Scholarly Edition, 613–75. Lincoln: The University of Nebraska Press.

Hubbard, Elbert, ed. 1895–1915. *The Philistine: A Periodical of Protest*. East Aurora, NY: The Society.

Kaplan, Wendy. 1987. *"The Art That Is Life": The Arts and Crafts Movement in America, 1875–1920*. Boston: Little, Brown.

Lears, T. J. Jackson. 1981. *No Place of Grace: Antimodernism and the Transformation of American Culture 1880–1920*. New York: Pantheon.

McClure, S. S., ed. 1893–1926. *McClure's* magazine. New York.

Moseley, Ann. 2003. "The Creative Ecology of Walnut Canyon: From the Sinagua to Thea Kronborg." In *Cather Studies 5*. Edited by Susan J. Rosowski, 216–236. Lincoln: University of Nebraska Press.

The Philistine. 1904 Volume 19 (4): 17.

Porter, David. 2008. *On the Divide: Willa Cather's Many Lives*. Lincoln: University of Nebraska Press.

Rosowski, Susan, with Kari A. Ronnig. 1997. "Historical Essay." In *A Lost Lady*, Scholarly Edition, 177–233. Lincoln: University of Nebraska Press.

Stout, Janis P. 2002. *A Calendar of the Letters of Willa Cather*. Lincoln: University of Nebraska Press.

Tisdale, Judy Jones. 1997. "Working Women on the Frontier: Capitalism and Community in Three Willa Cather Novels." In *The Image of the Frontier in Literature, the Media, and Society*, edited by Will Wright and Steven Kaplan, 177–84. Pueblo: University of Southern Colorado.

Trachtenberg, Alan. 1982. *The Incorporation of America: Culture and Society in the Gilded Age*. New York: Hill and Wang.

Willburn, Sarah. 1994. "Crafting Objects, Crafting Subjects: The Arts and Crafts Movement in Late Nineteenth Century America." *The Mid-Atlantic Almanac* 3: 55–63.

Chapter 7

Cather's "Twilight Stage"

Aestheticism, Tonalism, and Modernist Sentiment

Joseph C. Murphy

In an 1894 theater review, Willa Cather compares Julia Marlowe's acting to James McNeill Whistler's painting as examples of art that is "all very winning and beautiful, but . . . not the highest kind. . . . Mr. Whistler's nocturnes in color are ravishingly beautiful things, but they have not the power or the greatness of the old faded frescoes that told roughly of hell and heaven and death and judgment. After all, the supreme virtue in all art is soul, perhaps it is the only thing which gives art a right to be. . . . All prettiness for its own sake is trivial, all beauty for beauty's sake is sensual. No matter how dainty, how refined, how *spirituelle*, it is still a thing of the senses only" (Cather 1970, 37). Cather's statement is laced with the ambivalence that characterized American attitudes toward Whistler and Aestheticism generally during the 1890s. In advocating "soul" over "refine[ment]," Cather effectively joined a debate about the relationship between Whistler and American tonalism, a movement that dominated American landscape art at the turn of the century and looked to Whistler, searchingly but warily, for inspiration. Although their muted half-tones and twilit atmospheres suggested kinship with the avant-garde American expatriate, the tonalists stressed art's spiritual and emotional content rather than art for art's sake. Nevertheless, his technical similarities were too striking, and Whistler himself too outsized a figure, for the tonalists and their critical circle to ignore. Like Cather, these American artists and critics acknowledged Whistler's painting as "refined," even praised it as "beautiful"; increasingly, however, they turned a blind eye

95

to his Aestheticist intentions and viewed his works as mediums of soul and emotion—reading as deeply spiritual what Cather here dismisses as *"spirituelle."*[1]

As a writer and critic, Cather became an interested observer of tonalism; approving references to tonalist painters—George Inness, Dwight William Tryon, Birge Harrison, and others—are scattered through her early journalism. She viewed tonalist works in museums in the United States and abroad and met some of the artists at exhibits and at Connecticut's Cos Cob art colony. By the turn of the century, her mention of them had outpaced her notice of Whistler. Although we have no evidence that Cather herself participated in the tonalists' rereading of Whistler, she did come to recognize the higher possibilities in the tonal style all these artists shared. It was through tonalism that she eventually embraced a customized aestheticism—emotionalized, spiritualized, and Americanized. This spiritualized aestheticism helped Cather forge her own brand of American modernism comprising states of feeling, national references, and formal experiments beyond the scope of the English Aesthetic tradition.

Tonalism was the signature American landscape style between 1880 and 1920, although less recognized today than the broken brushstrokes and high-keyed colors of the contemporaneous impressionist school.[2] The concept of "tone" refers to two techniques: the use of a prevailing color, usually a cool shade of green, blue, violet, or grey (Corn 1972, 3); and glazing, "successive applications of thin washes of pigment suspended in oil or varnish, through which light could penetrate . . . and be reflected back" to form an atmospheric veil (Gerdts 1982, 26). Together, these strategies create blurring, vibrating, and shimmering effects through a narrow chromatic range—conveying, for many turn-of-the-century viewers, a sense of profound feeling diffused across the picture plane.

Tonalism was a typically American enterprise, at once conservative and experimental: its craftsmanship was the last stand of American academicism, while its subjectivity and abstraction anticipated postimpressionism (Gerdts 1982, 25–26; Corn 1972, 19–20). In addition to Whistler and English Aestheticism, tonalism channeled a range of transatlantic influences, all of which shaped Cather as well: the French Barbizon painters Jean-Baptiste-Camille Corot and Charles-François Daubigny, the German Barbizon or Hague school of Josef Israels and Anton Mauve, and the French Symbolists, including Pierre Puvis de Chavannes (Cleveland 2004, 13). New York's Lotos Club, which championed the style during the 1890s, mounted two exhibitions sketching a tradition: Some Tonal Paintings of the Old Dutch, Old English, Barbizon, Modern Dutch, and American School (1896) and Tonal Paintings: Ancient and Modern (1897) (Becker 2005, 31). Although Whistler was not represented in these shows, he

Figure 7.1. Dwight W. Tryon, American, 1849–1925, *Midsummer Moonrise*, 1892. Oil on wood, 48.7 × 65.1 cm (19 1/8 × 25 5/8 in.), Smithsonian American Art Museum. Gift of International Business Machines Corporation.

was, despite himself, a key personality in the tonalist movement (Merrill 2005, 61). As Wanda Corn observes, "Whistler's popularization of musical phraseology"—symphony, harmony, note, tone—"to emphasize the abstract nature of paintings was widely adopted by American painters and critics to describe tonalist works, although the paintings themselves were rarely informed with the same refined estheticism which was found in the master's work" (Corn 1972, 9).

The spiritualism the tonalists injected into Whistler's aestheticism was associated with the other guiding light of the movement: the American landscape master George Inness. Inness developed a late style, detectable from the 1870s, that overthrew the picturesque and narrative foundations of his midcentury work in the Hudson River School. His landscapes became, as critical commentary tracked them, "suggestive," "indefinite," "softened," and "ghost[ly]." He was first called a "tonalist" in 1884,[3] although Inness himself never adopted the label (he died in 1894 before its widespread use). Inness insisted on his art's philosophical depth, informed by his reading of the eighteenth-century Swedish mystic philosopher Emanuel Swedenborg and expressed in his own voluminous meditations on geometry, color, and divine truth (Cikovsky 2005, 53,

56–57). The tonalists and their critical retinue appreciated Inness's paint-ings for their "soul," "mood," "feeling," "sentiment," and "poetry."[4] If "sentiment" was a watchword for the tonalists, it was also a vexed term, to be carefully distinguished from Victorian sentimentality. Although the tonalists rejected Whistler's declaration that "[a]rt . . . should stand alone, and appeal to the artistic sense of eye and ear," they readily agreed with him that painters should not traffic in such storybook emotions "as devo-tion, pity, love, patriotism, and the like" (Whistler 1892/1967, 127–28). They pursued mysterious, inchoate feelings—not responses to narrative but to the dialectical tensions animating their paintings, between time and timelessness, place and placelessness, form and feeling.

In contrast to Whistler's aloof refinement (Merrill 2005, 69–70), tonal-ism's sentiment responded to American conditions, to the lingering trauma of the Civil War and the fresh upheavals of urbanization and industrialization. Corn characterizes the feeling communicated by tonalist works as "'loss'—a pervasive though understated melancholy that these artists felt as their familiar world succumbed to alien and mechanical forces" (Corn 1972, 2). However, tonalism went beyond nostalgia; it em-bodied a "progressive mindset" that was both "avatar of" and "antidote to" change (Cleveland 2010, 16, 353). By providing a kind of emotional

Figure 7.2. George Inness, American, 1825–1894, *The Home of the Heron,* 1893. Oil on canvas, 76.2 × 115.2 cm (30 × 45 in.), Edward B. Butler Collection, 1911.31, The Art Institute of Chicago. Photography © The Art Institute of Chicago.

conditioning for the shocks of modern life, tonalism moved closer than Whistlerian aestheticism to the mainstream of American modernism. In an essay on Cather's modernism, Richard H. Millington describes American modernist culture as a large-scale challenge to the simplifying dichotomies of the Victorian era, between civilization and barbarism, high and low, male and female, public and private, all of which served the end-driven ideology of progress.[5] Although the tonalist movement took shape from such Victorian dichotomies—the opposition between business and spirituality, for example—its alluring dreamscapes portrayed experience as unbounded and fluid. As such, tonalism was a harbinger of the modernist culture in which Cather would participate—a culture that, in art, science, and popular expression, would blur traditional distinctions, cast aside prudential narratives, and pursue what Millington identifies as Cather's central project: "the making of meaning itself" (Millingon 2005, 56). Tonalism's strangely scintillating surfaces, I contend, guided Cather's attention toward what Millington calls "acts of making and forms of feeling cut free from the depth-seeking, ending-hungry, explanation-driven trajectories of Victorian culture"—toward "a new sense of the sources of meaning and value . . . a new repertoire of response" (Millington 2005, 63).

Tonalism's influence on Cather is evident in her statements about how fiction should operate. "A novel should be like a symphony, developed from one theme, one dominating tone," she said in a 1931 interview (Cather 1986, 111). Her flagship essay, "The Novel Démeublé" (1922)— which commends authors who, "following the development of modern painting . . . present their scene by suggestion rather than enumeration"— casts even *The Scarlet Letter* in tonal terms: "[I]n the twilight melancholy of that book, in its consistent mood, one can scarcely ever see the actual surroundings of the people; one feels them, rather, in the dusk" (Cather 1922/1988, 40). For Cather tonal refinement is not only an aesthetic goal but a register of elusive feelings. By the climax of "The Novel Démeublé" Cather has shifted her attention from a novel's "tone" to its "over-tone," from the fine-tuned medium to the unnamable feeling suspended there: "It is the inexplicable presence of the thing not named, of the over-tone divined by the ear but not heard by it, the verbal mood, the emotional aura of the fact or the thing or the deed, that gives high quality to the novel or the drama, as well as to poetry itself" (Cather 1922/1988, 50). As the tonalist Henry Ward Ranger wrote in 1894, great art is distinguished by "the poetic impulse, the deep feeling, the suggestion of more than is expressed, the power of making you feel" (Ranger 1894, 25).

Cather became conversant with American tonalism by frequenting the places where the movement was taking shape. During her Pittsburgh years (1896–1906), the Carnegie Institute of Art provided ready access to major tonalist works by Inness, Tryon, and others.[6] Abroad in 1902,

Cather saw at the Luxembourg Gallery paintings by tonalists Ben Foster and John White Alexander, a Pittsburgh native, hanging beside works by Whistler, John Singer Sargent, and Winslow Homer, all of which appeared to her to be "comparable [in technical excellence] only to . . . the masters of modern France" (Cather 1970, 883). It was probably after her return from Europe that Cather began to visit the Cos Cob art colony on the Connecticut coast, where she hobnobbed on a scene that included tonalists Birge Harrison and Leonard Ochtman, as well as several impressionists who incorporated, at turns, the tonalists' misty atmosphere and muted color: J. Alden Weir, Theodore Robinson, John Twachtman, and Childe Hassam (Skaggs 2000, 43, 48; Larkin 2001, 212–17; Corn 1972, 4). After settling permanently in New York, Cather had access at the Metropolitan Museum to the full range of tonalism, from the decorative idylls of Thomas Wilmer Dewing to the cryptic nocturnes of Albert Pinkham Ryder (Metropolitan Museum of Art, collection database).

Cather's critical comments on tonalist painting demonstrate a trenchant appreciation of the movement's methods and principles. In a 1900 review of Pittsburgh's Carnegie Institute, she comments on Tryon's painting *May* (1898–99): "This is a windy May, of blues and violets and light greens and yellows, with the cleanest of color and treated with great elasticity and delightful enthusiasm and freshness." Cather's perception of these colors as both "[clean]" and "[elastic]" grasps the essence of Tryon's method, which introduced a range of colors and then toned them down, thus achieving a "complexity of . . . [surface] . . . responding to different intensities of light or angles of viewing" (Cleveland 2010, 280). Cather remarks generally of Tryon's works that "they keep the atmosphere in which they were done" (Cather 1970, 763)—hinting at the tonalist principle that the artist "convincingly [reproduce] not only what he saw in nature but his emotional response as well" (Corn 1972, 2). On another visit to the Carnegie, in 1901, she notes the subdued tone of Harrison's *Christmas Eve*, "representing a quiet village, shrouded in snow and a sort of holy stillness, under a blue winter night" (Cather 1970, 869).

Cather's most extended study of an individual tonalist, her 1901 essay "Joe Jefferson, the Painter"—reviewing a Washington, DC, exhibit of fifty-four landscapes by the actor-painter best known for his stage portrayal of Rip Van Winkle—values Jefferson's work for its disciplined color and mood. "One of the most striking canvases," Cather writes, "was a study of the Everglades, in sepia and Chinese white, with no other color discernible, with broken trees and grey mosses" (Cather 1970, 808). Another painting, *Forest and Streams*, was "especially poetic, being entirely submerged in [a] peculiar yellow shade of green . . . in which Jefferson delights as Inness did in the colder and bluer tint" (808). Of his *Moonrise*, she asserts in tonal-ese, "the sentiment of the piece is exquisite" (809), and of a Chicago view called

A Smoky City: "a long somber picture of the Chicago lake front, full of dull greys and reds. It is chiefly artistic through what it omits. . . . The grey of the slimy water, the soft colors of the smoke, the effect of height and murkiness are present, but beyond that I don't believe a Chicago merchant would know his town any more than a London cockney would recognize Whistler's picture of St. James, and that is the best I can say for it" (809). As Cather describes it, Jefferson's art answers Inness's call for painting to possess "both the subjective sentiment—the poetry of nature—and the objective fact" (Inness 1888), even when those facts are poeticized by a city's own smoke. Jefferson's Chicago makes a somber but fit companion to Cather's image in *The Song of the Lark* of Denver defamiliarized by a storm: "wrap[ped] . . . in dry, furry snow, ... muffled in snow," yet "full of food and drink and good cheer," making it, "more than other American cities, an object of sentiment" (Cather 1915/1999, 289).

Like the tonalists, Cather associates "sentiment" with the veiling of reality, as in these quiescent depictions of Chicago and Denver. However, in a 1901 review of Chicago's Art Institute she pushes the term's parameters—defending, for example, "domestic and sentimental subjects," if well executed, over works of "noblest sentiment" "shipwrecked" by poor technique (Cather 1970, 842). She invests "homely sentiment" with a power exceeding domestic sentimental cliché: the "Philistine"— her sympathetic caricature of the middlebrow museumgoer—"knows that sentiment is the most vital motive in society, in his own life and in the lives of his friends. That it wrecks banks and controls the markets, directly or indirectly, and he demands that the comings and goings and courtings and festivals and farewells that make up the gladness and sadness of his life be somehow put into art" (845). Conflating the artistic, domestic, and market connotations of sentiment, Cather breaks down the normative Victorian barriers between private and public spheres, high and low cultures. Further, she depicts the modern museum as a place where traditional boundaries between classes are being tested. Pointing, at Chicago, to "the Cyrus H. McCormick loan exhibition," which featured paintings from Inness's late, tonalist phase,[7] she goes on to observe: "When any one of the Deerings or McCormicks buys an Inness or a Corot, he exhibits it in the Art Institute and their workmen drop in to have a look at it some Sunday and decide that they could have done something better with the money, if it had been theirs" (843–44). For Cather, tonalism partakes of a culture where the meaning of art ranges across classes and social spheres, touching upon the domestic and economic realities that these strangely shimmering landscapes seem to escape.[8] "Tonalism's cool serenity is deceptive," observes David A. Cleveland. "[I]t was an art for uncertain times. It is this uncertainty and ambiguity that places tonalism at the fountainhead of American modernism" (Cleveland 2010, xiv–xv).

My case for the presence of tonalism in Cather's fiction, then, is focused on connections between the movement's two aesthetic trademarks—narrow chromatic range and scintillating effects—and the process of meaning-making that Cather came to associate with such imagery. Tonalist imagery gives rise in Cather's fiction to what I will call modernist sentiment: states of feeling relieved from historical, economic, and narrative forces but all the while inflected by the remote pressure of these same realities. Passages from *O Pioneers!* (1913), *My Ántonia* (1918), *One of Ours* (1922), *A Lost Lady* (1923), and *Lucy Gayheart* (1935) demonstrate how Cather employed tonalist imagery to fashion dreamscapes on the brink of awakening into history.

The impact of Cather's tonalist imagery is most readily apparent in *One of Ours*, which first showcases a Hudson River–style, narrative landscape before shifting to a tonalist vision. Book two opens with Claude Wheeler standing on the steps of the Colorado State Capital in Denver and searching for his destiny in the Rockies to the West: "Over there, in the golden light, the mass of mountains was splitting up into four distinct ranges, and as the sun dropped lower the peaks emerged in perspective, one behind the other. It was a lonely splendour that only made the ache in his breast the stronger" (Cather 1922/2006, 164). Such clarity of perspective, the antithesis of tonalist haze, is a hallmark of mid-nineteenth century American painters like Church, Bierdstadt, and the early Inness; it is the prospect of Manifest Destiny. However, in Claude's vision, the empire is fading from sight; the frontier is closed, its heroic narratives sealed off: "The statue of Kit Carson on horseback, down in the Square, pointed westward; but there was no West, in that sense, any more" (165). Joining the war effort on the French frontier, Claude enters a landscape where tonal economy, temporal suspense, and sudden revelation replace the programmatic progress of the old American frontier: "The light about him, the very air, was green. The trunks of the trees were overgrown with a soft green moss, like mould. He was wondering whether this forest was not always a damp, gloomy place, when suddenly the sun broke through and shattered the whole wood with gold. He had never seen anything like the quivering emerald of the moss, the silky green of the dripping beech-tops" (464). This tonal theme park relieves the narrative pressure of the war even while hinting at the lurking threat of violence in the sun's "shatter[ing]" assault.

O Pioneers! depicts tonal retreats similarly suspended over catastrophe. Murky light surrounds the lovers Emil Bergson and Marie Shabata as they languish in emotional frustration. In a night scene dappled with fireflies, Marie's "white dress looked grey in the darkness. She seemed like a troubled spirit, like some shadow out of the earth," or on another night, "like a white night-moth out of the fields" (Cather 1913/1992, 207–8, 222).

Cather had, from her formative years as a writer, witnessed such imagery in tonalist painting, where human figures, when they appear at all, "are depersonalized, inactive, and dissolved in the same murky penumbra as the ponds and fields" (Corn 1972, 2), much like Marie here. At the Carnegie Cather surely would have encountered, more than once, Inness's *The Clouded Sun* (1891) (fig. 7.3), which entered the permanent collection there in 1899 (Quick 2007, 305, 317). In this painting the viewer's eye follows a grey stone wall from the foreground toward a female figure whose indefinite shape and uniform grey color frustrate particular identification. Similarly "grey" and "shadow[y]," Marie treasures her feelings for Emil by receding into the landscape, identifying with the pond's lunar reflection: "She felt as the pond must feel when it held the moon like that; when it encircled and swelled with that image of gold" (Cather 1913/1992, 223–24). This reflected moonlight, a fixture in such tonalist landscapes as Tryon's *Midsummer Moonrise* (1893) (see fig. 7.1), conveys an emotional suspense ultimately blasted by Frank Shabata's Winchester rifle.

In *My Ántonia* Jim Burden seeks relief from the disappointments of his New York adulthood in the "central figure" of his Nebraska childhood, Ántonia Shimerda. "To speak her name," Cather writes in the introduction, "was to call up pictures of people and places, to set a quiet drama going in one's brain" (Cather 1918/1994, xii). On the tongue, "Ántonia

Figure 7.3.   George Inness, American, 1825–1894, *The Clouded Sun*, 1891. Oil on canvas, 77 × 115 cm (30 1/8 × 45 1/4 in.), Carnegie Museum of Art, Pittsburgh; Purchase. Photograph © 2011 Carnegie Museum of Art, Pittsburgh.

Shimerda" modulates delicately between "tone" and "shimmer," qualities that characterize the novel's landscape as well as Ántonia herself.
These qualities also constitute tonalism's overall effect, which was sometimes described in art circles "simply as 'tonal,' 'tonalistic,' or even 'tony'"
(Corn 1972, 3). "Tony," as Ántonia is called, is a Whistlerian arrangement
in brown against the brown earth: her eyes "like the sun shining on
brown pools in the wood," "skin . . . brown, too, and in her cheeks she had
a glow of rich, dark color. Her brown hair was curly and wild-looking"
(Cather 1918/1994, 22–23). At the end of book four Jim holds Ántonia's
"brown hands" and seeks her face "through the soft, intrusive darkness,"
charging it with redemptive meaning: "the closest, realest face, under
all the shadows of women's faces, at the very bottom of my memory"
(313–14). He promises to return—but ambition intervenes.

In *A Lost Lady* another idealistic man, Niel Herbert, fixes his nostalgia
upon a woman, Marian Forrester, who likewise merges with the landscape. For Niel, the "skeleton poplar" trees bordering the Forrester's road
serve conceptually as a ghostly barricade against the base materialism
that overtakes the early pioneer ideal and ultimately the Forrester home
itself (Cather 1923/1997, 40). These trees are awash with tonal light.
Before witnessing Mrs. Forrester's infidelity, Niel ascends "the poplar-
bordered road in the early light": "All over the marsh, snow-on-the-
mountain, globed with dew, made cool sheets of silver, and the swamp
milk-weed spread its flat, raspberry-coloured clusters. There was an
almost religious purity about the fresh morning air, the tender sky, the
grass and flowers with the sheen of early dew upon them" (80). In these
fields, "the quivering fans of light . . . seemed to push the trees farther
apart and make Elysian fields underneath them" (108–9). The marshy
meadowland is only a temporary preserve from the incursions of the vulgar materialist Ivy Peters, who rents and drains it to "[assert] his power
over the people who had loved those unproductive meadows for their
idleness and silvery beauty" (101–2). Still, the poplars stand in resistance,
their "black, plume-like shadows" falling "across the lane and over Ivy
Peters' wheat fields" (115).

A case can be made, I think, for the specific influence of Dwight Tryon's
landscapes on Cather's depiction of the Forrester grounds, especially two
paintings displayed at the Carnegie around the century's turn. Both are
delicate patterns of trees on meadowland: *May*, mentioned in Cather's
1900 review, and its prototype, *Early Spring in New England* (1897), which
won a Medal of the First Class (Merrill 1990, 128–29). (See fig. 7.4.) In 1909,
critic Charles Caffin wrote of *Early Spring*: "The structure . . . has grown
to music. The rhythm and relation of the values are so discernible that the
austerity of the scene melts into melody . . . the very air palpitates with
song. . . . It faintly stirs the awakening foliage and hovers like a sigh over

Figure 7.4. Dwight W. Tryon, American, 1849–1925, *Early Spring in New England*, 1897. Oil on canvas, 181.2 × 148.3 cm, Freer Gallery of Art, Smithsonian Institution, Washington, D.C.: Gift of Charles Lang Freer, F1906.77a-b.

the earth that after its long sleep begins again to be awake" (Caffin 1909, 32). Caffin's appreciation draws upon the established association between tonal landscapes and music, which Cather intuitively understood in her description of the Forrester meadow: "There was in all living things something limpid and joyous—like the wet, morning call of the birds, flying up through the unstained atmosphere" (Cather 1923/1997, 80).

To Niel, this is the proper setting for Mrs. Forrester's "inviting, musical laugh" (39).

Set in the modern city, *Lucy Gayheart* reflects explicitly upon a concern troubling all these novels: that tonal imagery might obstruct a clear vision of reality. On Lucy's "very individual map of Chicago," the "city of feeling rose out of the city of fact like a definite composition" (Cather 1935/1995, 20): "a blur of smoke and wind and noise, with flashes of blue water, and certain clear outlines rising from the confusion; a high building on Michigan Avenue where Sebastian had his studio—the stretch of park where he sometimes walked in the afternoon—the Cathedral door out of which she had seen him come one morning—the concert hall where she first heard him sing" (20). Upon examination, this web of "memories and sensations" is at once too fragmented and too storied to correspond strictly with the tonalist movement. Lucy finds this personalized city "beautiful because the rest was blotted out" (20), evincing a contempt for objective reality at odds with Inness's call for painting to synthesize "subjective sentiment" and "objective fact."

Lucy later achieves what is arguably a more authentic tonalist vision, in terms that Inness in particular would have understood. On the day before her final Christmas, she watches a snowstorm from the upper floor of the family house in Haverford. As the room turns "greyer and darker," she is seized by "a long forgotten restlessness . . . in pursuit of something she could not see, but knew" (154). Lucy does not blot out reality as before, but searches beneath it, for "something . . . in the breeze, in the sun . . . behind the apple boughs": "through the soft twilight, everything in her was reaching outward, straining forward" (154–55). In her mind, Lucy reaches beyond Haverford to crowded city streets and wonders "if Life itself were the sweetheart . . . waiting for her in distant cities" (155). This elasticity of vision corresponds to Inness's sense that reality is a "living motion," "indefinable" because always changing (Inness 1879, 377). As Nicolai Cikovsky proposes, Inness might have absorbed Swedenborg's insight that, at a spiritual level, spaces "are not fixed and constant . . . for they can be lengthened or shortened; they can be changed or varied" (Cikovsky 2005, 56–57; Swedenborg 1908, 7). Inspired by a similar revelation, Lucy resolves to "go back into the world and get all she could of everything that had made [Sebastian] what he was" (Cather 1935/1995, 155). This scene models how a tonalist landscape might function therapeutically, from a vision of spirit behind a twilit scene (inflected, here, by the musical association of the drowned singer Sebastian) to higher knowledge and restoration—albeit in Lucy's case, very temporary—into the world.

In these examples tonal imagery and modernist sentiment envelop characters caught between private dreams and historical facts. But in Cather's fiction tonal imagery is never the last horizon; significantly, the characters who indulge these moods do not survive or, in the cases of Jim Burden and Niel Herbert, they escape them. Drift and haze finally give way to historical consciousness in concrete acts of stewardship, domestication, and memory arising from the tonal interludes: Alexandra's marriage and land management after the young lovers' deaths; Jim's alignment of his own history with Ántonia's; Mrs. Wheeler's and Mahailey's toil at the kitchen stove, remembering Claude; an old Englishman's perpetual care of Captain Forrester's sundial tombstone; Harry Gordon's preservation of Lucy's sidewalk footprints. In *The Professor's House*, Godfrey St. Peter's boyish "half-awake" experience contemplating "the seven motionless pines" as they "drink up the sun" is a belated "twilight stage" succeeded by the mature example of Augusta and his acceptance of life "without delight" (Cather 1925/2002, 263, 282). Through the dreamwork of twilight, Cather's characters construct futures around loss, absence, and memory.

For Cather, twilight represents the suspension of history that makes new historical consciousness possible. The *Archbishop* retrospectively defines the period of aesthetic searching during the pre-Christian era as an extended "twilight" prefacing a new historical dispensation: "Long before [Mary's] years on earth, in the long twilight between the Fall and the Redemption, the pagan sculptors were always trying to achieve the image of a goddess who should yet be a woman" (Cather 1927/1999, 269–70). Cather's modernism breaks its own path through the dreamy lights of tonalism toward the deeper script that is the unnamed referent of her language.

NOTES

Research on this essay was funded by a grant from the National Science Council, Taiwan, during the 2008–09 academic year (NSC 97-2410-H-030-040).

1. Merrill (1990) details Whistler's complex relationship to tonalism, quoting Cather's comment on Whistler as an example of his reception in the United States (68). Cleveland (2010) defines a shift around 1900 from a decorative, Whistlerian "Aesthetic Tonalism" to a more symbolic and emotional "Expressive Tonalism" (xiv, xxv).

2. The crossbreeding between tonalism and other movements, including impressionism and aestheticism, has left its particular influence on Cather unnoticed, although critics have linked her to artists associated with the movement. See Duryea (1993) and Skaggs (2000). Miller (2008) detects the influence of tonalism on Cather's mentor Sarah Orne Jewett.

3. Cikovsky (2005) collects these comments from reviews published in the *New York Times*, the *New York Evening Post*, and the *Boston Advertiser* between 1875 and 1884.

4. These terms appear in Merrill (1990) and Cikovsky (2005).

5. Millington (2005, 52–53). Millington's essay draws upon the definition of American modernism in Singal (1987).

6. At the 1897 Founder's Day competition, which Cather reviewed, the judges included John La Farge, an early tonalist in the Barbizon mood whose fresco *The Ascension of Our Lord* she would later admire in New York's Church of the Ascension (Cather 1970, 512–14; Lewis 1953/2000, 151).

7. The McCormick loans included Inness's *Autumn* (1892), *A Breezy Day* (1893), and *The Lonely Pine* (1893). For a listing of the Inness paintings then on view at the Art Institute, see Quick (2007, 479, 481) and Art Institute of Chicago (1901, 180, 192).

8. The prominence of tonalist painting at American world's fairs in the early twentieth century is another indication of the movement's broad visibility among the general population. See Cleveland (2010), 441–43.

WORKS CITED

Art Institute of Chicago. 1901. *General Catalogue of Objects in the Museum, August 1901*. Chicago: Art Institute. http://archive.org/details/generalcatalogu01 chicgoog.

Becker, Jack. 2005. "Championing Tonal Painting: The Lotos Club." In *The Poetic Vision: American Tonalism*, edited by Ralph Sessions, 29–37. New York: Spanierman Gallery.

Caffin, Charles H. 1909. *The Art of Dwight W. Tryon: An Appreciation*. http://archive .org/details/artofdwightwtyro00caffricht.

Cather, Willa. 1913/1992. *O Pioneers!* Willa Cather Scholarly Edition. Edited by Susan J. Rosowski and Charles W. Mignon with Kathleen Danker. Historical essay and explanatory notes by David Stouck. Lincoln: University of Nebraska Press.

———. 1915/1999. *The Song of the Lark*. New York: Penguin.

———. 1918/1994. *My Ántonia*. Willa Cather Scholarly Edition. Edited by Charles W. Mignon with Kari A. Ronning. Historical essay by James Woodress. Explanatory notes by James Woodress with Kari Ronning, Kathleen Danker, and Emily Levine. Lincoln: University of Nebraska Press.

———. 1922/1988. "The Novel Démeublé. In *Willa Cather on Writing: Critical Studies on Writing as an Art*, 35–43. Lincoln: University of Nebraska Press.

———. 1922/2006. *One of Ours*. Willa Cather Scholarly Edition. Edited by Frederick M. Link with Kari A. Ronning. Historical essay and explanatory notes by Richard C. Harris. Lincoln: University of Nebraska Press.

———. 1923/1997. *A Lost Lady*. Willa Cather Scholarly Edition. Edited by Charles W. Mignon and Frederick M. Link with Kari A. Ronning. Historical essay and explanatory notes by Susan J. Rosowski with Kari A. Ronning. Explanatory notes by Kari A. Ronning. Lincoln: University of Nebraska Press.

———. 1925/2002. *The Professor's House*. Edited by Frederick M. Link. Historical essay by James Woodress. Explanatory notes by James Woodress with Kari A. Ronning. Lincoln: University of Nebraska Press.

———. 1927/1999. *Death Comes for the Archbishop*. Willa Cather Scholarly Edition. Edited by Charles W. Mignon with Frederick M. Link and Kari A. Ronning. Historical essay and explanatory notes by John J. Murphy. Lincoln: University of Nebraska Press.

———. 1935/1995. *Lucy Gayheart*. New York: Vintage.

———. 1970. *The World and the Parish: Willa Cather's Articles and Reviews, 1893–1902*. Selected and edited with a commentary by William M. Curtin. 2 vols. Lincoln: University of Nebraska Press.

———. 1986. *Willa Cather in Person: Interviews, Speeches, and Letters*. Edited by Brent Bohlke. Lincoln: University of Nebraska Press.

Cikovsky, Nicolai. 2005. "George Inness and Tonalist Uncertainty." In *The Poetic Vision: American Tonalism*, edited by Ralph Sessions, 51–59. New York: Spanierman Gallery.

Cleveland, David A. 2004. *Intimate Landscapes: Charles Warren Eaton and the Tonalist Movement in American Art 1880–1920*. [Groton, MA]: De Menil Gallery at Groton School.

———. 2010. *A History of American Tonalism, 1880–1920*. Foreword by John Wilmerding. Manchester, VT: Hudson Hills Press.

Corn, Wanda. 1972. *The Color of Mood: American Tonalism 1880–1910*. San Francisco: M.H. De Young Memorial Museum and California Palace of the Legion of Honor.

Duryea, Polly. 1993. "Paintings and Drawings in Willa Cather's Prose: A Catalogue Raisonné." PhD diss., University of Nebraska, Lincoln.

Gerdts, William H. 1982. "American Tonalism: An Artistic Overview." In *Tonalism: An American Experience*, edited by William H. Gerdts, Diana Dimodica Sweet, and Robert R. Preato, 17–28. N.p.: Grand Central Art Galleries Art Education Association.

Inness, George. 1879. "Mr. Inness on Art-Matters." *Art Journal* 5: 374–77. Quoted in Cikovsky 2005, 56.

———. 1888. George Inness to Ripley Hitchcock, March 23. Quoted in Montclair Art Museum 1964.

Larkin, Susan. 2001. *The Cos Cob Art Colony: Impressionists on the Connecticut Shore*. New Haven, CT: Yale University Press.

Lewis, Edith. 1953/2000. *Willa Cather Living: A Personal Record*. Lincoln: University of Nebraska Press.

Merrill, Linda. 1990. *An Ideal Country: Paintings by Dwight William Tryon in the Freer Gallery of Art*. Washington, DC: Freer Gallery; Hanover, NH: University Press of New England.

———. 2005. "The Soul of Refinement: Whistler and American Tonalism." In *The Poetic Vision: American Tonalism*, edited by Ralph Sessions, 61–72. New York: Spanierman Gallery.

Metropolitan Museum of Art. Collection database. http://www.metmuseum .org/collections/.

Miller, David C. 2008. "Sarah Orne Jewett's 'A White Heron' and Tonalist Painting." Lecture presented at Fu Jen Catholic Univerity, May 8.

Millington, Richard H. 2005. "Willa Cather's American Modernism." In *Cambridge Companion to Willa Cather*, edited by Marilee Lindemann, 51–65. Cambridge: Cambridge University Press.

Montclair Art Museum. 1964. *George Inness of Montclair*. Exhibition Catalogue. Montclair, NJ: Montclair Art Museum. Unpaginated.

Quick, Michael. 2007. *George Inness: A Catalogue Raisonné*. 2 vols. New Brunswick, NJ: Rutgers University Press.

Ranger, Henry W. 1894. "Basis for Criticism on Painting." *Collector* 6 (Nov. 15): 25. Quoted in Sessions 2005, 10.

Sessions, Ralph. 2005. Introduction. In *The Poetic Vision: American Tonalism*, 9–13. New York: Spanierman Gallery.

Singal, Daniel Joseph. 1987. "Towards a Definition of American Modernism." *American Quarterly* 39: 7-26.

Skaggs, Merrill Maguire. 2000. "Young Willa Cather and the Road to Cos Cob." In *Willa Cather's New York: New Essays on Cather and the City*, edited by Merrill Maguire Skaggs, 43–59. Madison, NJ: Fairleigh Dickinson University Press.

Swedenborg, Emanuel. 1908. *Angelic Wisdom Concerning the Divine Love and the Divine Wisdom*. New York: American Swedenborg Printing and Publishing Society. Quoted in Cikovsky 2005, 57.

Whistler, James Abbott McNeill. 1892/1967. *The Gentle Art of Making Enemies*. New York: Dover Publications.

Chapter 8

Willa Cather, the Nabi of Red Cloud

Mark Facknitz

As she aged, Willa Cather became increasingly aware that hers was a painterly art, and, always an accomplished draughtswoman, she became ever more confident as a pure colorist. At first attracted to the nostalgic realism of Barbizon, a school of painting named for a town near Fontaine-bleau that she visited in 1902 and whose painters once included Theodore Rousseau, Jean-Francois Millet, and in their tradition Jules Breton, she was later much inspired by the luminous allegories of symbolist and muralist Puvis de Chavannes. Finally, however, she is an impressionist—not in the broad sense but in the particular and later sense of impressionism as practiced by the Fauves and especially those emigrants from Pont Aven called the Nabis. My purpose here, is not, however, merely to emphasize the extraordinarily telling similarities between Cather and these exuberant and evocative painters—who, not incidentally, rediscovered the out of doors in bright, clean colors—but also to suggest that through the influence of these painters, Cather achieves a kind of transcendence in her style. Significantly, *fauve* means "wild" in French, and *Nabi* is from the Hebrew word for prophet: there is a uniquely American synthesis to the wilderness and prophecy in Cather's landscape art.

Willa Cather had clear opportunities to develop a first-hand familiarity with modern French painting. From 1886 to 1937 the Orangerie at the Palais du Luxembourg was the principal public gallery for works of living artists in France. It was there, for example, that Hemingway went to see the modern paintings, especially those by Cézanne that he recalled in *A Moveable Feast*:

> If I walked down by different streets to the Jardin du Luxembourg in the af-
> ternoon I could walk through the gardens and then go to the Musée du Lux-
> embourg . . . for the Cézannes. . . . I was learning something from the paint-
> ing of Cézanne that made writing simple true sentences far from enough to
> make the stories have the dimensions that I was trying to put in them. I was
> learning very much from him but I was not articulate enough to explain it to
> anyone. Besides it was a secret. (Hemingway 1964, 13)

If clear lines and simple planes in some respect suggest the narrative structures of Hemingway and their similarity to Cézanne, Cather's early effects tend more toward harmonies and coloratura. They suggest moments of vivid iconography—perhaps talismanic, perhaps transcendent—always remarkable as a sudden salience of bright image, a moment grasped because seen and held in heart and mind—moments like the bright gold of the palms on black lacquer of Harvey Merrick's coffin or, out of a swirl of relentless grays, the copper toes of the boy's boots at the beginning of *O Pioneers!* In this respect, and unlike the architectural undercoats of Cézanne or the spare girding of a Hemingway narrative, Cather's moments of visual lyricism tend to be exquisite, unique, ephemeral, and more vivid than angular, as if they were Cather's response to Pater's scandalous idea that "art comes . . . proposing frankly to give nothing but the highest quality to . . . moments as they pass, and simply for those moments' sake (Pater 1873/1986, 153). Unquestionably, Cather was a devotee of Walter Pater.

When Cather first visited Paris in 1902, she had her picture taken in front of the Palais du Luxembourg (fig. 8.1), a ten minute walk from the Pantheon where she was inspired by the Ste. Genevieve frescoes of Pierre Puvis de Chavannes from the 1890s.[1] In the weeks that followed, Cather visited Barbizon where realists Jean-Francois Millet and Theodore Rousseau died and where Corot and Courbet had been inspired. These were all artists whose homely fields and deep lights resembled Jules Breton, the painter whose *The Song of the Lark* (1884) afforded Cather an important title and whose work she had previously seen in Chicago. In other words, the evidence is strong that Cather was familiar with the realists, especially the romantic realists, as well as the allegorists and the symbolists who were active in France in the late nineteenth century. However, the surmise that she was learning also from the postimpressionist Fauves and Nabis relies on reading the evolution of her own descriptive method, recognizing that Conradian pictorial accuracy gives way to brighter swaths of color, the raised horizons, and the colors straight from the tube that characterized the visual libertinism of the Nabis: Paul Sérusier, Paul Gauguin, Maurice

Figure 8.1. Willa Cather at Luxembourg in 1902. Black/white print. 6.35 × 10.16 cm. Philip L. and Helen Cather Southwick Collection, Archives and Special Collections, University of Nebraska-Lincoln Libraries.

Denis, Edouard Vuillard, and Pierre Bonnard. These colorists influenced Cather heavily during her trips to Europe and eventually helped her to see the American southwest in its most elementally visual light and line.

In general I agree with Asad Al-Ghalith's contention that "Cather, like the impressionist painters, capitalizes on the transfiguring, emotionally evocative power of light as it plays upon objects in her work" (1996, 267). Yet I maintain that more can be averred about Cather as verbal painter than simple technical relations to the impressionist sense of light and sun. True, Cather progressed from dilettante to connoisseur, and over the arc of her career her descriptive art becomes increasingly distinctive. Her letters give us some few references by which to track the process. In May 1908 Cather wrote to Sarah Orne Jewett comparing the color of the water in the gulf of Salerno to the blue in a painting by Puvis de Chavannes (Cather 1908/2002, 23). In 1920 she wrote to Viola Roseboro' that she was staying on the Left Bank facing the Louvre (1920/2002, 78). Her hotel, then, would be on Quai Malaquais, near the Institut de France; more interesting than facing the Louvre, a half mile walk south would take her past the Ecole de Beaux Arts, diagonally across the square at Saint Sulpice, and up the narrow rue Férou to the museum across the rue de Vaugirard just inside the Luxembourg gardens. Soon after Leon Bakst started painting Cather's portrait in his studio, an August 11, 1923, letter to her sister (probably Elsie) indicates that Cather was less concerned with progress on the portrait than she was with the spacious and tidy rooms of the artist (Cather 1923/ 2007). In *The Professor's House* (1925), the Mesa, a bold stroke of blue standing out against sky and bolstered by deep shadow, is one of many expressions of Cather's confidence as colorist. In Leon Bakst's ample and exotic rooms Cather had plenty of time to ponder the dark, narrow, claustrophobic antithesis of the cramped space at the top of St. Peter's house, the clutter of the professor's life, and within that dismal clutter the bright aperture of Outland's story.[2] By the mid-twenties Cather had conceived of contrasting planes of color as structural metaphors.

From her early stories in *The Troll Garden* (1905)—four of which were revised and printed in *Youth and the Bright Medusa* (1920)—Cather was aware of line and contrast, opening "A Sculptor's Funeral" with a set of grays laid in long curves on the Kansas plains as "a group of the townspeople stood on the station siding of a little Kansas town, awaiting the coming of the night train" (Cather 1905b/1987, 34). About them is the night-time white, for "the snow had fallen thick over everything," and "in the pale starlight the line of bluffs across the wide, white meadows south of the town made soft, smoke-coloured curves" (34). Against this background, a chiaroscuro of grayscale, so to speak, "the men on the siding stood first on one foot and then on the other, their hands thrust deep into their trouser pockets, their overcoats open, their shoulders screwed up with the cold." And from this middle distance "they glanced from time to time toward the southeast, where the railroad track wound along the river shore" (34), this last descriptive gesture laying a pair of roughly parallel curves in opposition to the hard steel linearity of the railway tracks. Out of this variation of monotones, "the night express shot, red as a rocket," through the meadows with "escaping steam hanging in grey masses against the pale sky and blotting out the Milky Way" (35). Motion, heat, and color are sudden: "In a moment the red glare from the headlight streamed up the snow-covered track before the siding and glittered on the wet, black rails" (35).

Harsh, monotonic backgrounds also persist in "Paul's Case," the protagonist of which is drawn to painting as he is drawn to New York and the "red glory" (Cather 1905a/1987, 131) of the carnations he carries with him to the bleak site of his suicide, where their bright splashes of color—like the bright flash of Paul's short life, fall and are buried in the snow. Paul's mistake is to allow himself to be obliterated by the ordinary landscape, to have imagined it as limited and limiting: "As he fell, the folly of his haste occurred to him with merciless clearness, the vastness of what he had left undone" (131). In his instant of regret, images reminiscent of the Barbizon group compose his insight: "There flashed through his brain, clearer than ever before, the blue of Adriatic water, the yellow of Algerian sands"; then "the picture making mechanism was crushed, the disturbing visions flashed into black, and Paul dropped back into the immense design of things" (131).

In "Paul's Case" Cather's affinity appears to lie with the romantic realists of the Barbizon school, painters similar to Jules Breton, whose *The Song of the Lark* is perhaps the most important iconic allusion in all of Cather's fiction. Like the bright focal point of the setting sun in *The Song of the Lark*, the Barbizon painters tended to draw isolated and intense points of color out of broad washes of earth tones. For example, Jean-Francois Millet in *The Gleaners* (1857) draws a milky light from a distant and murky horizon to the rich blue and red head scarves of two women bending to pick grain from the harvested field. Similarly, Jean-Baptiste-Camille Corot in *Ville d'Avray* (1867) light up three points of bright white—a distant house, a walker's sleeve, and two trees in bloom—against earth tones and dusky water. But Cather appears to have wanted something more flamboyant than a bright and ironic flash of red on snow. Even before "Paul's Case," in "A Wagner Matinée" (1904), the attraction to the impressionists is explicit as Cather lays color next to color with no apparent concern for focus, horizon, or frame in describing the people in the streets of New York:

> One lost the contour of faces and figures, indeed any effect of line whatever, and there was only the colour of bodices past counting, the shimmer of fabrics soft and firm, silky and sheer; red, mauve, pink, blue, lilac, purple, ecru, rose, yellow, cream, and white, all the colours that an impressionist finds in a sunlit landscape, with here and there the dead shadow of a frock coat. My Aunt Georgiana regarded them as though they had been so many daubs of tube-paint on a palette. (Cather 1904/1987, 106)

Both lessons, the earthy linearities of Barbizon (and "Paul's Case") and the exuberant colorations of the Nabis fuse as elegant narrative models by the time she writes the opening paragraph of *O Pioneers!* (1913). Aloft in a strong cold wind, the eye of the story begins to swing downward where "a mist of fine snowflakes was curling and eddying about the cluster of low drab buildings huddled on the gray prairie, under a gray sky" (1913/1987, 139). Into the windswept grayness, Cather inserts her description of Hanover's main street—"a deeply rutted road, now frozen hard, which ran from the squat red railway station and the grain 'elevator' at the north end of the town to the lumber yard and the horse pond at the south end" (139). Splashed onto an ordinal vertical north-south line is one swipe of red. On either side cluster disorganized shapes of buildings in blurry gray snow and "a few rough-looking countrymen in coarse overcoats, with their long caps pulled down to their noses" (139). By now the perspective is on the ground, on the main street, and the attentive eye catches "a red or a plaid shawl [that] flashed out of one store into the shelter of another" (139). Waiting, grounded, centered—the eye is ready to place in its foreground the immigrant boy with his copper-toed boots who cries about his kitten up the telegraph pole. The effect is to begin the novel by finding the place within the matrix of the landscape from which best to portray—and view—the scene. It also creates an initial point of reference against which to measure strong dynamic and lucent contrasts. For example, when, after Amédée's death, Emil rides toward the Shabata farm, "he could feel nothing but the sense of diminishing distance. It seemed to him that his mare was flying, or running on wheels, like a railway train. The sunlight, flashing on the window-glass of the big red barns, drove him wild with joy. He was like an arrow shot from the bow. His life poured itself out along the road before him as he rode to the Shabata farm" (266). Here the line created by the speeding horse changes the horizon from the natural line of the distant divide to the near and bright sunlit mare dark like a train eclipsing, one after another, red barns in the middle distance. From contemplation of the earth, its hues, tones, and lines, we are offered instead a rushing impression of motion and color.

Cather's next novel, *The Song of the Lark* (1915), makes explicit the special presence of painting in her imagination. But, even as the novel derives its title from Jules Breton's picture (1884; fig. 8.2), so much in the nostalgic realist vernacular of Barbizon, the girl in the painting is—like Thea—most herself in her will to transcend the banality of the here and now by turning away from the west and the setting sun toward a darker, eastern horizon. It is as if she has seen—not simply heard—something unexpected and ineffable in the east. Both Cather and Thea leave behind the mannered banalities of Breton, preferring sudden and exuberant coloratura in the place of static duskiness. For example, in the "Panther Canyon" section Cather lets us know that Thea's "faculty of observation was never highly developed," for the roses "in the florists' shop windows in Chicago were merely roses" (1915/1987, 549)—clichés that are romantic and real, but still, static, and indiscriminately lighted. When Thea's memory and understanding attach to flowers from her own experience, however, the effect is different: "But when she thought of the moonflowers over Mrs. Tellamantez's door, it was as if she had been that vine and had opened up

Figure 8.2.   Jules Breton, 1827–1906, *The Song of the Lark*, 1884. Color postcard 14.8 × 10.5 cm from Chicago Art Institute. Digital image credit: Willa Cather Pioneer Memorial Collection, Nebraska State Historical Society.

in white flowers every night. There were memories of light on the sand hills, of masses of prickly-pear blossoms . . . of late afternoon sun pouring through the grape leaves and mint bed in Mrs. Kohler's garden . . ." (549). These memories provide focus, intensity, arrested movement, and a source of light like the setting sun on the horizon in the Breton painting.

Little in Chicago penetrated to the depth of Thea's most moving Moonstone memories; nothing had enough immediate authenticity to suggest itself as aesthetic and memorable experience to the young woman. But in Panther Canyon, escorted by the exquisite nostalgia of girlhood, Thea finds the landscape spontaneously yielding, not only of pleasure in sun and air but also of a depth and a kind of poignancy more usual to powerful memory than to immediate experience. Bathing with "ceremonial gravity" in the bright pool behind the cottonwoods, Thea suddenly sees that "any art [is] an effort to make a sheath, a mould in which to imprison for a moment the shining, elusive element which is life itself" (522). The recognition instantiates Thea's sense of the natural world as the ground and central moment of art. Here, in a scene that prefigures the plough and the sun image in *My Ántonia*, Thea watches morning spill into the arroyo:

> In a moment the pine trees up on the edge of the rim were flashing with coppery fire. The thin red clouds which hung above their pointed tops began to boil and move rapidly, weaving in and out like smoke. The swallows darted out of their rock houses as at a signal, and flew upward, toward the rim. Little brown birds began to chirp in the bushes along the watercourse down at the bottom of the ravine, where everything was still dusky and pale. At first the golden light seemed to hang like a wave upon the rim of the canyon; the trees and bushes up there, which one scarcely noticed at noon, stood out magnified by the slanting rays. . . . The red sun rose rapidly above the tops of the blazing pines. (560–61)

Thea, in other words, faces east at morning, not evening, seeing a new brilliance breaking—blindingly—over the clean, hard, and very high line of the horizon at the arroyo rim.

If *The Song of the Lark* is the story of how Thea finds her voice, it also shows us how Cather found her palette. By the time she writes *My Ántonia* (1918), her sense of color is well developed; and her distinctive visual technique is still characterized by powerful sinuosities of line and strong verticals, against which are placed intensely simple colors suggestive of motion and drama. To accomplish this, Cather lends her eye to Jim Burden. A bright orphan, he comes ready to the landscape, eager to "see what lay beyond that cornfield" where there is a sea of red grass and "the road ran about like a wild thing, avoiding the deep draws, crossing them where they were wide and shallow" and making a "gold ribbon across the prairie" where "the sunflowers grew" (1918/1987, 725). The effect is a strikingly simple movement from a plane of green into a tilted field of red crossed by a sinuous dark line edged in gold, a moment that seems to be informed by Sérusier's bright and tilting planes in *The Talisman* (fig. 8.3). Much later Burden follows the same road in a different season, a different moment. The place is the same, the colors brightly different: "It was a beautiful blue morning. The buffalo-peas were blooming in pink and purple masses along the roadside, and the larks, perched on last year's dried sunflower stalks, were singing straight at the sun, their

Figure 8.3.   Paul Sérusier, 1864–1927, *The Talisman, the River Aven in Pont-Aven*, 1888. Oil on wood, 27 × 21.5 cm. Museé d'Orsay, Paris. Photo credit: Erich Lessing / Art Resource, NY.

heads thrown back and their yellow breasts a-quiver" (795). Like Monet's various images of the cathedral at Rheims, only the geographical location is constant. Senses and mind—and hence people—are ever and always different, and so the eye relentlessly recolors and rebuilds.

Soon the landscape will show itself in storm, loud with quick shadows, as Jim and Ántonia watch the lightning from their perch on the sloping roof of a chicken house: "The thunder was loud and metallic, like the rattle of sheet iron, and the lightning broke in great zigzags across the heavens, making everything stand out and come close to us for a moment. Half the sky was checkered with black thunderheads, but all the west was luminous and clear: in the lightning flashes it looked like deep blue water, with the sheen of moonlight on it" (802). In these stormy washes of color, in hard contrasts of darkness and light, the middle distance tends to disappear; the breadth of the landscape can be comprehended in one glance of the active eye. Nowhere is Cather so entirely a primitive, Fauve, or Nabi, as in the most celebrated image in *My Ántonia*, perhaps in all of Cather:

> There were no clouds, the sun was going down in a limpid, gold-washed sky. Just as the lower edge of the red disc rested on the high fields against the horizon, a great black figure suddenly appeared on the face of the sun. We sprang to our feet, straining our eyes toward it. In a moment we realized what it was. On some upland farm, a plough had been left standing in the field. The sun was sinking just behind it. Magnified across the distance by the horizontal light, it stood out against the sun, was exactly contained within the circle of the disc; the handles, the tongue, the share—black against the molten red. (1918/1987, 865–66)

Here are two pure colors and black, no background, no foreground except that implied by the perceiver, and we see the temporary magnitude of the object, not at all the same as seeing the object itself. Cather has understood that making readers see depends not on careful, crafted complexities but on simple colors quickly applied or, more generally, on significance suddenly and solidly revealed.

The Nabi preferences for colors straight from the tube and collapsed middle distances—illustrated in Paul Sérusier's *Talisman* (1888), the Nabi manifesto in its argument for bright colors, clear contrasts, lifted lines of sight, and unambiguous focal point—are shown in Cather's preference for descriptive language that verbally represents an iconic tableau, arrested in time. After her 1920 trip to France, Cather's descriptive manner remains simple and bright like a Nabi's work. For example, in *One of Ours* (1922) she evokes the landscape of Lorraine: "Little black yew trees, that had not been visible in the green of summer, stood out among the curly yellow rakes. Through the gray netting of the beech twigs, still holly bushes glittered" (1922/1987, 1254).

Cather's application of colorist techniques in her earlier works became staples for the mature novels. In *The Professor's House* (1925) "the rays of sunlight fell slantingly through the little twisted piñons," the light was "as red as a daylight fire. . . . And the air, my God, what air!—Soft, tingling, gold, hot with an edge of chill on it, full of the smell of piñons—it was like breathing the sun, breathing the colour of the sky." The plain below was "streaked with shadow, violet and purple and burnt orange until it met the horizon" (1925/1990, 246). As evening deepens, Cather's description echoes the images of both the sun bursting above the eastern rim of the arroyo in *Song of the Lark* and the plough outlined by the sun in *My Ántonia*: "The sun got behind [the mesa] early in the afternoon, and then our camp would lie in its shadow. After a while the sunset colour would begin to stream up from behind it. Then the mesa was like one great ink-black rock against a sky on fire" (215). In her 1938 open letter "On *The Professor's House*," Cather explained that her "open[ing] the square window" of Professor St. Peter's study and "let[ting] in the fresh air that blew off the Blue Mesa" had been inspired by Dutch genre paintings she had seen in Paris before beginning the book (1938/1988, 31–32)—a declaration that she repeated in the spring of 1944 in a letter to Elizabeth Vermorcken stating that she conceived of the Blue Mesa as opening like a window on the sea in a Dutch genre painting (Stout, 2002, 261, #1666). To use a more modern analogy, she may also have connected—consciously or subconsciously—both the mesa and Tom's story with Bonnard's *The Open Window* (1921) or any number of other Nabi paintings which use the motif of a perspective defined by an open window—not merely for the blue exterior and spaciousness, but for the visual contrast of large exterior spaces and constricted and shadowy interiors. The effect, in painting and in prose, tends to associate darkness with interiors and suffocation, color and light with the outside air—whether subtly, as in the garden of the new house perceived through the open French doors of the parlor, or more emphatically, the distant horizons of ambition and youth perceived from the suffocating darkness of the professor's study in the old house.

In *Death Comes for the Archbishop* (1927) Cather is comparably bold in color and line in visualizing the heights above Rome:

> The light was full of action and had a peculiar quality of climax—of splendid finish. It was both intense and soft, with a ruddiness as of much-multiplied candlelight, an aura of red in its flames. It bored into the ilex trees, illuminating their mahogany trunks and blurring their dark foliage; it warmed the bright green of the orange tree and the rose of the oleander blooms to gold; sent congested spiral patterns quivering over the damask and plate and crystal. The churchmen kept their rectangular clerical caps on their heads to protect them from the sun. The three Cardinals wore black cassocks with crimson piping and crimson buttons, the Bishop a long black coat over his violet vest. (1927/1990, 277)

Here the light and contrasting colors create a landscape that transcends the pompous and prosaic cardinals. Much later in "The Mass at Acoma" Cather is sure enough of the memorable vividness of her opening scene to tell us that on the mesa, on "the Rock," "the Bishop found a loggia— roofed, but with open sides, looking down on the white pueblo and the tawny rock, and over the wide plain below" and to suggest that, though the places are continents apart, the images belong side by side. She writes that "from this loggia he watched the sun go down; watched the desert become dark, the shadows creep upward," and to complete the parallel, "in the plain the scattered mesa tops, red with the afterglow, one by one lost their light, like candles going out" (339). Here the Bishop feels a still sense of cosmic permanence.

In *Shadows on the Rock* (1931) Cather luxuriates in a way of seeing in which the intensity of sensual experience has become endowed with spir- itual profundity—perhaps a lasting endowment of the writing of *Death Comes for the Archbishop*. The painting eye can, so to speak, overcome the wilderness and the irregular topography of Quebec to create order on a rock or on a river. It can even make a place for Cécile and Jacques to play:

> Quebec is never lovelier than on an afternoon of late October; ledges of brown and lavender clouds lay above the river and the Ile d'Orléans, and the red-gold autumn sunlight poured over the rock like a heavy southern wine. Beyond the Cathedral square the two lingered under the allée of naked trees beside the Jesuits' college. These trees were cut flat to form an arbour, the branches interweaving and interlacing like basketwork, and beneath them ran a promenade paved with flat flagstones along which the dry yellow leaves were blowing, giving off a bitter perfume when one trampled them. Cécile loved that allée, because when she was little the Fathers used to let her play there with her skipping-rope,—few spots in Kebec were level enough to jump rope on. (1931/1990, 485)

Skipping as nimbly as the little girl on the level *allée*, refracted light high- lights the "crystal bowl full of glowing fruits . . . purple figs, yellow-green grapes with gold vine-leaves, apricots, nectarines, and a dark citron" that Cécile loves to study in Count Frontenac's home. These glass fruits "were hollow, and the light played in them, throwing coloured reflections into the mirror and upon the wall above" (501). Later, as the sun fades and au- tumn deepens, Cather again has readers look across the water at Quebec, recoloring and stratifying it, separating the spires and roofs of the city from the rock they are built upon with a heavy line of mist:

> The autumn fog was rolling in from the river so thick that [Cécile] seemed to be walking through drifts of brown cloud. Only a few roofs and spires stood out in the fog, detached and isolated: the flèche of the Récollet chapel and the slate roof of the Château, the long, grey outline of Bishop Laval's Seminary,

floating in the sky. Everything else was blotted out by rolling vapours that were constantly changing in density and colour; now brown, now amethyst, now reddish lavender, with sometimes a glow of orange overhead where the sun was struggling behind the thick weather. (502–3)

Cather achieves a painterly effect through the bowl of colored fruit, and the texture and colors of the landscape are truly impressionistic.

"Not the fruit of experience, but experience itself, is the end," wrote Walter Pater (1873/1986, 153). Mr. Rosen, in "Old Mrs. Harris" (1932), takes a line from Jules Michelet, yet changes little of Pater's message when he says "le but n'est rien; le chemin, c'est tout" ("the end is nothing, the road is all") (Cather 1932/1992, 657). To experience is to be, and to be as intensely as possible is the success of the Fauve or the Nabi. It was also the aesthete in Cather who struggled with the realist. That awash in color, with an exuberant eye, one might disappear into the vast landscape of America is the ideal of transcendence as Willa Cather came to conceive of it in such places as the Enchanted Bluff, Sand City, Hanover, Moonstone, Black Hawk, Lovely Creek, the Blue Mesa, Tesuque and Santa Fe, and Quebec—North American places where Cather sought color and found horizons of aesthetic completeness. The one God—the art about which Cather wrote to Mariel Gere—proved to be a God of sky, horizon, wild bright sweeps of color, prophetic urgency, and arrested evanescence.

NOTES

1. Nearly four decades later, as speaker at a dinner at the Plaza Hotel in New York (May 4, 1933) honoring the 1932 Pulitzer Prize winners as well as previous awards winners, Cather would call on novelists to have the courage to give "every story its own form, instead of trying to crowd it into one of the stock moulds on the shelf." In the next breath she would directly allude to the Luxembourg gallery, commenting: "there is a Latin inscription on the wall of the Luxembourg art gallery in Paris which expresses a sane and rational attitude toward Art. It reads something like this: 'Because of the past, we have hope for the future'" (Cather 1933/1986, 170).

2. Cather sat for Bakst between August and October of 1923; on October 23 she began her voyage home to America. Lewis reports that "she returned from Europe with the idea for the novel in her mind" (Woodress 1987, 339, 353), so this idea must have been incubating while she sat for Bakst.

WORKS CITED

Al-Ghalith, Asad. 1996. "Cather's Use of Light: An Impressionistic Tone." In *Cather Studies 3*, edited by Susan J. Rosowski, 267–82. Lincoln: University of Nebraska Press.

Cather, Willa. 1904/1987. "A Wagner Matinée." In *Early Novels and Stories*. Edited by Sharon O'Brien, 102–110. New York: Library of America.

———. 1905a/1987. "Paul's Case." In *Early Novels and Stories*. Edited by Sharon O'Brien, 111–31. New York: Library of America.

———. 1905b/1987. "A Sculptor's Funeral." In *Early Novels and Stories*. Edited by Sharon O'Brien, 34–48. New York: Library of America.

———. 1908/2002. "Letter to Jewett #138." In *A Calendar of the Letters of Willa Cather*. Edited by Janis P. Stout, 23. Lincoln: University of Nebraska Press.

———. 1913/1987. *O Pioneers!* In *Early Novels and Stories*. Edited by Sharon O'Brien, 133–290. New York: Library of America.

———. 1915/1987. *The Song of the Lark*. In *Early Novels and Stories*. Edited by Sharon O'Brien, 291–706. New York: Library of America.

———. 1918/1987. *My Ántonia*. In *Early Novels and Stories*. Edited by Sharon O'Brien, 707–937. New York: Library of America.

———. 1920/2002. "Letter to Roseboro' #507." In *A Calendar of the Letters of Willa Cather*. Edited by Janis P. Stout, 78. Lincoln: University of Nebraska Press.

———. 1922/1987. *One of Ours*. In *Early Novels and Stories*. Edited by Sharon O'Brien, 939–1297. New York: Library of America.

———. 1923/2007 "Letter to Her Sister #1960." In *A Calendar of the Letters of Willa Cather: An Expanded, Digital Edition*. Edited by Andrew Jewell and Janis P. Stout. *The Willa Cather Archive*. http://cather.unl.edu./index.calendar.html.

———. 1925/1990. *The Professor's House*. In *Later Novels*. Edited by Sharon O'Brien, 99–271. New York: Library of America.

———. 1927/1990. *Death Comes for the Archbishop*. In *Later Novels*. Edited by Sharon O'Brien, 273–459. New York: Library of America.

———. 1931/1990. *Shadows on the Rock*. In *Later Novels*. Edited by Sharon O'Brien, 461–641. New York: Library of America.

———. 1932/1992. "Old Mrs. Harris." In *Stories, Poems and Other Writings*. Edited by Sharon O'Brien, 619–72. New York: Library of America.

———. 1933/1986. "On the Novel." In *Willa Cather in Person: Interviews, Speeches, and Letters*. Edited by L. Brent Bohlke, 168–70. Lincoln: University of Nebraska Press.

———. 1938/1988. "On *The Professor's House*." In *Willa Cather on Writing: Critical Studies on Writing as an Art*, 30–32. Lincoln: University of Nebraska Press.

Hemingway, Ernest. 1964. *A Moveable Feast*. New York: Scribners.

O'Brien, Sharon, ed. 1987. *Early Novels and Stories*. New York: Library of America.

———. 1990. *Later Novels*. New York: Library of America.

———. 1992. *Stories, Poems, and Other Writings*. New York: Library of America

Pater, Walter. 1873/1986. *The Renaissance: Studies in Art and Poetry*. New York: Oxford University Press.

Stout, Janis P., ed. 2002. *A Calendar of the Letters of Willa Cather*. Lincoln: University of Nebraska Press.

Woodress, James. 1987. *Willa Cather: A Literary Life*. Lincoln: University of Nebraska Press.

Chapter 9

Blessed Damsels,
Lost Ladies, and
Cather's Real Women

Angela Conrad

On her first trip to Europe in 1902, Willa Cather tried to learn as much about art as she could. She visited homes of artists such as G. F. Watts, Dante Gabriel Rossetti, and Frederick Leighton. She chronicled in detail her visit to the studio of Edward Burne-Jones. As she stood before his unfinished works she thought, "Certainly there can be no question nowadays as to who was the master of all English painters. There is something that speaks from every canvas or study on the studio wall, from the long-limbed languid women, the wide, far-seeing eyes, the astonishingly bold, yet always delicate and tender experiments in composition and colour scheme which speak from no other canvas stretched in English land" (Cather 1902/1956, 73–74). Cather had noticed those remarkable women that make up the central focus of Pre-Raphaelite paintings. Their undeniable power lay in their captivating beauty, passionate looks, and implied stories.

All the Pre-Raphaelite painters demonstrate strong interest in the roles and power of women, though those of the later period, such as Dante Gabriel Rossetti and Edward Burne-Jones, aligned themselves more with the Aesthetic movement's focus on beauty rather than instruction as a purpose for art (Hilton 1970, 207). They broke with earlier Pre-Raphaelites who preferred moral lessons and focused instead on beautiful women of myth or legend (Prettejohn 2007, 98). The women depicted are all of the same physical type: tall women with large eyes, lips, and noses and a lot of hair (190). The titles of the paintings identify characters including Venus,

Guinevere, the Lady of Shallot, Ophelia, Beatrice, and many others—all women whose beauty and sensuality controlled men's desires. Most important, all these women come with a ready-made story that describes the results of this power.

Willa Cather, too, featured extraordinary female characters, and this quality of her work can be compared to the Pre-Raphaelite painters whose work she admired. Although Cather does not follow the same restricting avenue of representation of women as the Pre-Raphaelites, she could not leave their methods completely alone; she set up certain characters and plots to enter into dialog with the works of Pre-Raphaelite painters about what makes a real woman and who gets to decide that question. Cather explores a few favorite Pre-Raphaelite character types that I define as follows: the Lost Lady, who is first idealized but who later falls into sin because of her own passionate nature; the Temptress, who uses her femininity to trap and ruin men; the muse or Blessed Damsel who works for the salvation of her true love; and the Crushed Flower, spurned by her beloved and thus suicidal. The actions of these women all revolve around men, whether to love them or to destroy them; they never act independently of men. Of special interest are Cather's works that examine women through the male perspective: *A Lost Lady*, *My Ántonia*, and "Coming, Aphrodite!" In each of these works Cather presents a powerful woman seen and interpreted through the eyes of a young man, a type himself: the Aesthete. In addition to studying the women, Cather examines the male/artistic gaze and how it shapes the reader's view of women and appropriates women's power. The key to this relationship is captivity: the woman's beauty is described as "captivating," yet the artist's power is his ability to "capture," to lock-in the image by committing it to canvas as "his" work of art. The balance of power will be settled by who captures whom, who is able to control the viewer and tell the story of this power.

Cather begins each of these works by allowing the male interpreters to study the female subjects and cast each of them into one of the archetypal female roles glorified by Pre-Raphaelite artists. The young man has the woman all figured out as he captures her image to fit it into an archetype. Yet in all three works, Cather forces the women off course, veering sharply away from the idealized tragic plot set out for them by the archetype, allowing them to avoid possession under the male representational gaze. The real women retain their power over the men whose attention they captivate, while slipping out of the roles assigned to them. Cather ultimately places into the hands of the female subject the power to create her own roles and her own significance.

At the very beginning of *A Lost Lady*, we enter a feudal reality, with a title that hearkens back to medieval legend through characters like Captain Forrester, whose name evokes Robin Hood, and his lady-love Marian, whom the Captain calls "Maidy" (Cather 1923/1990, 49). From the start, Marian controls and creates her image, appearing stately to locals and in "dishabille" to the lords of industry. Her power is in her wealth and position but also in sexuality. She tempts the boys in the village to think about her body when she tells them seductively of her wading in the brook for flowers: "I can't resist it. I pull off my stockings and pick up my skirts and in I go!" (Cather 1923/1990, 8).

When Niel Herbert emerges as the key viewpoint character, Marian is cast into the idealized Lost Lady role, the first step on the road to her destruction. Niel, whose name suggests the kneeling posture of the devoted knight, becomes enchanted after a fall from a tree on her estate. The Lady nurses him in her boudoir: "He was in pain, but he felt weak and contented. What soft fingers Mrs. Forrester had, and what a lovely lady she was. Inside the lace ruffle of her dress he saw her white throat rising and falling so quickly. Suddenly she got up to take off her glittering rings,—she had not thought of them before,—shed them off her fingers with a quick motion as if she were washing her hands, and dropped them into Mary's broad palm" (13–14). In this intimate setting, Niel examines her body; her shedding the rings becomes a gesture of noblesse oblige and acceptance of him as suitor.

Cather's remarkable image matches closely an 1858 painting by William Morris titled *Guenevere or La Belle Iseult*. It shows the lady in the foreground of her bedroom, the unmade and curtained bed behind, with a small dog (medieval symbol of marital loyalty) curled up asleep (Hall 1974, 105). Guinevere is dressed in her gorgeous gown, though her eyes are downcast and pensive. Morris shows her in a lush and wealthy environment that creates part of her image, as Marian's surroundings do for Niel, who notes "heavy curtains looped back with thick cords," "the marble-topped washstand," and the "massive walnut furniture . . . all inlaid with pale-coloured woods" (Cather 1923/1990, 14). Morris used the setting to create the idealized woman, transforming working-class model Jane Burden into Guinevere. His depiction gives power to her sensuality.

According to legend, Guinevere, the chosen wife to the rightful king of Britain, was left alone with handsome and noble Lancelot and, weak as she was, succumbed to the temptation to become his lover, bringing about the ruin of her husband and her nation. Rossetti's 1857 watercolor *Sir Lancelot in the Queen's Chamber* depicts Lancelot and Guinevere discovered in their adultery in Guinevere's bedchamber (Treuherz, Prettejohn, and Becker 2003, 38); Lancelot leans out to the window from behind the curtains of the bed, angrily looking for approaching knights, a sword in his hand pointing back into the room and toward the standing figure of the Lady. Guinevere wears an elaborate dressing gown, her long hair loose, her head thrust backwards in despair (or ecstasy), her eyes almost closed, stroking her long neck passionately. In her fall, Guinevere is the most glorious, the most sensuous she can be. Her greatest power is destructive, and it comes not from taking action as much as from allowing herself to be overtaken by the passion that is her feminine nature.

Niel's view of his Lady after belatedly discovering her infidelity is similar to Rossetti's sensual portrayal of Guinevere. Like a good courtly lover, he at first most admires her "in her relation to her husband," in which he found "her loyalty to him, stamped her more than anything else" (Cather 1923/1990, 43). He realizes her affair with Frank Ellinger only after rushing to her at dawn, to pay homage with gifts of wild roses; while stooping to place the flowers on the sill of her bedroom window, he hears "a woman's soft laughter; impatient, indulgent, teasing, eager," answered by a man's, "fat and lazy." Though the narrator claims that in that instant Niel "had lost one of the most beautiful things in his life" (47), he clings to her almost more than he did before. Yet now he looks on her from the position of the Aesthete observer: "It was not a moral scruple she had outraged, but an aesthetic ideal. Beautiful women, whose beauty meant more than it said . . . was their brilliancy always fed by something coarse and concealed?" (48). At this point, he becomes the Aesthete, learning to savor the beauty of her iconic fall. He learns that through his re-imaging of her life, he can gain control over the poignancy of her destruction.

The archetypal Lost Lady ends her story in grief and repentance. Rossetti painted the end of Guinevere's story in *Arthur's Tomb* (1860) (Treuherz, Prettejohn, and Becker 2003, 39). It shows an aggressive Lancelot bending over the tomb of King Arthur to try to kiss the kneeling figure of Guinevere. She is dressed in the nun's habit. She and Lancelot are compressed into close proximity by overhanging trees that crowd the space above. But since Arthur's death, Guinevere shrinks from Lancelot's kiss. In order to salvage her feminine image, she must exile herself from sexuality, even though her love for Lancelot is genuine and her husband is now dead. Once she is stripped of her sensual power, she no longer captivates but becomes the image defined by a painter's imagination.

In contrast to Rossetti, Cather does not allow her Lost Lady to be forced into repentance and powerlessness. Marian follows the archetypal pattern to a point. She is wealthy, powerful, and seductive; and she allows her passionate nature to rule her. She accepts, even delights in, the adulation of a young devoted admirer such as Niel. Yet after her husband becomes disabled due to stroke, she continues to pursue Frank Ellinger and phones him desperately in the night. When her liege lord is dead, she does not make her way to the nunnery, nor does she repent her love for another man. She transfers her legal business and investing to the unethical Ivy Peters, who gets ahead through cheating Indians. She even looks for new youthful admirers in the uncouth young townsmen.

Niel, the Aesthetic onlooker, is repelled by her failure to stick to the script and transfers his loyalty to a trustworthy subject. He realizes it was not she, Marian Forrester, that he desired to preserve; it was the age she represented to him. "It was already gone, that age; nothing could ever bring it back." Indeed, "it was what he most held against Mrs. Forrester; that she was not willing to immolate herself, like the widow of all these great men, and die with the pioneer period to which she belonged; that she preferred life on any terms" (95). Niel wants to see Guinevere at the tomb, following her proper role of self-sacrifice to preserve the beauty of the moment for the audience. Like the Pre-Raphaelite artist, he preserves the image while rejecting a less beautiful reality. While Cather acknowledges the ways the male interpreter tries to nudge women into beautifully tragic plot lines, she also allows for the subject's rejection of those roles.

Similarly, in *My Ántonia*, narrator Jim Burden tries to claim Ántonia as a function of his own life: "I'd have liked to have you for a sweetheart, or a wife, or my mother or my sister—anything that a woman can be to a man. The idea of you is a part of my mind; you influence my likes and dislikes, all my tastes, hundreds of times when I don't realize it. You really are a part of me" (Cather 1918/1987, 910). While this affirmation seems to indicate that Ántonia is a very powerful character, it actually says that the *image* Jim has of her is what is powerful. As Susan Rosowski (1992) has shown, "Male, successful, and articulate, Jim assumes he is the subject, the creator and the source of power in 'his' story. He would make Ántonia an object, and he would impose his conventions on her." Moreover, he claims her as subject of his work of art, appropriating her power to his use. He must write about her by saying "a great deal" about himself; as he explains, "It's through myself that I knew and felt her" (Cather 1918/1987, 713).

It can be dizzying to trace all the conventional figures into which Jim tries to place his childhood friend. After her move to the Harling house in Black Hawk, she sheds her masculine traits of farm work and takes up what Jim considers women's work of domestic activity, stating to him, "Maybe I be the kind of girl you like better, now I come to town" (811). Yet here is also where she enters the category of "hired girls," with its obvious secondary suggestion of prostitution. These immigrant girls represent "a menace to the social order" (840) as their budding sexuality threatens to attract those of higher social class. When they go out dancing each night with different men outdoors at "the tent," Ántonia's employers threaten her: "You've been going with girls who have a reputation for being free and easy, and now you've got the same reputation" (843). Their ultimatum poses for her the dilemma of cloistering herself or losing her job.

Society brands Ántonia with the seductress image that matches one of the Pre-Raphaelite archetypes. Images of the mistress or prostitute abound in their paintings: Rossetti's painting *Found* (1859) shows a modern prostitute who has been found at dawn on a London street by her former country suitor. Rossetti describes the scene thus: "He has just come up with her and she, recognizing him, has sunk under her shame upon her knees . . . while he stands holding her hands as he seized them" (Treuherz, Prettejohn, and Becker 2003, 165). To a more neutral eye, the man appears to be angry, dragging her back to an unhappy marriage, an idea perhaps enhanced by the background image of a calf in a cart, trapped in a net. Other temptresses depicted on canvas by these painters seduce viewers by brushing their long wavy hair, like Rossetti's images of the voluptuous red-haired model Fanny Conforth in paintings such as *Bocca Bacciata* (1859), *Woman Combing her Hair* (1864), and *Lady Lilith* (1868) (Treuherz, Prettejohn, and Becker 2003, 66, 70, 63). Burne-Jones shows the siren dragging a sailor down to the depths before she has realized he is already dead in his 1886 painting *The Depths of the Sea* (Wildman and Christian 1998, 119).

Kathy Alexis Psomiades argues that this concentration on the prostitute figures reveals the Pre-Raphaelite disgust at the thought of selling femininity, which they parallel to commercializing passion through selling art. She points out, "unlike 'soul,' 'beauty' has a material existence: straddling spiritual and material realms, it draws attention to the double nature of art, priceless yet for sale" (Psomiades 1997, 38). Yet, the Pre-Raphaelite painters did capture beauty in art and sell it in the form of painting. Ántonia, however, does not work as a prostitute, and her beauty is not for sale. When Jim misreads her signals as a "hired girl" and tries to kiss her, she rejects him, telling him "it ain't right" (Cather 1918/1987, 853). When he argues that Lena lets him kiss her, we see Jim maintain the archetype of Temptress by transferring it onto a more likely person.

In fact, Lena Lingard, who does become involved with Jim sexually, is more easily cast into the sexual temptress role. Her pastoral sensuality tempts Ole Benson, a married farmer, to "wander off to wherever Lena was herding." Her "ragged" dresses and bare feet produce violence when Ole's wife "chased her across the prairie" with a corn knife (818). In this scene she resembles the sexually easy shepherdess in William Holman Hunt's 1851 painting *The Hireling Shepherd* (fig. 9.1). That woman, with red hair and skirt and bare feet, leans back toward the hireling shepherd, who casually embraces her from behind as if to show her a flower in his hand, bringing them cheek-to-cheek. Her sidelong glance says she is willing, and in the meantime, sheep are going astray and a lamb on her lap get itself sick on green apples. The "idealized Romantic pastoralism" is overthrown (Hilton 1970, 88), and, like Lena, the shepherdess, with her sensuality, has tempted the shepherd into creating chaos

Figure 9.1.   William Holman Hunt, 1827–1910, *The Hireling Shepherd,* **1851. Oil on canvas, 76.4 × 109.5 cm, Manchester City Galleries, Manchester, UK. Photo © Manchester City Galleries.**

Still, Lena resists characterization into types as well. As an adult, her commercial sensibility trains her to sell beauty in the form of dresses to elegant ladies; at the same time, she makes no effort to trap and keep men with her sexuality. Though he associates her with the Dumas' courtesan Camille, she rejects long-term relationships: "Men are all right for friends, but as soon as you marry them they turn in to cranky old fathers, even the wild ones" (Cather 1918/1987, 892). She is not, like the temptress archetype, trying to trap men.

After Ántonia comes home pregnant and unmarried, Jim attempts to read her story by the light of other archetypal models, though she never quite fits. The shame of an illegitimate child should signify the fall of the Temptress, yet Ántonia loves her baby, "was never ashamed of it," and is a "natural born mother" (906). She could appear as the Crushed Flower type, like Ophelia jilted and maddened by a faithless man, except that she does not commit a beautiful suicide as shown in John Everett Millais' painting of Ophelia; rather, she maintains her dignity and bears all her hardship sturdily. Eventually Jim plugs her into the muse archetype and rests at that. Though Jim would have her play some conventional role in relation to himself, seductress or muse, she creates her own roles, as "subject rather than object," as Rosowski argues, and she "has written her own script . . . far richer and more meaningful . . . than any that her narrator or her culture would impose upon her" (Rosowski 1992, 111). Though her beauty captivates Jim, she ultimately avoids capture, resists becoming *his* creation, *his* work of art, *his* Ántonia.

The work in which Willa Cather most evidently examines the male artistic gaze on the female subject is "Coming, Aphrodite!" the tale of a young New York painter in his passionate encounter with the beautiful aspiring singer. Both the goddess in the title and the name of the heroine (Eden Bower) signal the connection with Pre-Raphaelites. Edward Burne-Jones's beautiful works *Venus Discordia* (1872–73) and *Venus Concordia* (1872) (fig. 9.2) were among the unfinished paintings that thrilled Cather during her visit to his studio (Cather 1902/1956, 73), and the goddess of love turns up stunningly in the form of Astarte in Dante Gabriel Rossetti's later paintings as well. Moreover, the name Eden Bower is also the title of a poem by Rossetti about Lilith, the evil first wife of Adam of Talmudic tradition.

In the paintings by both artists, the goddess of love is hugely powerful, controlling and enchanting men. In Burne-Jones's *Venus Discordia* the goddess sits on her throne to left, legs crossed and chin on hand observing the chaos that passionate love engenders. At center, male nudes wrestle and fight to the death, while female nudes, right, huddle together, arms crossed before their breasts, frightened. In Rossetti's picture *Astarte Syriaca* (1877) and his accompanying sonnet, by the same name, Astarte or

Figure 9.2. Edward Burne-Jones, 1833–1898, *Venus Discordia*, 1872–1873. Oil on canvas, 128.2 × 209.8 cm, National Museums and Galleries of Wales. Photo credit: National Museum of Wales.

"Venus Queen/Ere Aphrodite was," holds the viewer transfixed, center stage, larger than life. All must be enthralled, as Rossetti writes, to "that face, of Love's all-penetrative spell/Amulet, talisman, and oracle" (Treuherz, Prettejohn, and Becker 2003, 214). These portraits show a temptress par excellence, whose power brings about ruin.

Lilith, from Rossetti's poem "Eden Bower," is all evil and jealousy. Her story originates from the existence in the Hebrew Bible of two stories of creation, one in which God creates man and woman simultaneously and the other in which he makes Eve from Adam's rib. This dual explanation gave rise to the tale of Lilith, the first wife of Adam, spurned and jealous at Adam's new love. In Rossetti's poem, Lilith takes the serpent's shape so that she can take revenge on Adam and Eve. Lilith, the speaker, uses the refrain "(Eden bower's in flower)," making use of that favorite Victorian word "bower" for a nature-oriented sexual couch (Merritt 1966, 62–70). Rossetti's 1868 painting entitled *Lady Lilith* emphasizes the physical (Treuherz, Prettejohn, and Becker 2003, 63) (fig. 9.3). The woman in a loose gown falling from her shoulders sits against a background of roses, watching herself in a hand mirror as she runs a comb outward through her long, wavy, red hair. Poisonous foxglove lies on the table to her right, where a standing mirror reflects the outdoor scene behind the viewer. In this very intimate seduction of the viewer, the woman seems not to be aware of the audience. She wants to captivate the male gazer, but to appear indifferent.

This image makes a lovely starting point for an examination of Cather's Eden Bower. The first time Don Hedger sees her—that is, really looks at her—is through a knot-hole in the wall of his closet that adjoins her apartment:

> Yonder, in a pool of sunlight, stood his new neighbor, wholly unclad, doing exercises of some sort before a long gilt mirror. Hedger did not happen to think how unpardonable it was of him to watch her. Nudity was not improper to any one who had worked so much from the figure, and he continued to look because he had never seen a woman's body so beautiful as this one,—positively glorious in action. The soft flush of exercise and the gold of afternoon sun played over her flesh together, enveloped her in a luminous mist which, as she turned and twisted, made now an arm, now a shoulder, now a thigh, dissolve in pure light and instantly recover its outline in the next gesture. (Cather 1920/1992, 366)

She appears, like Lilith, to be unaware of her viewer, though we find out later she knew about the knot-hole. Hedger immediately imagines drawing her and "the charcoal seemed to explode in his hand." When he gets off his knees in his dusty closet, he feels captivated by "a vision out of Alexandria, out of the remote pagan past." Though he claims her through

Figure 9.3.   Dante Gabriel Rossetti, 1828–1882, *Lady Lilith*, 1866–1868 (altered 1872–1873). Oil on canvas, 38 × 33 1/2 inches, Delaware Art Museum, Samuel and Mary R. Bancroft Memorial, 1935.

his gaze, he begins a period of thralldom, in which he is compelled to watch her each day and stops painting: "His brain held but one image now—vibrated, burned with it" (367). Her feminine power rules and isolates him. His artistic image of her cast into exotic roles controls him and makes him in turn want to depict her in order to capture her.

This story more than the others explains the relationship between the male gaze and the female subject matter of art, according to the Pre-

Raphaelite attitude. In the other tales, we see the young Aesthete trying to lay claim to the beautiful woman, possessing her through his duty and his loyalty—and we see her slip away from him by defying expectations. Here, however, we see the female image captivating and controlling the man. Thus we see Hedger as "the Captive" eunuch in the story of the Aztec Rain Princess that he recounts. The beauty of the princess's body drives a man to force himself upon her, and, as punishment, he is enslaved to her, emasculated, and made dumb. He becomes powerless, incapable of self-expression, just like the obsessed Don Hedger.

For the Pre-Raphaelite artists, the way to counter this feminine power was to claim it, to restrict it to the role of paint on canvas, and thus to use its power for the artist's expression. Indeed when Don and Eden come together sexually, he returns to painting. Her passion, which—like art—should not be cheapened by the marketplace, is given freely, and she smashes the locks on her side of the doors connecting their apartments as a symbol of releasing her slave and permitting him access to her. She is neither the blessed virgin, locked away from men, nor the unfaithful wife, who falls to her own passion. Yet, Don is angered by Eden's willingness to show her body off to please a crowd, as she does performing balloon stunts at Coney Island. Eden is perplexed at Don's unwillingness to paint what people like, to "make money" and "try to get a public" (389). They break up over the question of the right use of art: she believes the artist plays a role to please an audience, and Hedger stands firm that he, like the ideal Pre-Raphaelite painter, "works to please nobody but himself" (389). To readers, this may seem, as the narrator states, "an abstraction" (388). Yet, nothing could be more central to the gender issues in Pre-Raphaelite art.

The woman, following Aesthetic thinking, *is* the work of art, the object the viewer looks at, even if it is her artist's conception of her. Her value lies in the beauty of her body, the extent to which she meets the expectation of the viewer, and the tragic consequences of her passion. The man is the artist. His subject may captivate him, but it is he who creates her; his role is to please himself, not a public. She can be pure, like the Blessed Damsel, but only to please a public, so that her image can be sold on a canvas; thence she becomes tainted, prostituted for the gain of the artist.

Conversely, Eden, as a singer, is also an artist, but one whose existence is dependent on public pleasure. She must act out all the female roles, sell herself, place her name on a marquis for all to see, for a performance without an audience cannot qualify as a work of art. But it is in acknowledging that she is both artist and subject that the female (performing) artist captivates her audience. She plays roles according to her own strategy and, when the curtain comes down, goes back to being her authentic self. The power of the role, then, is not claimed by a painter who shapes her image according to his ideals but by the woman and artist herself, who thus retains the power of expression that her passion engenders.

This is why Don Hedger is confused when Eden leaves him. He had cast her into the role of temptress and escaped her snare, the world of commercialized art. Later he repents and returns, ready to submit to her power. When he comes home, however, she is gone, the knothole plugged up, a note left for him explaining how she has moved on. The curtain has fallen—the show is over. When Eden returns from Europe eighteen years later, her name is in lights. Don is not on display as she is, but he is "one of the first men among the moderns." Not having sold out, he still paints for himself and "for all the young men," and he is now "a great influence in art" (395). The male artist retains his authentic vision of the world. The female artist seems diminished, her now-aged face appearing "in the ugly orange light" of streetlamps, yet we are assured she will be revivified the following night in "the golden face of Aphrodite" (396).

Through these stories, Willa Cather allows readers to look through the eyes of the Aesthete male painter to see women as a series of possibly beautiful and tragic tales, meant to inspire pathos. The figures captivate and enthrall their viewers, as their images are captured and shaped by their artists' visions. But Cather also turns our gaze on the male artists, whose devotion to certain idealized archetypes prevents them from understanding a complete female person. These male artists are able to remain "pure" by selling not themselves but the passion and power of the women who figure in their works. Clearly, Cather also recognized and was drawn to the beauty and passion of the female form as it appears in the stop-frame of the Pre-Raphaelite painting; but she could not freeze the figure there. Her women write their own stories and resist characterization into familiar tragic plots. As her unfaithful wife survives, as her fallen farm girl redefines herself, as her beautiful female nude moves and exercises, they become even more powerful than the temptresses and fallen ladies of the canvas. Cather's heroines rise on their own power to create themselves, insist on themselves, and weave the web of their own stories.

WORKS CITED

Cather, Willa. 1902/1956. "London: Burne-Jones's Studio." In *Willa Cather in Europe: Her Own Story of the First Journey*. Edited by George N. Kates, 65–79. New York: Knopf.

———. 1918/1987. *My Ántonia*" In *Early Novels and Stories*. Edited by Sharon O'Brien, 707–937 . New York: Library of America.

———. 1920/1992. "Coming Aphrodite!" In *Stories, Poems, and Other Writings*. Edited by Sharon O'Brien, 357–96. New York: Library of America.

———. 1923/1990. *A Lost Lady*. In *Later Novels*. Edited by Sharon O'Brien, 1–98. New York: Library of America.

Hall, James. 1974. *Dictionary of Subjects and Symbols in Art*. Boulder, CO: Westview Press.

Hilton, Timothy. 1970. *The Pre-Raphaelites*. London: Thames & Hudson.

Merritt, James D., ed. 1966. *The Pre-Raphaelite Poem*. New York: E. P. Dutton.

Prettejohn, Elizabeth. 2007. *The Art of the Pre-Raphaelites*. London: Tate.

Psomiades, Kathy Alexis. 1997. *Beauty's Body: Femininity and Representation in British Aestheticism*. Stanford, CA: Stanford University Press.

Rosowski, Susan. 1992. "Willa Cather's Visions and Revisions of Female Lives." In *Images of the Self as Female: The Achievement of Women Artists in Re-Envisioning Feminine Identity*. Edited by Kathryn N. Benzel and Lauren Pringle, 107–17. Lewistown: Edwin Mellen.

Treuherz, Julian, Elizabeth Prettejohn, and Edwin Becker. 2003. *Dante Gabriel Rossetti*. London: Thames & Hudson.

Wildman, Stephen, and John Christian. 1998. *Edward Burne-Jones: Victorian Artist-Dreamer*. New York: Metropolitan Museum of Art.

Chapter 10

Fernand Léger and Willa Cather's "Coming, Aphrodite!"

Jacqueline H. Harris

In 1920, Willa Cather's second collection of short stories, entitled *Youth and the Bright Medusa*, included "Coming, Aphrodite!," a story focusing on the relationship between painter Don Hedger and opera singer Eden Bower and on their disagreements concerning the aesthetics of art. Cather, a so-called Francophile, had made her first trip to Europe with Isabelle McClung some eighteen years prior, to tour the English and French cultures and see artists she had for so long admired (Wagenknecht 1994, 29). It was during this journey that, "with all the fire and immediacy of the modern age, she first began to feel the admiration and love of French art [and] French form, which has set such an impress on her work" (Lewis 1953, 560), no doubt involving the great influence of the nineteenth-century Aesthetic movement, or the idea of *l'art pour l'art* that had so greatly penetrated European artists' lives (Abrams 1999, 3). Regarding the influence of France on Cather during her first visit to that country, Robert Thacker writes, "Poised as she was . . . on the verge of her most mature and complex writing, Cather was about to reach the goal she had set for herself while she was still living in Nebraska. Like Eden Bower in 'Coming, Aphrodite!' who knew early 'that she was to be Eden Bower,' Willa Sibert Cather . . . was about to become Willa Cather, author indeed, in the midst of her own major phase" (Thacker 2006, 45). Indeed, Willa Cather was strongly affected by the beauty of the French art she viewed, as demonstrated in the strong correlation between the artistic philosophies of France's burgeoning artistic icon, Fernand Léger, and her own character, Don Hedger.

The goal of immersing herself in French culture was one that greatly affected the work that Cather subsequently produced. French history, culture, art, and language influenced Cather's writings for the rest of her career. In "Coming, Aphrodite!" she may have pulled from her knowledge of French art and the French artist Fernand Léger for her New York–based story. The connection between Fernand Léger and Don Hedger lies in more than the coincidental sound of their names. The connection is also found in their similar artistic backgrounds and stylistic choices. In "Coming, Aphrodite!" Cather not only demonstrates the important influence of an artist's art on other artists but also re-reads male texts (such as Léger's paintings) within her own female-empowered story. While Fernand Léger is often identified with his exploration of artistic genres within his paintings, Léger was greatly influenced by his birth in the age of the French Aesthetic movement that was later introduced into Victorian England. His country's history and role in the birth of the Aesthetic movement are reflected in his beliefs about the need for art for art's sake that helped motivate his painting.

Fernand Léger, whose art has been called a "special achievement," was born in France in 1881 and would both participate within and continue to influence artistic movements and genres up until his death in 1955 (Faerna 1996, 5). Of Léger's legacy, Serge Fauchereau writes, "when he died, the world discovered to its stupefaction that the man who had quietly practiced his painterly craft with such calm passion was [such] a universal figure that his death left a major gap in the art of our century" (1994, 8). Léger himself argued for the ideals behind the Aesthetic movement and the need to see the "beautiful phenomena" that surround us when he wrote that "Every object, picture, piece of architecture, or ornamental organization has a value in itself; it is strictly absolute and independent of anything it may happen to represent. . . . Beauty is everywhere, in the arrangement of your pots and pans, [and] on the white wall of your kitchen" (1973, 505). Léger used his ability to see beauty in the world around him and to capture this allure on canvas. Considering Cather's love and appreciation for French art from 1902, along with Léger's artistic development and increasing influence during the years to follow as well as the similarities between his works and images created in "Coming, Aphrodite!," Léger could well have been the inspiration for Cather's artistic framing of Don Hedger. With his French exhibits coinciding with Cather's repeated trips to France,[1] it is likely that she would have been aware of his prominent rise in France's modernist art movement and would have kept up with his work after her return. Robert Thacker comments on Cather's need to see the world abroad, stating that "Cather had first gone to France in 1902, a young woman of very serious literary ambitions bent to absorb as much of France—and of Europe generally—as she could" (2006, 45).

Edward Wagenknecht comments on Cather's first trip to Europe and her fondness for impressionism, cubism, and the Fauves (1994, 38); all three of these painting genres are reflected in the span of Fernand Léger's work. Edith Lewis also wrote about the influence of the French on Cather, recording, "I think French culture, coming to it as she did in her most impressionable years, and finding it so new, so challenging and awakening, spoke . . . directly to her imagination, and . . . definitely influenced her writing" (1953, 56). Additionally, Cather once wrote that if France "were to take a landslide into the sea some day, there would not be much creative power of any sort left in the world" (Woodress 1987, 426; Wagenknecht 1994, 38). While Wagenknecht alludes to the French influence on Cather, verified by Edith Lewis, little literary criticism—except within this volume—has pointed to French painters directly influencing Cather's texts. However, Fernand Léger's devotion to Cézanne and his paintings and Léger's own work in cubism are echoed in the artistic idealism and imagery found in "Coming, Aphrodite!" Even though Léger himself is not a direct prototype for Don Hedger, his work is a palpable presence in Cather's short story.[2]

Cather begins "Coming, Aphrodite!" with an introduction to the painter Don Hedger and the city setting of his apartment studio. Wagenknecht refers to Cather's introduction of Hedger's home as her own "French postcard" (1994, 38). When Cather first traveled abroad to London and then France, she observed several different artist studios. When in Barbizon, she dined at Hôtel des Artistes, which she later recorded "derives its very attractive name from the fact that it has a studio to let, and that the walls of the bar are decorated with oil sketches, furnished mostly by painters who were unable to pay their accounts" (Cather 1956, 123). While Cather was depicting an artist in New York, she recalls her time abroad in her city setting. In the short story, Hedger lives "on the top floor of an old house on the south side of Washington Square" in which the owner "sublet her rooms, with their precious furniture, to young people who came to New York to 'write' or to 'paint'—who proposed to live by the sweat of the brow rather than of the hand, and who desired artistic surroundings" (Cather 1920, 11, 12)—a literal site where Cather once lived herself.

From 1908 to 1909, Léger also lived in an artists' studio, La Ruche ("The Beehive"), where he befriended painters Delaunay, Chagall, and Soutine (Léger 1973, xxxi). Don Hedger lives in a similar artistic atmosphere with a "studio window that looked upon a court and upon the roofs and walls of the other buildings" (Cather 1920, 11). When Cather wrote this scene, she may have been inspired by Léger's painting series that depicted a similar view from La Ruche—including *Fumées sur les toits* (*Smoke Over the Rooftops*), c. 1911, which would likely have been included within his exhibitions (Brunhammer 2005, 30), one she could relate to from her experiences at 60 South Washington Square in Greenwich Village and that she could have compared to the studios at Hôtel des Artistes in France. Perhaps such a studio seemed, in her own experience and in her observations abroad, to be an ideal artistic living quarters. If Hedger is to play the role of an influential painter, living the lifestyle of true artists such as Cather and Léger, his living in a similar physical setting helps to validate his commitment to the artistic lifestyle.

As Cather develops Hedger's character, the reader learns about his draughtsman experience and devotion to the French artist "C——" (Cather 1920, 36), both details that connect with the life of Léger and further suggest that Cather was aware of this artist, his life, and work. From 1897 to 1904, Léger was first apprentice and then draftsman to architects in France (Léger 1973, xxxi). Hedger is likewise an "expert draughtsman" who could use his skill for commercial work when he was in need of money to support his painting lifestyle (Cather 1920, 18). The "biggest man among the moderns," described only as "C——" in "Coming, Aphrodite!", is most likely Paul Cézanne, who greatly influenced Léger's cubist style. Originally painting in the impressionist style, Léger was struck by Cézanne's work after visiting one of his exhibitions in 1907. According to José Maria Faerna, Léger acknowledged that "it was from Cézanne's work that he learned to love abstract shapes as entities in themselves and to concentrate on creating a composition that would be both precise and utterly devoid of sentimentality" (1996, 10). The abstract shapes are reflected in the depiction of Don Hedger's painting—in his experimentation with "unusual lighting," for example (Cather 1920, 13). In recalling Cézanne's art, one might not think of his influence upon lighting, but his style was in fact very influential to new artists like Léger in this aspect of painterly composition. For example, Morgan Russell (1886–1953), one of Léger's contemporaries, pulled from Cézanne just as Léger and Don Hedger do (Stavisky and Rothkopf 2009, 284). Of his admiration for Cézanne, Léger wrote not only that "one painter among the impressionists, Cézanne, understood everything that was incomplete in traditional painting" but also that Cézanne "was the only one of the impressionists to lay his finger on the deeper meaning of plastic life, because of his sensitivity to the contrast of forms" (Léger 1973, 5, 17). Léger soon began experimenting with cubist styles, eventually creating his own "tubist" form, a cylindrical version of cubism (5). Aware of Léger's draughtsman background and connection to Cézanne, Cather may have been influenced by Léger to use him as a model for Hedger.

When Hedger first meets singer Eden Bower, they cross paths outside their rooms in the hallway where they share a bathroom. Before their conversation begins, Hedger sees her as an artist sees and observes Eden's stature as a "tall figure in a flowing blue silk dressing-gown that fell away from her marble arms" (Cather 1920, 23). Rather than arms of flesh and blood, hers are "marble," an artistic medium. Hedger initially sees Eden as a potential subject for his art, rather than as a living woman. Thus Hedger is enforcing his artistic, objective framework on Eden Bower, a woman who will never give herself completely to him but who will instead use her sexual power over him to please herself. In 1912 as Léger began to develop his own style, he painted *La Femme en bleu* (*The Woman in Blue*), an oil painting that can be interpreted as an abstract form of a woman in blue surrounded by multicolored (including marble-toned) surroundings. This Fernand Léger painting is one from which Cather may have derived some of her artistic imagery for this moment in her short story.

Before Hedger becomes acquainted with Eden, he discovers a cleared knot-hole in the wall of his closet dividing his apartment from hers. "Without realizing what he was doing," Don begins watching Eden through the hole as she either exercises or lounges "wholly unclad" (Cather 1920, 26). Hedger becomes transfixed with Eden and her body: "Nudity was not improper to any one who had worked so much from the figure, and he continued to look, simply because he had never seen a woman's body so beautiful as this one,—positively glorious in action" (Cather 1920, 26). Hedger sees Eden's body as one of movement, suggesting that his painting or sketching of her would likewise try to convey a sense of action. Léger's early nude sketches likewise depict women amidst multiple curving and abstract lines that might suggest movement, as seen in his 1909–11 *Seated Female Nude* and 1913 *Seated Nude*. While one might hastily assume the subject in *Seated Female Nude* was stationary, deeper analysis suggests that the woman is in the midst of moving or transitioning her body. The subject's leg appears to have just been pulled to her chest, and yet the ink strokes around her arm, thigh, and calf suggest that she is about to move yet again. In Léger's *Seated Nude*, the long vertical stroke depicting the female's neck appears to be stretching and extending upwards, almost off of the canvas.

Hedger's obsession with Eden grows as he repeatedly watches her through the hole as she reclines undressed in her apartment. Her body and sexuality hold a power over him that he cannot understand. Afterwards, Hedger looks at the rest of the world without pleasure and says, "Everything here [is] different; he hated [it] . . . . He felt desperate" (28). He will later say that Eden's body has him "completely possessed" and that he is unable to continue his work: "He was not painting at all now. This thing, whatever it was, drank him up as ideas had sometimes done, and he sank into a stupor of idleness as deep and dark as the stupor of work" (30). Hedger's sexuality leaves him impaired and unable to pursue his work. Thus Cather begins to turn the tables on her male character, for he is now losing his power and sense of self to a woman.

Hedger later invites Eden to accompany him to Coney Island, where one of his painting models is going up in a balloon. Upon arriving at the location for the event, Cather inserts a key description of the Coney Island circus setting: "A red-faced man in a linen suit stood in front of the tent, shouting in a hoarse voice and telling the people that if the crowd was good for five dollars more, a beautiful young woman would risk her life for their entertainment. Four little boys in dirty red uniforms ran about taking contributions in their pillbox hats" (46). After Cather establishes this circus background, complete with red-faced announcers and red-uniformed boys, the balloon begins to rise, and we see Hedger's model, Molly Welch, for the first time. As Molly begins to perform her aerial acrobatics, she is twice described as wearing green tights while moving about the trapeze.

The themes of circus and acrobatics reappear throughout Fernand Léger's art, just as they play a key role in "Coming, Aphrodite!" Limiting ourselves solely to Léger paintings that Cather would have been aware of before the 1920 publication of "Coming, Aphrodite!," three paintings contain subjects and settings similar to Cather's descriptions of Molly Welch, her costume, and her circus background. In 1914 Léger painted *La Femme en Rouge et Vert* (*The Woman in Red and Green*), a portrait that is echoed in Molly Welch's red and green costume. In 1918, he painted *Médrano*, which depicts a circus within a city setting, a background similar to Cather's Coney Island scene. In 1918, Léger also painted *Les Acrobates dans le Cirque* (*The Acrobats at the Circus*), which depicts an acrobatic spectacle at a circus setting. These three paintings, when paired with the "Coming, Aphrodite!" text published just a couple of years later, suggest a clear connection between Léger's work and Cather's subtle allusions to him and his art.

But these circus scenes are also important in what they say about Eden's control over her body as a commodity. The Coney Island scene in "Coming, Aphrodite!" shows Eden within a sexualized spectacle in which she is a willing participant, and her open showcase of her body makes Don Hedger the uncomfortable one, as he would only violate her sexuality in private while peering at her through the hole in his closet wall. But Eden displays her body and participates in the circus and the scene in the hot air balloon because it not only puts her body physically and symbolically on display but also puts it out of Hedger's reach. Eden resists letting Hedger, the artist, define or control who she is. Eden refuses to be objectified in Hedger's sketches of her, choosing instead to be a three-dimensional force in real life.

Part of Hedger's purpose in telling "The Forty Lovers of the Queen" to Eden later that evening is to reassert his power over Eden, power that he lost at the circus, or perhaps realized he never had. Hedger wants to show Eden he can shape a female's story from his own perspective through his verbal storytelling as another type of creative depiction separate from his visual art. But Eden will once again show Hedger that she will not allow him, or any other male, to ever have that control. When Eden later comes up to join Hedger on the rooftop, Cather describes the commencement of their love affair: "Standing against the black chimney, with the sky behind and blue shadows before, they looked like one of Hedger's own paintings of that period; two figures, one white and one dark, and nothing whatever distinguishable about them but that they were male and female. The faces were lost, the contours blurred in shadow, but the figures were a man and a woman, and that was their whole concern and their mysterious beauty—it was the rhythm in which they moved, at last, along the roof and down into the dark hole; he first, drawing her gently after him" (62–63). Even as suggested by Cather's word choice, Hedger views Eden as something to be objectified as, in a clever pun, he "draw[s] her gently after him."

This scene and, as the narrator comments, its resemblance to one of Hedger's own paintings (62), could, in fact, be an allusion to *La Noce* (*The Wedding*), painted in 1910 by Léger, although the title *La Noce* would have been ironic for Cather as there certainly will be no marriage or spiritual union between Don and Eden. Fauchereau describes *La Noce* as "a multiple perspective which disperses the subject and breaks it up with non-representational planes. . . . [T]hose elements are still indicated by shading . . . [and] they become flatly geometrical areas of pure colour" (1994, 10). Even an unskilled eye can find mysterious aesthetic beauty in the abstract forms in Léger's painting. As Hedger tells his story of the consequences of female desire to Eden, a woman he wants to control, the artistic framing of their conversation connects to an artist's depiction of a wedding, the ultimate commitment of men and women. But Eden will never submit herself to Hedger or give him power over her by uniting with him; when Eden ultimately realizes their deep-rooted disagreements about art and life, she will leave him, never having lost her passion or desire for her own form of aesthetic expression despite Hedger's attempts to control her.

Cather recasts French art with the descriptions in her short story, thus giving Fernand Léger's artwork another form in her writing. But how is Cather re-reading women within the same space? Cather gave great capacity and agency to her character Eden Bower. In her article "Coming, Willa Cather!," Marilyn Arnold points toward this freedom when she states that, "Eden Bower is the *whole* woman. . . . Eden is all of them and more; she is elemental woman, she is sexual . . . but her sexuality is more open, joyous, harmonious, unconscious, essential. . . . Almost nowhere else in modern American fiction has elemental passion, the mystery of innate feeling between men and women, been described with more grace and sensitivity" (1984, 248). Additional consideration, however, needs to be given to how Eden Bower defies Hedger and his telling of "The Forty Lovers of the Queen" and how she keeps agency over her sexuality, never fully surrendering it to Hedger, while at the same time continuing to pursue her art.

"The Forty Lovers of the Queen" tells the story of a woman who is punished for her sexual promiscuity by ultimately being burned at the stake. Hedger presumably tells the tale as a warning but, in a twist, actually for his own personal interest. To him, Eden should not, cannot be sexually promiscuous, as he interprets her actions at the circus, although these actions are acceptable for his model Molly. In other words, he believes that Eden's sexuality ought to be used only for his personal pleasure. His hypocrisy continues in his attempt to frighten Eden by insinuating she will have a nasty end if she, too, follows that path. But Eden is not thwarted, choosing never to submit herself or control over her actions to Hedger. After Hedger's telling of the story, the narrative voice switches to Eden, declaring, "Now she was looking at the man he really was. Nobody's eyes had ever defied her like this. . . . He was testing her, trying her out" (Cather 1920, 59). While Eden is definitely disturbed by Hedger's machismo, she still knows what she wants and will proceed anyway, now even more determined that she will never submit to Hedger's plan for her to play an objective role in his life and his life alone.

Hedger and Eden's relationship continues, but they ultimately fight about their conflicting definitions of success. Years later when Eden inquires about the painter, she learns "he is one of the first men among the moderns. That is to say, among the very moderns . . . [h]e is a great name with all the young men, and he is decidedly an influence in art" (77). This description of Hedger could be the concluding paragraph in any biography on the life of Fernand Léger. By participating in various movements from impressionism to cubism, creating tubism (Léger's cylindrically shaped version of cubism), and then moving more completely toward abstraction following the publication of Cather's "Coming, Aphrodite!" Léger clearly fits the artist Hedger becomes, one who was "original, erratic, and who is changing all the time" (Cather 1920, 77). Cather's subtle allusions to Fernand Léger throughout "Coming, Aphrodite!" serve as a tribute to both the "special achievement" of his art (Faerna 1996, 5) and the life-changing influence of the French on Willa Cather.

It has often been said that Cather believed that one could not be both an artist and a sexual being at the same time, that only one pathway could be pursued. This conclusion is supposedly demonstrated by Eden's leaving Hedger in order to travel to Paris. What has been ignored, however, are the subtle implications throughout "Coming, Aphrodite!" suggesting not only that Eden is in control of her sexual influence over Hedger but also that he holds no power over her. She, in fact, wields her own power over Hedger, and when she tires, she moves on, thus never abandoning her power but rather abandoning one of her subjects. Thus Hedger becomes the objectified one, with the sexual roles reversed. Eden, the female, is now the one in control, and the male artist, Hedger, is the one unable to create an objectified portrait of an unwilling subject.

"Coming, Aphrodite!" ends with Eden fully in control. When Hedger finds the empty knothole in his closet wall and watches Eden exercise and recline in the nude, she is both aware of his peeping and purposefully performing for him, knowing the power she will have over him once he becomes transfixed with her and her Aphrodite, goddess-like control over him. After Eden leaves and Hedger finds one of her dressing gowns in his closet, he also finds that the knothole has been refilled with the same paper on which Eden wrote the note. Eden wanted Hedger to watch her. Eden is no longer, and in fact never was, the victim; it is Hedger who is fooled.

The story of "The Forty Lovers of the Queen" has often been read as a warning to women to avoid domination over men, a path that will supposedly and ultimately end in death. However, Eden never suffers for her control over Hedger, as the Queen of the Aztecs does in Hedger's story. Instead, Eden uses Hedger. She gets what she wants from Hedger, but when she has finished with him, she is still able to travel to Paris to pursue her singing career, and she becomes very popular and successful. Additionally, Eden is never limited by Hedger's sly use of her as a sexual model for his art because she refuses to pose for him and thus refuses to be molded by Hedger's interpretation of her, true or not. Hedger, too, finally returns to his painting after Eden leaves and also has great artistic success. However, there is never an indication within "Coming, Aphrodite!" that during their relationship Eden set aside her singing with the same abandon that Hedger does his painting. Hedger's submission to Eden leaves him powerless to create art whereas Eden's control of Hedger never interrupts her artistic pursuits. She is able to have the best of both worlds.

But what is to be made of the final scene, of Eden's triumphant return to New York and her discovery of Hedger's success? Many would say that the "hard and settled" appearance of Eden's face upon learning of Hedger's success points to her disappointment and that Cather's final sentence, "But a 'big' career takes its toll, even with the best of luck" (78), shows that Eden could not have it all. However, women—and Eden in particular—are more complex than this interpretation suggests. The description of Eden's face as looking like a "plaster cast" (78) suggests, in fact, that Eden is still in control, for a plaster cast is a rendition or interpretation of a face—not the face itself. Hedger sought to control Eden, but she never succumbed to his attempts. As a beautiful woman with a lovely form, Eden may inspire *l'art pour l'art*. However, by not sitting for Hedger's drawings or disregarding her artistic dreams and staying in New York with him, Eden is able to remain true to herself. Perhaps in the end, Eden is playing a role, the role of a thwarted lover, but she remains the actor behind the mask, the one always in control. She lured Hedger to her, she transfixed him with her body, she made him worry when she traded places with Molly Welch, and she left him when he would have held her back from pursuing her dreams. Eden Bower is an actress, capable of fulfilling whatever role she needs to play for the moment; at the end of the story, she plays the role of someone who is disappointed, but in actuality "Tomorrow night the wind would blow again, and this mask would be the golden face of Aphrodite" (78).

Time and time again, Willa Cather invites us to re-read her texts and characters just as she has been re-reading art, history, and humanity in her own writing. Just as Fernand Léger was greatly influenced by the Aesthetic movement's pursuit of beauty and art for its own sake and later created his own artistic forms, so too is Eden Bower representative of a complicated artist choosing when to explore and when to reject the variety of roles and opportunities that lie before her. Indeed, the artistic talent and control exhibited by Fernand Léger can be seen not only in Don Hedger but also in Eden Bower.

NOTES

1. While Léger's artwork would eventually merit solo exhibits in Paris, he first began exhibiting painting submissions in the famous Salon d'Automne in 1907 and continued to exhibit there through the early 1920s. Cather, who visited Paris multiple times during the course of her life (in 1902, 1920, 1927, and 1934), would have also been there during the painter's exhibitions and would have been able to view his work and recognize his growing impact in the Cubist movement (Dantini 2008, 31; Woodress 1987, 156, 310, 420, 457).

2. The extensive body of Fernand Léger's work is housed in a number of museums and private collections. The works discussed in this essay can be found online: "Seated Nude" (1913) through The Museum of Modern Art, "La femme en

rouge et vert" (1914) through Christie's, and "Les Acrobates dans le cirque" (1918) and "Medrano" (1918) through general internet search engines.

WORKS CITED

Abrams, M. H. 1999. *A Glossary of Literary Terms*. 7th ed. New York: Harcourt.

Arnold, Marilyn. 1984. "Coming, Willa Cather!" *Women's Studies, An Interdisciplinary Journal* 11 (3): 247–60.

Brunhammer, Yvonne. 2005. *Fernand Léger: The Monumental Art*. Milan: Grafiche.

Cather, Willa. 1920. "Coming, Aphrodite!" In *Youth and the Bright Medusa*, 11–78. New York: Knopf.

———. 1956. *Willa Cather in Europe: Her Own Story of the First Journey*. Introduction and notes by George N. Kates. Lincoln: University of Nebraska Press.

Dantini, Michele. 2008. *Modern and Contemporary Art*. Translated by Timothy Stroud. New York: Sterling.

Faerna, José María, ed. 1996. *Great Modern Masters: Léger*. Translated by Alberto Curotto. New York: Abrams.

Fauchereau, Serge. 1994. *Fernand Léger: A Painter in the City*. New York: Rizzoli.

Léger, Fernand. 1973. *Functions of Painting*. Translated by Alexander Anderson, edited by Edward F. Fry. New York: Viking.

Lewis, Edith. 1953. *Willa Cather Living: A Personal Record*. New York: Knopf.

Stavisky, Gail, and Katherine Rothkopf. 2009. *Cézanne and American Modernism*. New Haven, CT: Yale University Press.

Thacker, Robert. 2006. "Object Lesson: Cather's 1923 Passport." *Willa Cather Newsletter and Review* 50 (2): 44-45.

Wagenknecht, Edward. 1994. *Willa Cather*. New York: Continuum.

Woodress, James. 1987. *Willa Cather: A Literary Life*. Lincoln: University of Nebraska Press.

Part III

MOVEMENT TOWARD MODERNISM

Chapter 11

"The Nude Had Descended the Staircase"

Katherine Anne Porter Looks at Willa Cather Looking at Modern Art

Janis P. Stout

The phrase quoted in my title, "the nude had descended the staircase," comes from Katherine Anne Porter's essay "Reflections on Willa Cather." Its allusion is of course to the painting *Nude Descending a Staircase, No. 2* (1912) by Marcel Duchamp, first exhibited in the United States at the 1913 Armory Show in New York (see fig. 11.1). In making her passing reference, Porter assumed that readers would recognize the allusion and understand its significance. And it was a good assumption. Duchamp's cubist nude has long served as an icon of modernism's break with traditional concepts and praxis in art.

I have argued elsewhere that "Reflections on Willa Cather" is an essentially duplicitous essay in which the ever insecure Porter, herself an icon of literary modernism but fearful that her halting production would erode her future place in literary history, sought to strengthen her position in that prospective history by weakening that of her slightly older contemporary. Invoking the nude on the staircase as a touchstone, she sought to position Cather outside the project of modernism altogether where, she strongly implied, Cather persevered in a stodgy and backward-looking aesthetic (Stout 1994).

Porter's essay on Cather was first written as a book review in the *New York Times* of Cather's posthumous collection *On Writing* (Cather 1949); the review was entitled "The Calm, Pure Art of Willa Cather." When the review reappeared in greatly expanded and revised form three years later in *Mademoiselle*, it bore the title "Reflections on Willa Cather"—a title that

153

Figure 11.1.   Marcel Duchamp, 1887–1968, *Nude Descending a Staircase (No. 2)*, 1912. Oil on canvas. 57 7/8 × 35 1/8 inches (147 × 89.2 cm), Philadelphia Museum of Art: The Louise and Walter Arensberg Collection, 1950. © 2012 Artists Rights Society (ARS), New York / ADAGP, Paris / Succession Marcel Duchamp.

well describes both the loosely associative form of the essay and its shift in emphasis from appreciation to assessment. It appears under this latter title in Porter's *Collected Essays and Occasional Writings* (1952/1970). The passage in which the nude makes her appearance asserts Cather's indifference to modernism in music and literature as well as visual art:

> Stravinsky had happened; but she went on being dead in love with Wagner, Beethoven, Schubert, Gluck, especially *Orpheus*, and almost any opera. She was music-mad, and even Ravel's *La Valse* enchanted her; perhaps also even certain later music, but she has not mentioned it [in the essays collected in *On Writing*].
>
> The Nude had Descended the Staircase with an epoch-shaking tread but she remained faithful to Puvis de Chavannes, whose wall paintings . . . inspired the form and tone of *Death Comes for the Archbishop*. . . . She loved Courbet, Rembrandt, Millet and the sixteenth-century Dutch and Flemish painters, with their "warmly furnished interiors" but always with a square window open to the wide gray sea. . . .
>
> Joyce had happened: or perhaps we should say, *Ulysses* . . . [but] that subterranean upheaval of language caused not even the barest tremor in Miss Cather's firm, lucid sentences. (37–38)

There can be little question that Porter genuinely admired the "firm, lucid sentences" that characterized Cather's style and paid tribute to her as a stylist and a formalist in her review-turned-essay. At the same time, she reinforces her own position of prominence as a "writers' writer" admired within a circle of other literary modernists—Glenway Wescott, Robert Penn Warren, Allen Tate, Cleanth Brooks, Eudora Welty—while removing Cather to a different category altogether. As a result of such mixed purposes, her "reflections" are skewed, partly right but often very wrong.

Much of the evidence that it is wrong is provided by Cather's letters, which were of course unavailable to Porter. Since the time of her writing, however, hundreds of Cather's personal letters have become available at university libraries. Today's scholars are privileged to read Cather's own expressions of her likes and dislikes, experiences and goals. In contesting Porter's construal of Cather as a writer whose "plain" face was turned squarely toward the past (1952/1970, 30), I will draw freely on these materials and on Cather's nonfiction. Moreover, the enormous theoretical and historical literature on modernism of recent decades has enriched the definitional basis for revisiting the issue of Cather's relationship to modernism in the arts. Three works in particular seem to me both exceptionally cogent and directly pertinent to my discussion here, in that they form linkages among the arts. They are Martha Banta's "The Excluded Seven: Practice of Omission, Aesthetics of Refusal" (1995); Joyce Medina's *Cézanne and Modernism* (1995); and Marc Manganaro's *Culture, 1922* (2002).

My purpose is only secondarily, however, to dispute Porter's contention that Cather was no modernist. She has long since lost that argument as scholars such as Richard Millington (2005), Phyllis Rose (1983), Jo Ann Middleton (1990), and myself (1994, 1995), among others, have demonstrated Cather's place within modernism.[1] More important, Porter's argument relating to Cather and modernism provides a useful point of reference for sharpening our own definitions and perspectives. In any event, the comments of one writer on another are almost always of interest, especially since both were women writers at a time when it was still a real struggle to achieve parity of attention with men. Neither Porter nor Cather was eager to make claims based on gender, but both left passages in their letters indicating their awareness that literary publication was very much a man's business. Porter experienced gender exclusivity as a writer primarily as a matter of genre (the short story or sketch versus the more "masculine" novel), while Cather experienced it most directly with respect to admissible or inadmissible subject matter, in reviews of her war novel *One of Ours*. For all these reasons, I find it both interesting and beneficial to place the two in conversation *as modernists* by way of Porter's truly intriguing essay and to use her essay as a springboard for exploring what we can know of Cather's interest in modern art, especially visual art.[2]

A BLURRED REFLECTION

At the time she wrote "Reflections on Willa Cather," Porter was well established as a master of the short story and a stylist whose elegantly crafted sentences and rich symbolism placed her among an elite of contemporary writers. Her stories had appeared in, for example, *Century, Transition, Hound & Horn*, the *Virginia Quarterly Review*, and the *Southern Review*. But she had yet to achieve a wide popular following; it would be another decade before the publication of *Ship of Fools* (1962) brought her that. She used her essay, then, to reinforce her position as a high-art modernist writer by invoking the names of celebrated modernists in literature, music, and visual art and linking them anecdotally with her own life and artistic maturation. It is a rhetorical strategy implying that the aesthetic represented by this litany of names is to be taken as a measure of artistic status. And by this standard she finds Cather wanting—a kind of mirror reversal of herself. Indeed, we might read the word "reflections" in the title as having dual meanings, referring both to Porter's process of reflecting on (thinking about) Cather and to the likeness or unlikeness between the two of them. The primary unlikeness suggested in the essay, other than an *ad feminam* sniff that Cather was not glamorous (Porter most assuredly was), is that she was not truly modern.

Porter was not alone in thinking of Cather in that way. By 1940, largely through the efforts of Marxist critics such as Granville Hicks, she had been relegated to a kind of pleasant literary backwater. Yet one would think that Porter might have recognized in Cather's work some of the principles and techniques that characterized her own and that, in various combinations, have come to be seen as defining attributes of "high" modernism. These would include gaps and fragmented surfaces, minimalist sculpting, resistance to conventions of form or manner, and a conception of art as a reality of its own counterpoised against an outer world drained of meaning. Readers both then and now would be likely to associate such characteristics with the names Porter invokes in her "Reflections": Henry James, W. B. Yeats, Joseph Conrad, Gertrude Stein, James Joyce; in the visual arts, Klee, Gris, Modigliani; in music, Bartók, Poulenc, Stravinsky. Keeping the focus as much on herself as on Cather, she reminisces about her own first encounter with Stein's *Tender Buttons* and the "great day" (33) on which she picked up a copy of Joyce's *Dubliners*, and recalls her years in Paris during the 1930s as the time when she encountered the work of painters such as Modigliani and became mad for "music hot from the composer's brain."[3]

She associates a very different set of names with Cather. It is true, as she states, that Cather turns to Shakespeare and Beethoven as exemplars of the highest achievement in art. She does so in several of the essays in *On Writing*, the 1949 volume Porter was initially reviewing, and had been since her earliest days of newspaper writing. But when Porter goes on to mention Cather's "lov[ing]" Shelley, Wordsworth, and Walter Pater, the accuracy of her assessment becomes problematic. Cather's references to Shelley in *On Writing* are not precisely expressions of adulation. At one point she takes "Citizen Shelley" to task for his mistaken involvement in politics (Cather 1988, 20), and at another simply mentions his name along with Wordsworth's in making the point that writers can treat traditional subjects without imitating traditional styles such as theirs (27). She makes a similar point in praising Sarah Orne Jewett, a writer Porter might well have cited, but did not, as evidence of a pre-modern aesthetic taste. Cather praises Jewett, though, not for being traditional but for being independent. Young writers and visual artists alike, she says, should be faithful to their own vision, as Jewett was, not model their work on what has already been done, however fine (51). None of these passages indicates a retrograde devotion to past masters.

Turning next to music, Porter reports that Cather was "dead in love with Wagner . . . Schubert, Gluck . . . and almost any opera" (37). This is essentially correct; she loved opera. In an undated 1913 letter to Elizabeth Shepley Sergeant she stated (with possible hyperbole) that she was attending operas more often than weekly (Cather 1913/1914). To be sure, she was beginning a novel about an operatic singer at the time, and her statement to Sergeant may have been meant as an indication of how devotedly she was preparing for the book. As to Wagner and Schubert, she refers to them with a frequency that indicates particular preference. But where Porter got the idea, as she goes on to assert, that Cather was "enchanted" with Maurice Ravel's *La Valse*—by which I believe she meant to suggest deplorable taste—I am unable to determine. I have found no reference to Ravel either in *On Writing* or in any of the letters, and Ravel's name is not indexed in either *The World and the Parish* or *The Kingdom of Art*, which reprint much of Cather's newspaper commentary on the arts. As for Porter's musing that Cather may even have liked "certain later music" than Ravel but if so "has not mentioned it in these papers" (37), that too is true, strictly speaking. But with increased availability of her letters we know that in 1934 she attended and enjoyed the New York premiere of *Four Saints in Three Acts*, with text by Gertrude Stein and music by Virgil Thomson (Cather 1934).

In the visual arts, my primary emphasis here, Porter was entirely correct in recognizing Cather's great affinity for the work of Pierre Puvis de Chavannes. She clearly indicates that affinity in "On *Death Comes for the Archbishop*," one of the most frequently cited of the pieces in *On Writing* (1927/1988, 9). Porter does not seem to have recognized, however—as I believe Cather did—that Puvis, with his stylized flattening of figures, was a significant precursor of modernism. In *The Louvre: French and Other European Paintings*, Michel Laclotte and Jean-Pierre Cuzin write that Puvis's *The Poor Fisherman* (1881, purchased by the Louvre in 1887) "shows how great an innovator" he was. They see in "the subtle arrangement of the simplified and rather stilted forms and the limited range of low-keyed, soft colours" an anticipation of "the young Picasso a few years later" (Laclotte and Cuzin 1982, 126). Porter may also have been correct in stating that Cather "loved Courbet" (38), but the only reference to Courbet in the pages of *On Writing* comes in a paragraph deploring the notion that an artist should be so committed to a political cause as Courbet was (1936a/1988, 20)—one of Cather's most firmly held ideas and one that she in fact shared with Porter, at least so far as politically oriented fiction was concerned. I find no reference to Courbet in any of Cather's letters, nor in either *The Kingdom of Art* or *The World and the Parish*, as indexed.

When singling out Jean-François Millet as an indicator of Cather's aesthetic, Porter is on firmer ground. Cather had in fact expressed an admiration for Millet as well as Jules Breton long before she wrote "On the Art of Fiction," one of the essays Porter was reviewing in her first version of the essay. Cather particularly admired the representation of ordinary life in the works of these painters, and as early as January 1898, in a column in the *Lincoln Courier*, praised their "technical mastery" and "elemental power" (1898/1970, 574–75). She singled out Breton's *The Song of the Lark* in a column of August 10, 1901, for its affective power and its appeal to ordinary museum-goers who saw it at the Art Institute of Chicago (Cather 1901b/1970, 843). She was still thinking of the broad humanity of Millet's work the following year, 1902, when she made her first trip to Europe. In one of the travel pieces she sent back to the *Nebraska State Journal* she observed that women working in the fields near Barbizon appeared tired toward evening and "grew to look more and more as Millet painted them, warped and bowed and heavy" (1902/1988, 123).

It is surprising that the travel reports Cather sent back to the *State Journal* did not mention going to art museums. Yet we have to believe she did. Indeed, James Woodress points out that her claim in "On *Death Comes for the Archbishop*" to have seen Puvis's "frescoes of the life of Saint Geneviève in my student days" actually refers to her 1902 trip (Woodress 1987, 399). We know from numerous letters that she was a frequenter of museums and galleries throughout her adult life, and her trip in 1902 was her first opportunity to enjoy a European museum. In addition to visits to the Art Institute of Chicago, to be examined more closely below, her letters record museum visits in Pittsburgh (Cather 1896a); in London, where she more than once stayed across the street from the British Museum (Cather 1909); in Paris, where she stayed near the Louvre (Cather 1923a, Cather 1930); and in New York, where she was particularly fond of the Frick Collection (Cather 1938).

Cather would obviously have singled out the Louvre as a destination in Paris. We can only wish we knew how many times she went there, how long she stayed, and what pictures stopped her in her tracks, to stand and look. But we do have two letters that give clues. In 1923 she wrote to Edith Lewis that she had stayed for an entire morning and mentioned two seventeenth-century paintings as favorites, a Murillo *Virgin* and a Ribera *Nativity* (Cather 1923a). She might well have singled out different ones on another day, and indeed she made that same point herself in a 1940 letter, saying that we all know our responses to art vary continually from one time to another (Cather 1940). In 1930, in the other letter referred to above as having a bearing on her preferences at the Louvre, she felt familiar enough with its vast collection to give Carrie Miner Sherwood some advice on how to see it. Don't try to do it all, she advised, but stay mainly in the Grande Galerie to see the best of the collection (Cather 1930). Which of the many paintings exhibited in the Grande Galerie she numbered among the very best we cannot know. Historical records indicate, however, that there would almost certainly not have been any from the nineteenth or twentieth century. A guide to the Louvre published in 1927 gives detailed indication of what was to be found in the various bays of the Grande Galerie and shows that the few impressionist works owned by the Louvre, along with paintings of the Barbizon School so loved by Cather, were hung on the third floor (Heywood 1927, xv-xvi, 333-54; see also Laclotte and Cuzin 1982, 103).[4]

CATHER AND THE ART INSTITUTE

The interest in Millet and Breton that Cather expressed in newspaper columns around the turn of the century and in her musings while in Europe in 1902 would have begun at the Art Institute of Chicago in either 1895 or 1896. The Institute had opened in its present site at Michigan Avenue and Adams Street in 1893. With a bequest from Mrs. Henry Field in 1894, consisting of a collection of French paintings, primarily mid-nineteenth-century landscapes and genre paintings, it quickly gained the foundation of a developing strength in French art. This early bequest, designated the Henry Field Memorial Collection, included Breton's *The Song of the Lark* as well as two paintings by Millet and one by Corot (*Wounded Eurydice*). The Breton painting would have a major impact on Cather's career when she borrowed its title for her third published novel and used its image on the cover. She would later regret having done so, but her choice reflected a genuine liking for the painting and more generally a belief in the importance of hearing the voice of beauty and inspiration ("the song of the lark") whatever one's circumstances. It is one of the great themes of her work.

Cather made her first trip to Chicago in April 1895, at the age of twenty-one. It is reasonable to suppose that the young Nebraskan, intent on absorbing as much high culture as possible, would have made time in her schedule to see the new museum, which had opened to considerable fanfare sixteen months earlier; but I have found no record that she did. There *is* definite record, though, that only a little over a year later, in 1896, she visited the Art Institute when she passed through Chicago on her way to Pittsburgh to begin her job at *Home Monthly*. Writing to her college friend Mariel Gere in July of that year, she says that she saw a Gustave Doré exhibit (Cather 1896b). She dismissed it as a splashy extravaganza on the order of billboards for "The Last Days of Pompeii."[5] Even at that date, to have admired Doré, a French Romantic artist of the nineteenth century, would not have indicated avant-garde taste. But her letter did not indicate admiration.

Fortunately, as we have seen, the Institute had much to offer in 1896 besides splashy romantic canvases like Doré's. It also had available for viewing the more realistic and restrained paintings of Millet, Breton, and others of the Barbizon School that would remain favorites of Cather's over the years. In columns published in the same turn-of-the-century years when she was praising Millet and Breton, she also called her readers' attention to Jean Baptiste-Camille Corot, 1796–1875 (1901a/1970, 808), generally regarded as a transitional figure, an anticipator of impressionism, and Alfred Sisley, 1839–1899 (1900/1970, 761), who belongs solidly among the impressionists. For her to have noticed and praised the play of light in Corot's and especially Sisley's paintings by 1900 and 1901 (the dates of columns she published in short-lived Pittsburgh periodicals, reprinted in *The World and the Parish* [1970]) was by no means to turn her back on what was new in visual art.

Writing almost half a century afterward, Porter may not have recalled that the works of truly innovative and demanding painters like Cézanne had not even been shown in the United States at century's end. In any event, she took Cather's fondness for Breton and Millet as an indicator of a conservative taste. But Cather's comments on Millet in *On Writing* do not so much emphasize either his realism or his accessibility as his simplification of the field of vision by eliminating extraneous reportage—a characteristic of decided pertinence both to her own work and to modernism itself. Porter either missed or chose to ignore this when writing her review and essay.

It is easy to understand that the representational canvases of Breton, Courbet, Corot, and Millet would have been more readily accessible to an early-twentieth-century viewer such as Cather, while the more obviously challenging and nontraditional works of the postimpressionists, futurists, and abstract painters would have been less readily appreciated. Even the late-nineteenth-century impressionists were more challenging for early-twentieth-century museum goers than the narrative realists who came only slightly earlier. They demanded a real readjustment of appreciative vision. Clearly, though, Cather's liking for the Barbizon painters was not exclusive; she did not refuse to make that adjustment or to appreciate other styles. When she bought prints for her brother Roscoe and his wife Meta in 1908, for their house in Wyoming, her selections were fairly eclectic. We know this from a letter to Roscoe in which she dutifully lists her purchases and what she paid. They included prints of Breton's *The Song of the Lark*, two by N. C. Wyeth (then only five years past his first commission), one by Remington, two eighteenth-century Dutch paintings, and an illustration by Maxfield Parrish, *The Dinkey Bird Is Singing in the Amfalula Tree*—all narrative works, none of them very innovative, but her selection was, after all, designed for a domestic space, and not her own.

The familiarity with the Art Institute of Chicago that Cather initiated in 1895 or 1896 was almost certainly maintained in subsequent years. She had reason to travel between New York and Nebraska or destinations farther west with some frequency, and Chicago was a major rail center. Letters show that *after* 1896 she either visited or passed through Chicago a minimum of ten times (in 1897, 1921, twice in 1924, in 1926, 1927, 1931, twice in 1932, and in 1935). Many of these visits were motivated by the need to make train connections, but she sometimes stopped off for a day or more to visit friends; and these stays would have provided opportunities to drop in and see what was being featured at the Art Institute or to revisit her favorites.

By the late 1920s, as a result of deliberate decisions about collection development, the Art Institute of Chicago was a major center of modern art. In 1913 it had been the only American museum to host an exhibition of a large subset of the Armory Show paintings. Indeed, its hosting of this controversial show had produced an outpouring of newspaper commentary, much of it negative.[6] Nevertheless, the Institute not only exhibited the show but purchased several of the works. Additional investments in modern art followed, as well as such major bequests as fifty-two paintings given by Bertha Honoré Palmer in 1924 and the Helen Birch Bartlett Memorial Collection in 1925–27. We do not know to what extent Cather was aware either of the Institute's exhibit of the Armory Show or the arrival of these later major bequests. Given her habit of voracious newspaper reading and the presence of friends in Chicago, it is hard to imagine she did not see the reports, but that is of course conjectural. In any event, we do know that she continued to visit Chicago and that during the years she did, the Institute came to house a permanent collection strong in impressionists and other moderns. Which of these she particularly liked or disliked we do not know.

We do, however, have one very strong indication—a letter stating her wish to see a particular show there that she was unfortunately missing. Her express wish to see this specific exhibit suggests, then, the direction in which her interest was turning in her later life—a direction that included the moderns. On May 16, 1941, she wrote to her longtime friends Irene Miner Weisz and Carrie Miner Sherwood, jointly, lamenting that she had not been able to join them in seeing a major exhibit of French paintings about to close at the Institute. That same exhibition had earlier visited New York, she said, but due to illness and matters of business she had not been able to see it there either.

The show she was referring to was "Masterpieces of French Art Lent by the Museums and Collectors of France," exhibited by the Art Institute from April 10 to May 20, 1941.[7] By consulting the catalog of this exhibit, still available from rare book dealers or at the Institute itself, we learn what it was that Cather so wished she could have seen. It was indeed a feast of modern art: 170 paintings plus 100 drawings and watercolors that collectively constituted, according to Daniel Catton Rich's introduction to the catalog, "an unforgettable picture of the background and development of modern art." Among the artists represented were Braque,

Cézanne, Corot, Courbet, Degas, André Derain (then still living and active), Gauguin, Van Gogh, Matisse, Millet (Cather's old favorite), Monet, Picasso, Pissarro, Puvis de Chavannes (whose presence in such company testifies to his status in relation to modernism), Renoir, Seurat, Sisley, Toulouse-Lautrec, and Vuillard. Obviously, we have no way of knowing which of the paintings in this challenging modern mix Cather would especially have liked, since she never got to see it. But the very fact that she expressed a wish to see this "great" (as she called it) exhibit, almost the whole of it given to recent art, indicates that her interests were not at all so focused on the past as Katherine Anne Porter believed when she wrote "Reflections on Willa Cather."

COMPETITIVE LITERARY SISTERHOOD

Again, one writer's comments on another are almost always of interest. Certainly that is true of Porter's essay on Cather. Contemporaries at a time when women writers were struggling for recognition on par with men, both were serious artists determined to be recognized as such. Both had emerged from social situations that might not have seemed conducive to literary eminence. Such commonalities might well have positioned them for mutual understanding and appraisal—indeed, for fruitful discussions of technique or of how the fact of gender had affected their experience of the literary profession. Yet so far as I have found, Cather never commented on Porter at all, the two never exchanged letters, and as we have seen, Porter's "reflections" on her sister writer's aesthetic affinities are marred by misunderstandings, perhaps even willful ones. If she had not been so eager to think of Cather as a rival for a position of future eminence, Porter might well have discerned, out of her own practice as a literary modernist, the aspects of Cather's work that share an affinity with that same movement in the arts.

What we see in the varied and complicated record provided by Cather's journalism, literary essays, and letters is not a regressive taste but an eclectic one. At various times Cather expressed a liking for religious art of the Renaissance, realism, and impressionist innovations, and at least an interest in postimpressionism. True, she once expressed to Elizabeth Shepley Sergeant the idea that cubist painting was not comfortable to look at (Cather 1914), and conveyed to Dorothy Canfield Fisher, in a letter of 1922, a negative reaction to the futurists. On the other hand, she used the word "modern" with no trace of pejorative implication in a letter to Irene Miner Weisz explaining her choice of Leon Bakst as her portraitist (Cather 1923b). And as David Porter has demonstrated, she admired the stylized, fully modern paintings of Edith Lewis's friends Earl Brewster and Achsah

Barlow Brewster, whose work has been described as having "eliminat[ed]
. . . 19th century 'realistic, romantic, sentimental, literary, and scientific'
accretions" in favor of "austere, formal, understated" images (D. Porter
2008, 149–50). If not an outspoken advocate of the nude who descended
the staircase, she was in any event responsive to modern art and recogniz-
ably modernist in her own work.

In 1896, when, twenty-three years old and a year out of college, Cather
went to Pittsburgh to accept her first job after college, stopping on the
way at the Art Institute of Chicago, she was feeling bedeviled by a label
that would not occur to us: her friends were calling her a bohemian. And
with good reason. She had exhibited "bohemian" irregularities in her personal life (she smoked, drank cocktails, and sometimes dressed oddly),
and her columns in the *Nebraska State Journal* had expressed enthusiasm
for the expatriate American painter James McNeill Whistler as well as
British Aestheticism. To us, the kind of friendly name-calling she experienced as a result may not seem like a very dire problem, but it is clear
from her letters that she did not want to be labeled in that way—or indeed
in any way. She is still resistant to labeling. It is useful to identify the
traces of particular aesthetic systems in Cather's (or any other writer's)
work, as I have sought to do here, but we err when, in the effort to define
a Catherian aesthetic, we try to place her in one and only one category,
for whatever reason.

Katherine Anne Porter, in her "Reflections on Willa Cather," did not
seek to place her in a category but to exclude her from one. She did so by
construing the evidence of Cather's artistic vision selectively, choosing
to mention some expressions of her taste but to omit contrary evidence
even within the few pages of the book she was initially reviewing, *On
Writing*. I think, for instance, of Cather's tribute to Katherine Mansfield's
"virtuosity" (1936b/1988, 107); her discernment that certain aspects of
Stephen Crane's work made him "one of the first post-impressionists"
(1926/1988, 69); and most of all her insistence that, even while revering
the Beethovens and the Wordsworths of our heritage, art should not per-
petuate "conventional poses" (1925/1988, 51). Porter noted none of these
in her review. Nor did she recognize in print any of the abundant evidence of Cather's engagement with the very modernist project of recon-
ceiving the nature of the novel, even though that engagement is evident
in her experiments with form throughout her career. It was evident too in
the *On Writing* essays Porter was reviewing, in her repeated questioning
of the definition of the novel as a genre.

Even with the resources we have available today which Porter did
not—some three thousand letters and the collected, albeit fragmented,
journalism—it is not possible to know precisely what Cather thought of

the nude's descending of the staircase. She apparently did not go on record about that "epoch-shaking" event. Yet we have other good reasons to believe that she listened attentively to the nude's tread on the stairs and did not find it unwelcome. Katherine Anne Porter's construal of her as a kind of premodern, not so much hostile as immune to the new in the arts, may well have been influenced by the fact that Porter did conceive of herself in modernist terms. Granted that the space among the serious moderns open to occupation by women was limited (though unless they became *too* successful in the marketplace they were welcome to take as much space as they wanted among the middlebrow writers) and that Porter fully meant to reserve space there for herself, she had every motivation, conscious or not, to position Cather elsewhere. A zero-sum game enforces competition, and Porter was a fairly devious competitor. She had no intention of giving up her seat.

NOTES

Reprinted with minor revisions (with appreciation) from Stout, Janis P. 2011. "The Nude Had Descended the Staircase." In *Cather Studies, Volume 9*, edited by Melissa J. Homestead and Guy J. Reynolds, 225–43. Lincoln: University of Nebraska Press.

1. Among other fine studies that bear on this subject, I would particularly call attention to Goldberg, which is perhaps only glancingly pertinent but in important ways.

2. With regard to Cather's taste in art, Bernice Slote's groundbreaking essay "First Principles: The Kingdom of Art" in *The Kingdom of Art* (1966, 31–112), remains of general interest here, even though it has very little to say about visual art. Of somewhat more pertinence is my own *Picturing a Different West* (2007). See also Keeler (1965), Al-Ghalith (1996), and D. Porter (2008).

3. In fact, Porter's interest in music also embraced French songs from the twelfth through eighteenth centuries. She spent a considerable portion of her time during 1932 and 1933 translating songs of this period for *Katherine Anne Porter's French Song Book*, published in 1934 by Harrison of Paris.

4. In fact, Porter's interest in music also embraced French songs from the twelfth through eighteenth centuries. She spent a considerable portion of her time during 1932 and 1933 translating songs of this period for *Katherine Anne Porter's French Song Book*, published in 1934 by Harrison of Paris.

5. Cather may be referring here to *The Last Day of Pompeii* by Russian painter Karl Briullov (1799-1852), which Edward Bulwer-Lytton said had inspired his novel of almost the same title but in the plural, as Cather uses it: *The Last Days of Pompeii*.

6. See Martinez (1993); also the web site of the Art Institute of Chicago.

7. I am grateful to Susan Augustine (2008) for confirming this.

WORKS CITED

Al-Ghalith, Asad. 1996. "Cather's Use of Light: An Impressionistic Tone." *Cather Studies 3*, edited by Susan J. Rosowski, 267–84. Lincoln: University of Nebraska Press.

Art Institute of Chicago website, http://www.artic.edu/aic/collections/index.php.

Augustine, Susan (Head of Reader Services at the Art Institute of Chicago). 2008. E-mail to the author, November, 2008.

Banta, Martha. 1995. "The Excluded Seven: Practice of Omission, Aesthetics of Refusal." *Henry James's New York Edition: The Construction of Authorship*, edited by David McWhirter, 249–60. Stanford, CA: Stanford University Press, 1995.

Cather, Willa. 1896a. Letter to Ellen Gere, 27 July. Willa Cather Foundation, Red Cloud, NE.

———. 1896b. Letter to Mariel Gere, July. Willa Cather Foundation, Red Cloud, NE.

———. 1898/1970. "The Death of Daudet." In *The World and the Parish: Willa Cather's Articles and Reviews, 1893–1902*. 2 vols. Edited by William M. Curtin, 572–76. Lincoln: University of Nebraska Press.

———. 1900/1970. "A Philistine in the Gallery." In *The World and the Parish: Willa Cather's Articles and Reviews, 1893–1902*. 2 vols. Edited by William M. Curtin, 760–64. Lincoln: University of Nebraska Press.

———. 1901a/1970, "Joe Jefferson, the Painter." In *The World and the Parish: Willa Cather's Articles and Reviews, 1893–1902*. 2 vols. Edited by William M. Curtin, 806–10. Lincoln: University of Nebraska Press.

———. 1901b/1970. "The Chicago Art Institute." In *The World and the Parish: Willa Cather's Articles and Reviews, 1893–1902*. 2 vols. Edited by William M. Curtin, 842–48. Lincoln: University of Nebraska Press.

———. 1902/1988. "Barbizon." In *Willa Cather in Europe: Her Own Story of the First Journey.* Edited by George N. Kates, 119–27. Lincoln: University of Nebraska Press.

———. [1908]. Letter to Roscoe and Meta Cather, 2 March. Roscoe and Meta Cather Collection, Archives and Special Collections, University of Nebraska, Lincoln.

———. 1909. Letter to Elsie Martindale Hueffer, 20 May. Division of Rare and Manuscript Collections, Cornell University Library, Ithaca, NY.

———. [1913, 1914]. Letters to Elizabeth Shepley Sergeant. Morgan Library, New York.

———. [1922]. Letter to Dorothy Canfield Fisher. [17 June]. Bailey Library, University of Vermont, Burlington.

———. [1923a]. Letter to Edith Lewis [summer]. Susan J. and James R. Rosowski Collection, Archives and Special Collections, University of Nebraska, Lincoln.

———. 1923b. Letter to Irene Miner Weisz, 11 August. Newberry Library, Chicago.

———. 1925/1988. "The Best Stories of Sarah Orne Jewett." In *Willa Cather on Writing*, 47–59. Lincoln: University of Nebraska Press.

———. 1926/1988. "Stephen Crane's Wounds in the Rain and other Impressions of War." In *Willa Cather on Writing: Critical Studies on Writing as an Art*, 67–74. Lincoln: University of Nebraska Press.

——. 1927/1988. "On Death Comes for the Archbishop." In *Willa Cather on Writing*, 3–13. Lincoln: University of Nebraska Press.

——. 1930. Letter to Carrie Miner Sherwood, 17 July. Willa Cather Foundation, Red Cloud, NE.

——. 1934. Letter to Mabel Dodge Luhan, 1 May. Beinecke Library, Yale University, New Haven, CT.

——. 1936a/1988. "Escapism." In *Willa Cather on Writing : Critical Studies on Writing as an Art*, 18–29. Lincoln: University of Nebraska Press.

——. 1936b/1988. "Katherine Mansfield." In *Willa Cather on Writing: Critical Studies on Writing as an Art*, 107–20. Lincoln: University of Nebraska Press.

——. 1938. Letter to Yaltah Menuhin, 11 January. Firestone Library, Princeton University, Princeton, NJ.

——. 1940. Letter to Paul Keppel, 6 February. Butler Library, Columbia University, New York.

——. 1941. Letter to Irene Miner Weisz and Carrie Miner Sherwood, 16 May. Willa Cather Foundation, Red Cloud, NE.

——. 1949. *On Writing: Critical Studies on Writing as an Art*. New York: Knopf.

——. 1988. *Willa Cather on Writing: Critical Studies on Writing as an Art*. Lincoln: University of Nebraska Press.

——. 1966. *The Kingdom of Art: Willa Cather's First Principles and Critical Statements, 1893–1896*. Edited by Bernice Slote. Lincoln: University of Nebraska Press.

——. 1970. *The World and the Parish: Willa Cather's Articles and Reviews, 1893–1902*. 2 vols. Edited by William M. Curtin. Lincoln: University of Nebraska Press.

Goldberg, Jonathan. 2001. *Willa Cather and Others*. Durham, NC: Duke University Press.

Heywood, Florence. 1927. *The Important Pictures of the Louvre*. 3rd ed. London: Methuen.

Hicks, Granville. 1933/1967. "The Case against Willa Cather." *English Journal*, November 19. In *Willa Cather and Her Critics*, edited by James Schroeter, 139–47. Ithaca, NY: Cornell University Press.

Keeler, Clinton. 1965. "Narrative without Accent: Willa Cather and Puvis de Chavannes." *American Quarterly* 17: 119–26.

Laclotte, Michel, and Jean-Pierre Cuzin. 1982. *The Louvre: French and Other European Paintings*. Translated by Diana de Froment and Frances Roxburgh. Paris: Scala; London: Philip Wilson.

Loire, Stéphane (Conservator in Chief of the Department of Paintings and Chief of Research Service and Documentation, Musée de Louvre). 2009. E-mail to author, 12 February.

Manganaro, Mark. 2002. *Culture, 1922: The Emergence of a Concept*. Princeton, NJ: Princeton University Press.

Martinez, Andrew. 1993 "'A Mixed Reception for Modernism': The 1913 Armory Show at the Art Institute." *Art Institute of Chicago Museum Studies* 19.1. *One Hundred Years at the Art Institute: A Centennial Celebration*. Chicago: Art Institute of Chicago. 30–57, 102–5.

Medina, Joyce. 1995. *Cézanne and Modernism: The Poetics of Painting*. Albany: State University of New York Press.

Middleton, Jo Ann. 1990. *Willa Cather's Modernism: A Study of Style and Technique.* Madison, NJ: Fairleigh Dickinson University Press.

Millington, Richard H. 2005. "Willa Cather's American Modernism." In *The Cambridge Companion to Willa Cather*, edited by Marilee Lindemann, 51–65. Cambridge: Cambridge University Press.

Porter, David. 2008. "'Life is very simple—all we have to do is our best!': Willa Cather and the Brewsters." In *Willa Cather: New Facts, New Glimpses Revisions*, edited by John J. Murphy and Merrill Maguire Skaggs, 141–57. Madison, NJ: Fairleigh Dickinson University Press.

Porter, Katherine Anne. 1952/1970. "Reflections on Willa Cather." In *Collected Essays and Occasional Writings*. Boston: Houghton Mifflin.

Rich, Daniel Catton. 1941. Introduction. In *Masterpieces of French Art Lent by the Museums and Collectors of France* (exhibit catalog).

Rose, Phyllis. 1983. "Modernism: The Case of Willa Cather." In *Modernism Reconsidered*, edited by Robert Kiely, 123–45. Cambridge: Harvard University Press.

Slote, Bernice, ed. 1966. *The Kingdom of Art: Willa Cather's First Principles and Critical Statements, 1893–1896.* Lincoln: University of Nebraska Press.

Stout, Janis P. 1994. "Katherine Anne Porter's 'Reflections on Willa Cather': A Duplicitous Homage," *American Literature* 66: 719–35.

———. 1995. *Katherine Anne Porter: A Sense of the Times.* Charlottesville: University Press of Virginia.

———. 2000. *Willa Cather: The Writer and Her World.* Charlottesville: University Press of Virginia.

———. 2007. *Picturing a Different West: Vision, Illustration, and the Tradition of Cather and Austin.* Lubbock: Texas Tech University Press.

Woodress, James. 1987. *Willa Cather: A Literary Life.* Lincoln: University of Nebraska Press.

Chapter 12

With the "Hand, Fastidious and Bold"

Bridging Walter Pater's Aestheticism and Willa Cather's Modernism

Olga Aksakalova

There is a spirit of general elevation and enlightenment in which all alike communicate. —Walter Pater

In the body of Willa Cather's critical accounts of art and artists, Walter Pater is rarely mentioned. When Cather does make direct references to Pater's work, they are not elaborate analytical discussions, but cursory remarks about his literary stature. We grasp in a column written in 1895 an open disregard for Oscar Wilde's (mis)interpretation of Pater's philosophy of art as a model to be sought in life (Cather 1895/1966, 389–90). We also begin to see a strong allegiance to Pater's credo that "every truly great drama must, in the end, linger in the reader's mind as a sort of ballad," as well as Cather's expansive implementation of it: "Probably the same thing might be said of every great story" (Cather 1925/1988, 49–50). But to delineate the full extent of Pater's presence in Cather's Kingdom of Art, we must examine her criticism more carefully and turn to her fiction. In this essay, I explore how Cather deploys the aesthetic and social platforms of her time to articulate and grapple with Pater's major tenets. Namely, I propose to view Cather's novel *The Professor's House* as a map of meta-commentary on the nature of art, one that illustrates several intersections between Pater's thought and modernist aesthetic.

In the "Conclusion" to his major work *The Renaissance*, Pater describes aestheticism as the richest form of existential pleasure. Specifying that "[n]ot the fruit of experience, but experience itself, is the end," Pater concludes, "art comes to you professing frankly to give nothing but the highest quality to your moments as they pass, and simply for those moments' sake" (Pater 1868/1974, 60, 62). As such, art stands its own autonomous ground, delighting in beauty and remaining unresponsive to practical, moral, or religious laws. In a 1920 essay "On the Art of Fiction," Cather fervently engages with Pater's fundamental idea that true art should not be "serviceable" (Pater 1888/1974, 106) but remain free from utilitarian constraints and committed to "a search for something for which there is no market demand, something new and untried, where the values are intrinsic and have nothing to do with standardized values" (Cather 1920/1988, 103). In this search, according to Cather in 1894, "An artist should not be vexed by human hobbies or human follies; he should be able to lift himself up into the clear firmament of creation where the world is not. He should be among men but not one of them, in the world but not of the world" (Cather 1894/1966, 407). Pater delivers the same point in his epigraph to *The Renaissance* taken from the Book of Psalms: "Though ye have lain among the pots, / Yet shall ye be as the wings of a dove covered with silver, / And her feathers with yellow gold."[1]

Following Pater's direction, Cather opens and persistently maintains a great divide between art and common experience in her early fiction. In her first short story collection, *The Troll Garden*, the nature of art indisputably demands a total disavowal of ordinary life—and sometimes life itself—as most protagonists here face the chiaroscuro of choice between aesthetic fulfillment and domestic preoccupations. A striking example is the figure of an artist as a young man in "Paul's Case," an adolescent who has "something of a dandy about him" (Cather 1905/1987, 111). Paul reveres the glamour of the theater, where he works as an usher, and loathes the boredom of school and home life: "It was at the theatre and at Carnegie Hall that Paul really lived; the rest was but a sleep and a forgetting. This was Paul's fairy tale, and it had for him all the allurement of a secret love. . . . After a night behind the scenes, Paul found the school-room more than ever repulsive" (120–21). What is already at work here is Cather's narrative technique of juxtaposition ,which sharpens the contrast between Paul's two worlds; in *The Professor's House*, this principle will gain not only narrative but also structural prominence (Middleton 1990, 104–16). Paul is clearly on the quest outlined by Pater: to "be present always at the focus where the greatest number of vital forces unite in their purest energy" (Pater 1868/1974, 60). Ultimately, in seeking beauty, Paul finds his place in "the immense design of things" (Cather 1905/1987, 131) but loses an essential touch with humanity.

Fast-forwarding to 1925, the publication year of *The Professor's House*, we notice that Pater's idealistic notes begin to produce a great deal of uneasiness in Cather. The novel indicates that while longing for escape, Cather's artist can no longer dissociate himself from life. If "Paul's Case" features an alienated artist seeking withdrawal from the material world, here we encounter a disillusioned professor who tries but does not succeed at abandoning life—its domesticity, commercialism, and temporality—for the sake of a sacred bond with the world of beauty and adventure. A major character in the novel, Tom Outland, is a young scholar, inventor, and writer. With his disdain for material values and appreciation of beauty, Tom can be seen as a vague prototype for Paul. He pioneered an important invention in aviation and earned a vast amount of money, which was inherited by his fiancée Rosamond, the professor's daughter. After Tom's death Rosamond married rich and practical Louie Marsellus. As the Marselluses are planning to build a new house named Outland, the omniscient narrator relates Professor St. Peter's tacit endorsement of Tom's death: Tom's artistic hand, "had he lived, must have been put to other uses." Spared this unfortunate destiny, Tom continues to dwell in St. Peter's memory as a romantic: "He had made something new in the world—and the rewards, the meaningless conventional gestures, he had left to others" (Cather 1925/1990, 236–37).

Another artist in the novel, Professor St. Peter himself, is almost ready to take the same route when he chooses to be asphyxiated in his old and empty house. Yet, Cather lets him live and ends her novel on the ambivalent note of St. Peter's muted nostalgia for the past and a firm determination to face the future:

> He had let something go—and it was gone: something very precious, that he could not consciously have relinquished, probably. He doubted whether his family would ever realize that he was not the same man they had said good-bye to. . . . At least, he felt the ground under his feet. He thought he knew where he was. . . . (258)

Let us compare this passage to the concluding lines of "Paul's Case" that describe the moment of suicide:

> There flashed through his brain, clearer than ever before, the blue of Adriatic water, the yellow of Algerian sands.
> He felt something strike his chest, and that his body was being thrown swiftly through the air, on and on, immeasurably far and fast, while his limbs were gently relaxed. Then, because the picture making mechanism was crushed, the disturbing visions flashed into black, and Paul dropped back into the immense design of things. (Cather 1905/1987, 131)

The two endings offer a good insight into how Cather's reading of Pater's aestheticism and her general understanding of art evolved over time: in the 1920s, she was not as categorical as before about separating aesthetic and material domains. In the post–World War I years, the prospect of retreat—artistic, temporal, spatial, existential—was alluring but somewhat troubling for Cather. While she shared her contemporaries' impulse to attain the spirit of the primitive in the enchanting vistas of the Southwest, she wrote her major novels in New York.[2] As John H. Swift and Leona Sevick have shown, the presence of the exotic Southwest in her two major 1920s novels, *The Professor's House* and *Death Comes for the Archbishop*, does not attest to Cather's categorical escapism. Rather, it calls attention to what Swift has identified as "the tension of contemporary experience and escape in Willa Cather's thinking" (Sevick 2005, 191–204; and Swift 2005, 175–90). In *The Professor's House*, Cather projects this tension onto her two artist characters, one of whom escapes the sweeping forces of modernity and the other who accepts them, however uneasily.

The intensity with which the society was changing after the war was simply dizzying and too real to be ignored. The decade of the 1920s was experienced not as a gradual continuum of change but as a series of drastic juxtapositions of uncompromising values and experiences: small town vs. metropolis, America vs. Europe, bohemianism vs. social reality, war vs. peace, past vs. present, high vs. low art.[3] In the historical sense, the war divided the world into the before and after; as Cather famously stated in her "Prefatory Note" to *Not under Forty*, "[t]he world broke in two in 1922 or thereabouts" (Cather 1936/1992, 812).The sense of rupture permeates *The Professor's House*, as evident in its tripartite structure and juxtapositions of old and new houses, the primitive past and the cynical present, contrasting landscapes, and colliding selves. With the massive social and political changes, Cather found it increasingly difficult to feel in tune with her contemporary life. But equally difficult was letting her artist "cling close to the skirts of his art, forsaking all others, and keep unto her as long as they two shall live" (Cather 1894/1966, 407). Maintaining a clear line between the world of art and the world of commerce became a real challenge, and in *The Professor's House* Cather is quick to register it; as Swift's analysis of the novel indicates, "[m]aterialism and idealism blur at their points of contact; Louie Marsellus and Tom Outland trade moral places disconcertingly (who is the businessman, who the dreamer?); the Blue Mesa itself acquires final significance in its status as commodity" (Lindemann 2005, 176).

Like her modernist contemporaries William Butler Yeats and T. S. Eliot, Cather began a dialogue with Pater regarding this unsettling conflict between life and art. As Edmund Wilson observes, Yeats realized its existence, though he still chose to plunge into the world of imagination, facing the consequence of being "thrown fatally out of key with reality" and "incur[ring] penalties which are not to be taken lightly" (Wilson

1931/1996, 40). Eliot blatantly called Pater's belief in art's exclusive power to constitute meaning and pleasure "demonstrably untrue" and insisted on discerning the moral underpinnings in Pater's ideas (Eliot 1932/1964, 390). Like Yeats, Cather perceives in Pater's thought a friction between art and life, but instead of probing it with a new interpretation as Eliot does, she uses the space of her novel to work out a more nuanced reading of Pater, in which art and life are inherently ontologically connected. She addresses the issues of perception and craftsmaking as envisioned by Pater, namely the process in which the outside world is refracted through the artist's subjective prism and then rendered in the ensuing artifact. The following passage from Pater's essay "Style" is particularly vivid in its description of the artistic process, from its inception to execution:

> Into the mind sensitive to "form," a flood of random sounds, colours, incidents, is ever penetrating from the world without, to become, by sympathetic selection, a part of its very structure, and, in turn, the visible vesture and expression of that other world it sees so steadily within, nay, already with a partial conformity thereto, to be refined, enlarged, corrected, at a hundred points; and it is just there, just at those doubtful points that the function of style, as tact or taste, intervenes. (Pater 1888/1974, 118)

Keeping faith in his "art for art's sake" principle, Pater focuses here on how the artist selects particles of the outside world in accordance with his inner aesthetic value system. The resultant works of art then become subjectively colored and stylistically formulated impressions of life. In these terms, Pater posits that the artist's picture of the world, while creatively rendered, is made of worldly material; only this material may be made unfamiliar and therefore, as Wolfgang Iser explains, more exciting: "And so instead of imitating a given world, art defamiliarizes in order to arouse new interest" (Iser 1987, 34). What art provides then is a reassembling of existing reality in a way that gives it a novel focus at the end.

Cather's professor fulfills the same task when he muses upon the arrangement of autumn flowers inside his drawing room:

> There was, in the room, as he looked through the window, a rich, intense effect of autumn, something that presented October much more sharply and sweetly to him than the coloured maples and the aster-bordered paths by which he had come home. It struck him that the seasons sometimes gain by being brought into the house, just as they gain by being brought into painting, and into poetry. The hand, fastidious and bold, which selected and placed—it was that which made the difference. In Nature there is no selection. (Cather 1925/1990, 61)

The elements of nature are manipulated skillfully by the artist who gives them a new form and a new meaning but by no means deprives them of their solid grounding in the physical reality. As Bernice Slote notes, for Cather "[a]rt is no longer nature, but is created according to the *laws* of nature" (Slote 1966a, 46; italics in the original). We can view the floral scene as a lucid metaphor for Cather's modernism: while exposing the artificiality of art, Cather still seeks harmony, not mimetic but perceptual, and this is where her criteria for art coincides with Pater's: at its heart lies sensual pleasure. While Cather agrees that art is "a game of make-believe, of re-production," she is mindful of excessive artificiality (Cather 1949/1988, 125). She spots it in Oscar Wilde's *Lady Windermere's Fan* and deems the play "a lie, a malicious lie upon human nature" (Cather 1895/1966, 390). In her pursuit of beauty, Cather is envisioning a refined, not a distorted reality. She is after that beauty which "in the long run [is] only *fineness* of truth," as Pater put it (Pater 1888/1974, 106; italics in the original).

Cather's rendition of the floral scene also reinforces her understanding of realism as discussed at length in her two essays "On the Art of Fiction" and "The Novel Démeublé," written in 1920 and 1922 respectively. Young writers, Cather points out, have inherited a long-standing tradition in mimetic representation; they are used to reading "stories that surprised and delighted by their sharp photographic detail" (Cather 1920/1988, 101) Simplification and omission should constitute a new tradition, she insists, that would redirect emphasis in realist fiction from the objective world of facts to a subjective pallet of impressions: "But is not realism, more than it is anything else, an attitude of mind on the part of the writer toward his material?" (Cather 1922/1988, 37).

Such a strong note of subjectivity in Cather's conception of realism echoes a major trope in Pater's aesthetic philosophy: perception as a central element of artistic endeavor. In his "Conclusion," Pater develops a telling analysis of the interaction between the outside world and the perceiving mind: "At first sight experience seems to bury us under a flood of external objects. . . . But when reflexion begins to act upon those objects they are dissipated under its influence; the cohesive force seems suspended like a trick of magic; each object is loosed into a group of impressions—colour, odour, texture—in the mind of the observer." Taking this process a step further, Pater insists on the observer's immersion in the sea of "impressions unstable, flickering, inconsistent" that ultimately bring the experience "to the narrow chamber of the individual mind." The objective picture of the world loses its significance, in Pater's view, as "each mind [is] keeping as a solitary prisoner its own dream of a world." In the aesthetic realm, the process continues with the artist's need to convey his/her "dream of a world" (Pater 1868/1974, 59–60). The vision must be materialized into a work of art, a transformation that requires a high level of crafting. All resources of language and imagination must serve the effort, so there can occur "the finer accommodation of speech to that vision within" (Pater 1888/1974, 106).

In revisiting this important trope, we must invite Gustave Flaubert into the discussion, as it was Flaubert who inspired Pater's vision of *ascêsis* (McGrath 1986, 217)—the epitome of "[s]elf-restraint, a skilful economy of means" (Pater 1888/1974, 110) in creative expression. Yet, as Wolfgang Iser explains, Flaubert's vantage point is realism understood as a quest for factual transparency between experience and its literary representation, and therefore Flaubert's commitment to style is anchored in "a passionless reproduction of the facts." Pater, on the other hand, concentrates on the individual artist's perception of the world and thus his "problem was how to objectify the inner vision, and the search for the right word, phrase etc. is the result of this need." Iser concludes, "[i]t is this search, and not the cause for the search, that links Pater to Flaubert" (Iser 1987, 48). With respect to Cather, several critics have observed Flaubert's influence in her delineation of form and style.[4] I would add that her reading of Flaubert was probably considerably mediated by Pater's ideas vis-à-vis the role of perception in realism. Cather's creative process is "the voyage perilous" whose course begins with a serious commitment to "keep[ing] an idea living, intact, tinged with all its original feeling, its original mood, preserving in it all the ecstasy which attended its birth, to keep it so all the way from the brain to the hand and transfer it on paper" (Cather 1896/1966, 417). She shares Pater's primary allegiance to feeling and mood, and to the task of epitomizing them in a written form.

In wanting to convey a vision of the fact rather than the fact itself, Cather is fully invested in seeking a harmonious relationship between form, language, and content. The magnitude of this investment transpires in both the genesis and the final text of *The Professor's House*. The novel's form was suggested by the Dutch paintings that featured a packed, furnished room with a window looking out to ships and the sea:

> In my book I tried to make Professor St. Peter's house rather overcrowded and stuffy with new things; American proprieties, clothes, furs, petty ambitions, quivering jealousies—until one got rather stifled. Then I wanted to open the square window and let in the fresh air that blew off the Blue Mesa. . . . (Cather 1938/1988, 31–32)

In her comprehensive study *Willa Cather's Modernism*, Jo Ann Middleton has identified juxtaposition as a governing principle in the novel. One form of juxtaposition occurs, as Cather originally intended, on the structural level: "By putting her Rock—the Blue Mesa—squarely in the center of her novel, everything else must be seen in relation—or in juxtaposition—to it" (Middleton 1990, 107). In the course of the narrative, however, particularly striking to the reader are the recurring shifts in setting. Exhibiting no physical beauty or comfort, the old house epitomizes creativity, purity, and a solid thread to the past. Its aura is permeated by the presence of Tom Outland, who brings with him the fresh air of the Blue Mesa and channels it freely into St. Peter's life. It is a place that fosters artistic impulses and genuine feelings. St. Peter writes his books here; Augusta sews her dresses; Tom Outland begins his education. In opposition, the new house has the comfort of big closets and a private bath, but contains no source of spiritual and creative sustenance.

Another level of juxtaposition is temporal; Cather contrasts St. Peter's past and present through the juxtaposition of Lake Michigan, symbol of his childhood, and the old house, symbol of his family life and professional growth. Observing the lake from his study in the old house, St. Peter catches a glimpse of the past, distant yet always accessible. In other words, the past and the present stand in immediate contrast while remaining in close physical proximity and in the same field of vision, as do the two scenes in the Dutch painting. The same principle is at work in the organization of the novel: two distinct narratives are brought into the same space of the book. These and other forms of juxtaposition indicate an artistic vision in which form and structure blend with the thematic texture so seamlessly that it is no longer possible to see them apart.

To establish her aesthetic principles, Cather transcends genre boundaries of criticism and fiction and articulates in and through *The Professor's House* her philosophy of writing. Middleton notes a resemblance between Cather's and St. Peter's "acute and intense capacity of observation" and continues, "[a]s Cather creates this made work of art, as she turns the reality of her own experience into the unreality of fiction, she also divulges the process by which she is able to do so" (1990, 106, 111). Cather remains sensitive to the shared preoccupation of her contemporary artists to expose the device—to use the space of art to comment on its nature. A self-conscious artistic discourse is a common feature in the fiction of Marcel Proust, James Joyce, Virginia Woolf, Andre Gide, and Gertrude Stein. To see a full picture of this modernist technique, it is useful to consider Richard Millington's recent study "Willa Cather's American Modernism," for it illuminates Cather's part in a modernist endeavor to construct narratives about art and artists. With the disappearance of enduring belief systems, no structures remained to bestow meaning onto human endeavors, Millington notes. In such a world, literary modernists sought to represent human beings through the figures of artists who engage in creative acts; thus, they imparted a dictum "we are—or we mean—because we make" (Millington 2005, 59). Cather's attitude to the old belief systems, such as religion, is not unequivocally negative; after all, it is Augusta, the devout Catholic, who saves St. Peter's life. But Cather finds in both religion and art the common virtues of creation and creativity; St. Peter assures his students that art and religion are "the same thing, in the end" (Cather 1925/1990, 55).[5]

Cather fills her work with artifacts of various kinds—pottery and jewelry, tapestry and remnants of ancient architecture, St. Peter's books, and Tom Outland's manuscript made available to the reader in the middle of the novel. Along with these aesthetic objects, Cather introduces different stages of the composition process. In her criticism, she makes a note of how a writer gestates his or her artistic vision by citing a passage from Sarah Orne Jewett's letter: "*The thing that teases the mind over and over for years, and at last gets itself put down rightly on paper—whether little or great, it belongs to Literature*" (Cather 1925/1988, 47; italics in the original). In the novel, she describes the next stage: the moment of epiphany when the idea reveals itself to the artist. For St. Peter, this happens when he is in Spain, his heroes' homeland:

> All day long they were skirting the south coast of Spain; from the rose of dawn to the gold of sunset the ranges of the Sierra Nevadas towered on their right. . . . St. Peter lay looking up at them from a little boat riding low in the purple water, and the design of his book unfolded in the air above him, just as definitely as the mountain ranges themselves. And the design was sound. He had accepted it as inevitable, had never meddled with it, and it had seen him through. (Cather 1925/1990, 89)

The word "design" signals the beginning of the following stage of crafting the artifact, as it recurs in yet another narrative in the novel, one that belongs to Father Duchene and is cited in Tom's story. In his "study" of the Cliff City, Father Duchene observes: "There is unquestionably a distinct feeling for design in what you call the Cliff City. Buildings are not grouped like that by pure accident." Tom himself comments on the stillness and permanence of the Mesa as if it were a sculpture exhibiting a profound sense of design: "It all hung together, seemed to have a kind of composition: pale little houses of stone nestling close to one another, perched on top of each other, with flat roofs, narrow windows, straight walls, and in the middle of the group, a round tower" (Cather 1925/1990, 196, 197, 179–80).

In making us aware of the artist's effort in these passages, Cather exposes her own conscientious work in weaving her narrative. Even the epigraph to the novel points us back to the novel: Cather uses Louie Marsellus's description of a "turquoise set in dull silver"—nature made into art, just like the flowers in the drawing room. What intensifies the sense of immediate, experiential reality of Cather's creative effort is the recurring image of the artist's hand. It comes up not only in the flower scene but also in the description of Tom Outland's exceptional hand, "fine long hand with the backspringing thumb, which had never handled things that were not the symbols of ideas" (Cather 1925/1990, 236). Further, after reading Tom's story, we are offered a careful analysis of his démeuble writing from the point of view of the professor: "If words had cost money, Tom couldn't have used them more sparingly. The adjectives were purely descriptive, relating to form and colour" (Cather 1925/1990, 238). This self-reflexive comment is deeply reminiscent of a line in "The Novel Démeublé": "The higher processes of art are all processes of simplification" (Cather 1922/1988, 40). The brevity of language and unadorned scene portrayal became emblematic of Cather's writing and helped to place her into the echelons of American modernism next to such writers as Ernest Hemingway and Gertrude Stein, and such Precisionist artists as Georgea O'Keeffe and Charles Sheeler (Rose 1985,155–58). Yet, another important parallel must be drawn to Pater. In his essay "Style," Pater, too, reaches to visual art for a fruitful analogy in making a strong case for avoiding "uncharacteristic or tarnished or vulgar decoration. . . . As the painter in his picture, so the artist in his book, aims at the production by honourable artifice of a peculiar atmosphere. 'The artist,' says Schiller, 'may be known rather by what he *omits*'; and in literature, too, the true artist may be best recognised by his tact of omission" (Pater 1888/1974, 110; italics in the original).

Indeed, when speaking about this minimalist literary technique, Cather obliges us to understand her aesthetic stance in connection to both her contemporaries and forerunners. In the literary milieu of her time, Hemingway's iceberg theory stands out as a comparable paradigm that emphasizes omission as a way of involving the reader and making him or her grasp the deeper meaning of what is on the page (Trout 2007). When Cather articulates her goal in fiction to create through omission the "inexplicable presence of the thing not named" (Cather 1922/1988, 41), she reveals the same preoccupation as Hemingway. Pater was more geographically and temporally remote, but his views regarding style and the relationship between author and reader were familiar to Cather, as she admits in the passage I quoted earlier: "Pater said that every truly great drama must, in the end, linger in the reader's mind." In Cather's writing, this lingering is often produced by what is not said on the page.[6]

Cather's rendition of this and other aspects of the artistic vocation in *The Professor's House* clearly points to the intertextual and international facets of the modernist aesthetic. Walter Pater remains a key figure at this crossroad. An aesthetician devoted to finding and delineating how art can transcend ordinary experience and imbue life with essential meaning, Pater stands behind the most salient markers of modernism: rejection of mimesis, subjectivity, autonomy of art, and a heightened sensitivity to style and technique. A trace of his aesthetic can be discerned in the works of many modernist writers, but it plays a very particular role in Cather's art: it helps to define her engagement with modernism. In her "Prefatory Note" to *Not under Forty*, Cather finds Thomas Mann's "backwardness" "more gratifying" than his "forwardness" (Cather 1922/1992, 812). In approaching Pater, she is comfortably looking backward, but going certainly forward.

NOTES

1. Psalm 68 Authorized (King James) Version. In his epigraph, Pater uses only one line from the Psalm: "Yet shall ye be as the wings of a dove."

2. I thank Morris Dickstein for bringing this important fact to my attention.

3. See Allen (1931), Douglas (1995), Hilfer (1969), and Hegeman (1999) for an overview of different aspects of the postwar period.

4. See Rose (1985) and Middleton (1990).

5. Later, Cather will establish this view in her essay "Escapism": "Religion and art spring from the same root and are close kin. Economics and art are strangers" (Cather 1936/1988, 27).

6. In her essay "'The Thing Not Named': Willa Cather as a Lesbian Writer," O'Brien (1984) interprets Cather's elusiveness in narration—her affinity for "the thing not named"—in connection to her reticence about her lesbian identity.

WORKS CITED

Allen, Frederick Lewis. 1931. *Only Yesterday: An Informal History of the Nineteen-Twenties*. New York: Harper & Row.

Bloom, Harold, ed. 1974. *Selected Writings of Walter Pater*. New York: Columbia University Press.

Cather, Willa. n.d./1988. "Light on Adobe Walls." In *Willa Cather on Writing: Critical Studies on Writing as an Art*, 123–26. New York: Knopf.

———. 1894/1966. "Commitment." In *The Kingdom of Art: Willa Cather's First Principles and Critical Statements, 1893–1896*, edited by Bernice Slote, 406–7. Lincoln: University of Nebraska Press.

———. 1895/1966. "The Aesthetic Movement." In *The Kingdom of Art: Willa Cather's First Principles and Critical Statements, 1893–1896*, edited by Bernice Slote, 389–90. Lincoln: University of Nebraska Press.

———. 1896/1966. "A Mighty Craft." In *The Kingdom of Art: Willa Cather's First Principles and Critical Statements, 1893–1896*, edited by Bernice Slote, 415–17. Lincoln: University of Nebraska Press.

———. 1905/1987. "Paul's Case." In *Willa Cather: Early Novels and Stories*. Edited by Sharon O'Brien, 111–31. New York: Library of America.

———. 1920/1988. "On the Art of Fiction." In *Willa Cather on Writing: Critical Studies on Writing as an Art*, 101–4. Lincoln: University of Nebraska Press.

———. 1922/1988. "The Novel Démeublé." In *Willa Cather on Writing: Critical Studies on Writing as an Art*, 35–43. Lincoln: University of Nebraska Press.

——. 1936/1992. "Prefatory Note" to *Not under Forty*. In *Willa Cather: Stories, Poems, and Other Writings*. Edited by Sharon O'Brien, 812. New York: Library of America.

——. 1925/1990. *The Professor's House*. New York: Vintage Classics.

——. 1925/1988, "The Best Stories of Sarah Orne Jewett." In *Willa Cather on Writing: Critical Studies on Writing as an Art*, 47–59. Lincoln: University of Nebraska Press.

——. 1936/1988. "Escapism." In *Willa Cather on Writing: Critical Studies on Writing as an Art*. Lincoln: University of Nebraska Press.

——. 1938/1988. "On *The Professor's House*." In *Willa Cather on Writing: Critical Studies on Writing as an Art*, 30–32. Lincoln: University of Nebraska Press.

——. 1949/1988."Light on Adobe Walls." In *Willa Cather on Writing: Critical Studies on Writing as an Art*, 123–26. Lincoln: University of Nebraska Press.

——. 1988. *Willa Cather on Writing: Critical Studies on Writing as an Art*. Lincoln: University of Nebraska Press.

Douglas, Ann. 1995. *Terrible Honesty: Mongrel Manhattan in the 1920s*. New York: Farrar, Straus and Giroux.

Eliot, T. S. 1932/1964. "Arnold and Pater." In *Selected Essays*, 382–93. New York: Harcourt, Brace & World.

Hegeman, Susan. 1999. *Patterns for America: Modernism and the Concept of Culture*. Princeton, NJ: Princeton University Press..

Hilfer, Anthony Channell. 1969. *The Revolt from the Village: 1915–1930*. Chapel Hill: University of North Carolina Press.

Iser, Wolfgang. 1987. *Walter Pater: The Aesthetic Moment*. Translated by David Henry Wilson. Cambridge: Cambridge University Press.

Lindemann, Marilee, ed. 2005. *The Cambridge Companion to Willa Cather*. Cambridge: Cambridge University Press.

McGrath, F. C. 1986. *The Sensible Spirit: Walter Pater and the Modernist Paradigm*. Tampa: University Presses of Florida; University of South Florida Press.

Middleton, Jo Ann. 1990. *Willa Cather's Modernism: A Study of Style and Technique*. London: Associated University Press; Rutherford, NJ: Fairleigh Dickinson University Press.

Millington, Richard H. 2005. "Willa Cather's American Modernism." In *Cambridge Companion to Willa Cather*, edited by Marilee Lindemann, 51–65. Cambridge: Cambridge University Press.

O'Brien, Sharon. 1984. "'The Thing Not Named': Willa Cather as a Lesbian Writer." *Signs* 9 (4). *JSTOR*. http://www.jstor.org/stable/3173612 (accessed September 1, 2010).

Pater, Walter. 1868/1974. "Conclusion to *The Renaissance*." In *Selected Writings of Walter Pater*. Edited by Harold Bloom, 58–63. New York: Columbia University Press.

——. 1888/1974. "Style." In *Selected Writings of Walter Pater*. Edited by Harold Bloom, 103–25. New York: Columbia University Press.

Rose, Phyllis. 1985. *Writing of Women: Essays in a Renaissance*. Middletown, CT: Wesleyan University Press.

Sevick, Leona. 2005. "Catholic Expansionism and the Politics of Depression in *Death Comes for the Archbishop*." In *The Cambridge Companion to Willa Cather*.

Edited by Marilee Lindemann, 191–204. Cambridge: Cambridge University Press.

Slote, Bernice. 1966a. "First Principles: The Kingdom of Art." In *The Kingdom of Art: Willa Cather's First Principles and Critical Statements, 1893–1896,* edited by Bernice Slote, 31–112. Lincoln: University of Nebraska Press.

Slote, Bernice, ed. 1966b. *The Kingdom of Art: Willa Cather's First Principles and Critical Statements, 1893–1896.* Lincoln: University of Nebraska Press.

Swift, John N. 2005. "Fictions of Possession in *The Professor's House.*" In *The Cambridge Companion to Willa Cather.* Edited by Marilee Lindemann, 175–90. Cambridge: Cambridge University Press.

Trout, Steven. 2007. "Antithetical Icons? Willa Cather, Ernest Hemingway, and the First World War." *Cather Studies* 7. Lincoln: University of Nebraska Press. http://cather.unl.edu/cs007.html (accessed August 8, 2011).

Wilson, Edmund. 1931/1996. *Axel's Castle: A Study of the Imaginative Literature of 1870–1930.* New York: Modern Library.

Chapter 13

From British Aestheticism to American Modernism

Cather's Transforming Vision

Jo Ann Middleton

The pursuit of pure beauty and the strenuous dedication of the artist to art itself, tenets of both Continental and British Aestheticism, inform Willa Cather's criticism and her fiction throughout her life, beginning with her youthful essay on Carlyle, in which she declares, "Art of every kind is an exacting master, more so than even Jehovah" (Cather 1891/1966, 423), and continuing in such essays as "Escapism," in which she says that "[t]he condition every art requires is, not so much freedom from restriction, as freedom from adulteration and from the intrusion of foreign matter" (Cather 1936/1988b, 26–27). She was steeped in Flaubert and Emerson, and, in a 14 January 1931 letter to Norman Foerster, still cited Pater and James as her favorite critics (Woodress 1987, 423). Nothing was ever wasted on her, and she seems to have forgotten nothing. In "Miss Jewett," Cather says, "The artist spends a lifetime in pursuing the things that haunt him, in having his mind 'teased' by them" (Cather 1925/1988a, 80), and she was fond of repeating Henry James: "How much life it takes to make a little art!" (Cather 1900/1970, 658). She told Eva Mahoney that "[a] book is made with one's own flesh and blood of years. It is cremated youth. It is all yours—no one gave it to you" (Cather 1921/1986, 36). George Seibel believed that "like Goethe, [she] had eyes in every pore," recalling that "Willa was interested in the study of human nature. She was avid of the world, always wondering, always questing, always digging, a prospector in the deep and quiet lodes of the soul. For her the proper study of mankind was man" (Hoover 2002, 18). When

Willa Cather says of Tom Outland, "The boy's mind had the superabundance of heat which is present when there is rich germination" and that "To share his thoughts was to see old perspectives transformed by new effects of light" (Cather 1925/1990, 234), she might have been describing the way in which her own mind worked. Cather's close attention to the world and its people revealed itself in the details and characters of her novels; after rich germination, the impressions of a lifetime of vibrant memories coalesced in the vivid scenes of her novels and in memorable characters like Ántonia, Marian Forrester, and Old Mrs. Harris.

But impressions and observations were not the only elements in the fertile mix that fueled Cather's imagination, enlisted her sympathy, and contributed to her art. Books were, in fact, central to her development as a critic and artist. In *The Kingdom of Art,* Bernice Slote makes the observation that Cather created something new, organic, and different out of everything she read (1966a, 42); and it has been well documented by scholars that Cather was a voracious reader throughout her life.[1] Sharon O'Brien notes that the Cather household was a bookish one and suggests that Cather learned her love of novels, including those of Scott, Ouida, and Marie Corelli (though she, like George Seibel, came to "despise her") from her mother (1987, 40). James Woodress tells us that, as a girl in Red Cloud, "[Cather] read constantly and indiscriminately, good books, trashy books, whatever came her way . . . no brief summary can do justice to her huge, eclectic consumption of books" (1987, 50). For Cather, Slote proposes, books and the reading of books constitute "the stream of experience most central to her own creativity" (1966a, 35), a stream of experience that included the Bible and Shakespeare, "the great essayists Carlyle, Ruskin, Pater, Arnold, and Emerson," as well as myth, fairy tales, the nineteenth-century classics, ladies magazines, Civil War novels, and popular romances of the day (37), an extraordinarily rich mixture of styles, ideas, and aesthetics.

Initially, Cather absorbed the principles of continental Aestheticism through her love of German and French writers. As a girl she read from the Wieners' collection of continental literature; in college she took four semesters of German and French, reading Daudet, Gautier, Balzac, and Racine, and spent two semesters studying the influential philosopher-critic Hippolyte Taine (Woodress 1987, 72). Later, Cather's enjoyment of all kinds of continental literature was nurtured and her taste refined through her friendship with the Seibels in Pittsburgh. Seibel reports:

We read uproarious trifles like Edmond About's *Roi de Montagnes,* pathetic romances like Pierre Loti's *Pêcheur d'Islande.* If we sometimes touched pleasant pastry like Emile Souvestre's *Philosophie son les Toits,* we indulged oftener in devil's food like Anatole France's *Le Lys Rouge.* We plunged into vats of color like Theophile Gautier's *Une Nuit de Cléopâtre*, and scaled towers of alexandrines in Victor Hugo's *Hernani*. Verlaine and Baudelaire were among the poets we discovered, Bourget and Huysmans among the novelists. . . .

[W]e ploughed through our adored Flaubert. *Madame Bovary* wasn't so hard, but *La Tentation de Sainte Antoine* and *Salammbô* proved most refractory until I discovered that a Latin lexicon and classical dictionary were more help than Littré. (Hoover 2002, 13)

Cather memorialized her love of French and German literature in "Old Mrs. Harris." Vickie Templeton, a portrait of the adolescent Cather, recapitulates her youthful pleasure in the Wiener library as Vickie lingers among the treasures of the Rosens': "a complete set of the Waverly Novels in German, for example; thick dumpy little volumes bound in tooled leather, with very black type and dramatic engravings printed on wrinkled yellowing pages. There were many French books, and some of the German classics done into English, such as Coleridge's translation of Schiller's *Wallenstein*" (Cather 1932/1974, 102). Vickie's enchantment with those books stayed with Cather throughout her life.

In addition to her natural predilection for books, reading was a necessity for Cather's career. One of the "front page girls" of the turn of the century, Cather joined the ranks of newspaperwomen, who "emerged as an icon of American Culture, a figure of modernity that promised to alleviate some of the alienating effects of the mass media that made possible her very existence" (Lutes 2006, 10). As a journalist, critic, and editor in Lincoln, Pittsburgh, and New York, Cather was required by the very nature of her job to see every theater production, to attend important social functions, to interview celebrities of all stripes, and to read everything, both popular and "literary" books, the news in the papers for which she worked, the articles in the magazines she edited, as well as the "thousands" of manuscripts submitted to the *Home Monthly* and *McClure's*.[2] Willa Cather was very much a part of her times and her culture, a culture both responsive to and horrified by the specter of British aestheticism. Slote describes the intellectual milieu of Cather's newspaper days as

a time distractingly, glitteringly "modern" as any time is when its years are new and change is more noticeable than permanence. But this "modernity," in particular, had that end-of-the-century, hectic flush that seemed part promise and part disease. It eloped in terms of "the Decadence," "Bohemianism," Philistinism; in continuing games of Wilde's lily and sunflower, living pictures, Beardsley's cartoons; a widening range of magazines from the more ponderously serious *Century* to the special elegance and color of the *Yellow Book* and the *Chap Book,* the flashing new *McClure's,* and the hundreds of plain and puritan home journals. The literary world was handsomely illustrated, described, and discussed in the *Critic.* "Modern" writers were still

Arnold, Ruskin, and Browning, as well as Shaw, Verlaine, Ibsen, Kipling and Hardy. (1966a, 32)

However, Slote concludes that Cather appropriated what she wanted from this heady mix for purposes of allusion and illustration, not for the formation of her principles. I would argue that, in fact, Cather's engagement in these very compelling cultural debates, her appreciation of style and assimilation of technique in the works she read, and, particularly, her attention to the lessons of Henry James ultimately led her to an aesthetic of her own, an artistic sensibility that, in fact, germinated into something new, a very American form of modernism that not only shares some of the characteristics with what we now call high modernism but is expansive enough to retain, renew, and incorporate the best of other literary traditions, such as classicism, realism, romanticism, and naturalism.

Jonathan Freedman is helpful in understanding how, at the turn of the century, "the tastes, the perceptions, the very attitudes of British Aestheticism had thoroughly penetrated the American cultural consciousness," particularly how "the aestheticist project of the beautification of everyday life, its privileging of sense experience, its evocation (particularly in its Paterian and Pre-Raphaelite phases) of a redemptive world elsewhere where such experiences could be ceaselessly realized" became issues in the "new social and ideological configurations" of late-nineteenth and early-twentieth-century American culture (1990, 79–80). As editor of the *Home Monthly*, new competitor to the wildly successful *Ladies' Home Journal*, Cather was well aware of these cultural trends and conflicts; in her magazine, she promised, "every phase of home needs will receive attention, together with work of the reviewer, while the best story writers of the country will furnish entertainment for the idle hour" (Byrne and Snyder 1980, 4). The clash between high and low culture, between the elite and the popular, was very real to Cather, who needed to make her living (another thorn in the side of the aesthetes) in journalism while at the same time she was trying to create something worthy of the kingdom of art. Although scholars have long acknowledged the apprenticeship Cather served as a journalist, none has so thoroughly investigated the culture of journalism at the turn of the century and its influence on Cather as M. Catherine Downs in *Becoming Modern: Willa Cather's Journalism*. Downs makes clear that Cather's experiences as "a woman in an office, writing journalism, editing journalism" (1999, 12) shaped her attitudes towards gender roles, technology, and consumer capitalism, the last especially vexing as it related to the question raised by the paradox of an artist devoted only to art making a living through the offering of that art to the marketplace.

In later years, Cather disparaged her newspaper writing: "It was a painful period in which I overcame my florid, exaggerated, foamy-at-the-mouth, adjective-spree period. I knew even then it was a crime to write like I did, but I had to get the adjectives and the youthful fervor worked off" (1915b/1986, 12–13). But it is her early *style* that she denigrates here, not the content of her work. If a book could be made of "cremated youth," then artistic vision could arise from digested books and stories. In the context of her journalism, Cather learned to rely on emotional response as a measure of successful art and to distinguish between the fine and the merely amusing, a distinction she would insist upon for the rest of her life. In a 1915 interview she said, "[I]n my course of reading thousands of stories, I was strengthened in the conclusion that I had come to before; that nothing was really worth while that did not cut pretty deep, and that the main thing was always to be honest" (1915a/1986, 8). She warns against "the dazzling journalistic successes of twenty years ago, stories that surprised and delighted by their sharp photographic detail and that were nothing more than lively pieces of reporting" (Cather 1920/1988b, 101). And in "The Novel Démeublé," she makes the point that "[i]n any discussion of the novel, one must make it clear whether one is talking about the novel as a form of amusement, or as a form of art; since they serve very different purposes and in very different ways" (1922/1988b, 93–94).

Cather also learned from these busy, hectic days that Sarah Jewett was right: an artist had to write from her own quiet center of life, guarding her energy for art. Aestheticism's ideal of the artist separate from society, devoted only to the pursuit of "art for art's sake," informs the part of Willa Cather who, in a crowded childhood home, had a room of her own, who rented the apartment above her so that she could have quiet, who snuck out of the Shattuck Inn to write undisturbed in the Jaffrey woods, who said of the writer: "He must spend thousands of uncounted hours at work. He must strive untiringly while others eat and sleep and play. Some people are more gifted than others, but it takes brains in the most gifted to make a success" (Cather 1915b/1986, 14). Willa Cather herself had the gift, the brains, the determination, and the work ethic to create, out of all she read and experienced, something fine and organic, something both new and lasting. And she was able to do so, in large part, because she internalized and built upon the lessons of "the keenest mind any American ever devoted to the art of fiction," Henry James (Cather 1925/1988a, 91).

Certainly James's importance to Cather cannot be overestimated. She considered him "the first living writer of pure English and the highest exponent of refined literary art" (Cather 1896/1970, 551n6), "that mighty

master of language and keen student of human actions and motives"
(1895/1970, 275), "one of the most subtle analysts, perhaps the greatest
living English master of the counterpoint of literary style" (551). She read
his novels, stories, and essays with her perceptive, questioning intellect,
and, although she and George Seibel disagreed about James's style, they
agreed that he was "a great critic" and pored over *Partial Portraits* and
French Poets and Novelists. Cather read James to discover "something of
what it means to really be an artist" (Cather 1895/1966, 361), imitating
his "pure prose" in her early stories and, most notably, in the style and
substance of *Alexander's Bridge*. Her understanding of the reader's role in
the creation of literary art can be traced to James, as well as her insistence
on the importance of the telling detail. Her later experiments with point
of view, particularly in *A Lost Lady* and *My Mortal Enemy*, arise from her
re-visioning of the Jamesian observing consciousness. Although Cather's
characteristically elegant and impenetrable style seems alien to James's
sometimes (to a modern sensibility) convoluted language, it also owes a
debt to the Master. In 1895 Cather wrote of James:

> And then his sentences! If his character novels were all wrong one could read
> him forever for the mere beauty of his sentences. He never lets his phrases
> run away with him. They are never dull and never too brilliant. He subjects
> them to the general tone of his sentence and has his whole paragraph partake
> of the same predominating color. You are never startled, never surprised,
> never thrilled or never enraptured; always delighted by that masterly prose
> that is as correct, as classical, as calm and as subtle as the music of Mozart.
> (Cather 1895/1970, 275)

When she describes Tom Outland's prose in 1925, Cather describes
her own "calm, pure style": "If words had cost money, Tom couldn't
have used them more sparingly. The adjectives were purely descriptive,
relating to form and colour, and were used to present the objects under
consideration, not the young explorer's emotions. Yet through this austerity one felt the kindling imagination, the ardour and excitement of the
boy, like the vibration in a voice when the speaker strives to conceal his
emotion by using only conventional phrases" (Cather 1925/1990, 238).
Echoes of James's novels appear throughout Cather's oeuvre; recently
Merrill Skaggs showed that "not only minor details, but major themes,
in *every one* of her novels, stretching throughout her writing life, can be
traced to Henry James's first 'serious' novel," the 1876 *Roderick Hudson*
(Skaggs 2007b, 160).

But it seems to me that Cather also learned from James what to do
with all that rich cultural experience and all those contradictory theories
of art she absorbed. Although she was, by nature, particularly attracted
to Aestheticism's privileging of the artist, she was too much a child of

her times to condone the decadent behavior of some of its practitioners, particularly Oscar Wilde, or the forbidden subjects they dared explore. (We should note, however, that she carried on her own rebellion against the social mores and dress codes of Red Cloud and Lincoln and chose to live in the bohemian Greenwich Village when she moved to New York.) She valued the romantic over the real, but wanted her romance to be honest. She asked the artist to avoid charged language, but she wanted art, above all, to evoke great emotion. James gave her a model for reconciling her own contradictions, permission to straddle the popular and the artistic, and a challenge to make of it all something uniquely American. Freedman's analysis of James's response to British Aestheticism is crucial to understanding the significance of his contribution to her subsequent freedom as an artist. Through his fiction, Cather learned how James "organized, structured and brought under firm control the uneasy and often uncanny play with contradictory possibilities that marks the British Aesthetic movement" (Freedman 1990, 132). Initially, like Cather, James was repelled by the decadent aspects of the Aesthetic movement; like her he also agreed with many of its artistic premises. Like Cather, he approved of Ruskin; unlike her, he never came to accept Pater. Like Cather, James continued to poke back at the things that teased his mind; his "work registers a sustained interrogation of the virtues and vices of aestheticism itself" (1990, 130). Following his example, Cather probes the worth and dangers of Aestheticism for herself in *The Troll Garden*, particularly in "Paul's Case."

Cather's use of the term "case" in her title can signal, as Claude J. Summers suggests, the 1905 discourse on homosexuality, which couched the discussion in legal or medical terms (1990, 109). But it can also be seen as Cather's nod to James's "The Art of Fiction," in which he defines the novel as "a personal, a direct impression of life," whose "execution belongs to the author alone" (1884/1948, 8, 9); in which he says "Try and be one of the people on whom nothing is lost!" (11); and, in which he argues that "[i]f we respect the artist at all, we must allow him his freedom of choice, in the face, in particular *cases*, of innumerable presumptions that the choice will not fructify" (15, emphasis added). One of the most important lessons Cather learned from James was flexibility, as Sarah Daugherty says, his "willingness to bend his principles to accommodate individual cases" (Daugherty 1981, 194). James reinforced what Cather learned from Emerson, that inconsistency *was* the hobgoblin of small minds, that great minds could accommodate paradox, and that she, like him, could maintain artistic independence while drawing what she needed from every "case" she studied, ignoring arbitrary distinctions among literary "schools," and refusing to become predictable. Over the years, James publicly changed some of his opinions, especially (probably to Cather's delight) about Maupassant and Flaubert. He sought the middle ground between the moral and the aesthetic, between romance and realism, between the necessity of form and the freedom of imagination. If James could mediate between opposites and select only what he needed from *his* teeming mind, then she could do the same with impunity.

For Cather's generation, Freedman points out, James was "the elite novelist par excellence—the internationally acclaimed but rarely read master of the art of fiction" (Freedman 1990, 82). However, Cather did not fail to recognize what he also makes clear: that although both the aesthetes and Henry James "consciously set themselves in opposition to the market economy, and particularly to the commodification of art and literature wrought by such an economy; both, however, participated in this as they critiqued this process, largely through what we might want to call the concomitant commodification of the artistic vocation, the professionalism of the literary and artistic practice—or what I call the rise of aesthetic professionalism" (xii). On the one hand, part of "Anglo-American aestheticism's social, artistic and intellectual sphere," James was also "an intimate part of the aestheticist revision of gentry values," joining the "Nortonian/ Ruskinian critique of the crudity, ugliness, and materialism of his society" and publishing in both the first issue of *The Yellow Book* "with all that implies" as well as in *The Chap Book* and in a number of its own imitators (129–30). Despite his status as culturally elite, despite his perceived disregard for popular approbation, James was not averse to popular success. Cather calls James to task for this in her comments on *What Maisie Knew*: "If it is indeed upon 'attractive houses' that Mr. James must base his claims to immortality, the author of *The Tragic Muse* and *The Princess Casamassima* had better study without delay the *Ladies' Home Journal*'s 'Interior of a Hundred Homes' and thus make his calling and election sure. O, Mr. James, this after all that we had hoped from you!" (Cather 1898/1970, 542). Reviewing *The Other House*, she marvels: "[O]f all men under heaven Henry James is the last man who would be expected to arouse any excited admiration in the mind of the public at large, yet he has done it. Yes, I repeat, Henry James has made a sensation! Will wonders never cease?" (1896/1970, 551). Cather herself wanted to make a sensation in the marketplace with her art, though she wanted her market to be made up of "fine readers." But she, too, became part of the literary profession, and she was very good at it. Alfred Knopf points out that she cared very much about the way her books looked and the way they were marketed: "Like many intelligent authors, she had a shrewd idea of the relative value of her own work, and when she brought me the manuscript of *Death Comes for the Archbishop* she said that our son would one day be paying royalties to her niece, and asked for special terms" (Hoover 2002, 136). If Henry James could stand with one foot in each world, then so could she.

Freedman proposes that "the influence of British aestheticism seems crucial to the formation of American modernism in a number of ways" (Freedman 1990, 127); for Willa Cather, Henry James was the conduit through which this version of aestheticism passed, a version which emphasized "the notion of the self-sufficiency of the work of art, the autonomy or autotelic nature of the poetic object . . . [t]he privileging of intense moments of special perception; the dialectical interplay of visual immediacy and representational distance; the concern with the purification of language and style; the simultaneous desire to evade or annul history and an intense, even obsessive, historicism" (127–28). James "helped shape the terms in which writers of the next century were to think about the nature and office of fiction" (131). Not the least of these writers was Willa Cather.

I have previously detailed at great length the characteristics and sources of Cather's modernism (Middleton 1990), focusing primarily on her style and the techniques that produce it, and others have since extended that discussion. Now we should consider how much of her modern aesthetic developed as a result of James's handling of Aestheticism. Cather met James on a rarefied plane of native intelligence and shared "book" knowledge; she knew her way around the books he valued; she was confident enough to review his work, challenge his opinions, and even judge him patronizing (Stout 2002, 251). Cather was uniquely suited to assimilate and make something new of his stunning contributions to the art of fiction because, unlike him, she chose to write "the Americans" from within. Her theme was not the clash of cultures, the American confronted with the European. She instead asked Americans to confront their own, a project in which she might be most modern. As she said, "The arts can not stand still; if they mark time, they die. There must be experimenting, if that is the right word for it" (Cather 1986, 110). After *Alexander's Bridge*, which too obviously announced its debt to the Master, Cather wrote eleven modern novels; each was an experiment, each distinctly her own, and each grounded in the New World, which transformed British Aestheticism into something organic and new, beginning, of course, with *O Pioneers!*, in which she showed that, indeed, she was *not* Henry James, but Yance Sorgeson (Stout 2002, 137). She was not T. S. Eliot nor Ezra Pound nor Hilda Doolittle either; hers was a modernism that arose when, like Alexandra, she set her face to the land with love and yearning, when she brought the muse to her own country, when she turned her genius to the quiet creation of American masterworks. For Yehudi Menuhin, "Willa Cather was the embodiment of America" even though she cared deeply for "the old, the European, the multilayered, and above all music." "But" he continues," her reverence did not cause her to stray into the self-doubt which some Americans used to show when confronting Europe" (Hoover 2002, 184–85). In 1936 she wrote him: "[I]t is the problem which every American artist confronts. If we remain always in our own land we miss the companionship of seasoned and disciplined minds. Here there are no standards of taste, and no responses to art *except emotional* ones." She continues, "On the other hand, if we adopt Europe altogether, we lose that sense of *belonging*, which is so important, and we lose part of our reality. . . . The things his own country makes him feel (the earth, the sky, the slang in the streets) are about the best capital a writer has to draw upon" (185–86). Late in her life, Cather still fed her art with "the slang of the streets," with the particulars of American life, just as she did as a journalist, and she remained a critical reader of classic and contemporary literature, taking from books what she needed to fuel her own creativity, as Merrill Skaggs's *Axes: Willa Cather and William Faulkner* (2007a) conclusively demonstrates.

At the end of her life, Willa Cather left an unpublished fragment, which was published in *Willa Cather on Writing* as "Light on Adobe Walls" (Cather n.d./1988b). In it she writes, "Art is a concrete and personal and rather childish thing after all—no matter what people do to graft it into science and make it sociological and psychological; it is not good at all unless it is let alone to be itself—a game of make-believe, of re-production, very exciting and delightful to people who have an ear for it or an eye for it. Art is too terribly human to be very 'great,' perhaps" (Cather 1988b, 125). Henry James gave Willa Cather permission to make great, terribly human art out of the richness of her own experiences, out of the artistic principles that she culled from a lifetime of reading and writing, out of an aestheticism that gave her permission to experiment, to "escape," in the very best sense of the word, and to explore human values using techniques that she continually honed into a pellucid style designed to engage the reader with the text itself. She repaid him by becoming the silent, detached, impersonal, and modern creator of American works that exist simply as aesthetic objects of great beauty and completeness.

NOTES

1. For detailed lists, see Woodress (1987, 50-51); Slote (1966a, 35–42); and O'Brien (1987, 78–84.

2. Also see Moseley (2009) for a full discussion of Cather's life as a journalist in turn-of-the-century Pittsburgh.

WORKS CITED

Bennett, Mildred. 1951/1961. *The World of Willa Cather*. Lincoln: University of Nebraska Press

Byrne, Kathleen D., and Richard C. Snyder. 1980. *Chrysalis: Willa Cather in Pitts-burgh 1886–1906*. Pittsburgh: Historical Society of Western Pennsylvania.

Cather, Willa. n.d./1988. "Light on Adobe Walls." In *Willa Cather on Writing: Critical Studies on Writing as an Art*, 123–26. Lincoln: University of Nebraska Press.

———. 1891/1966. "Concerning Thomas Carlyle." In *The Kingdom of Art: Willa Cather's First Principles and Critical Statements 1893–1896*, edited by Bernice Slote, 421–25. Lincoln: University of Nebraska Press.

———. 1895/1966. "James." In *The Kingdom of Art: Willa Cather's First Principles and Critical Statements 1893–1896*, edited by Bernice Slote, 360–62. Lincoln: University of Nebraska Press.

———. 1895/1970. "The Literary Situation in 1895." In *The World and the Parish*. Edited by William M. Curtin, 273–79. Lincoln: University of Nebraska Press.

———. 1896/1970. "Henry James: 'A Really Great Artist.'" In *The World and the Parish*. Edited by William M. Curtin, 551–54. Lincoln: University of Nebraska Press.

———. 1898/1970. "Women's Worlds" In *The World and the Parish*. Edited by William M. Curtin, 538–44. Lincoln: University of Nebraska Press.

———. 1900/1970. "Three Operas." In *The World and the Parish*. Edited by William M. Curtin, 655–58. Lincoln: University of Nebraska Press.

———. 1915a/1986. "Willa Cather Talks of Work." In *Willa Cather in Person: Interviews, Speeches, and Letters*. Selected and edited by L. Brent Bohlke, 7–11. Lincoln: University of Nebraska Press.

———. 1915b/1986. "The Vision of a Successful Fiction Writer" interview by Ethel M. Hockett. In *Willa Cather in Person: Interviews, Speeches, and Letters*. Selected and edited by L. Brent Bohlke, 12–16. Lincoln: University of Nebraska Press.

———. 1920/1988b. "On the Art of Fiction." In *Willa Cather on Writing: Critical Studies on Writing as an Art*, 101–4. Lincoln: University of Nebraska Press.

———. 1921/1986. "How Willa Cather Found Herself" interview by Eva Mahoney. In *Willa Cather in Person: Interviews, Speeches, and Letters*. Selected and edited by L. Brent Bohlke, 33–39. Lincoln: University of Nebraska Press.

———. 1922/1988b. "The Novel Démeublé." In *Willa Cather on Writing: Critical Studies on Writing as an Art*, 35–43. Lincoln: University of Nebraska Press.

———. 1925/1988a. "Miss Jewett." In *Not Under Forty*, 76–95. Lincoln: University of Nebraska Press.

———. 1925/1990. *The Professor's House*. New York: Vintage Books.

———. 1932/1974. *Obscure Destinies*. New York: Vintage Books.

———. 1936/1988b. "Escapism." In *Willa Cather on Writing: Critical Studies on Writing as an Art*, 18–29. Lincoln: University of Nebraska Press.

———. 1986. *Willa Cather in Person: Interviews, Speeches, and Letters*. Edited by L. Brent Bohlke. Lincoln: University of Nebraska Press.

———. 1988a. *Not under Forty*. Lincoln: University of Nebraska Press.

———. 1988b. *Willa Cather on Writing: Critical Studies on Writing as an Art*. Lincoln: University of Nebraska Press.

Curtin, William M., ed. 1970. *The The World and the Parish: Willa Cather's Articles and Reviews, 1893–1902*. Edited by William M. Curtin. Lincoln: University of Nebraska Press.

Daugherty, Sarah B. 1981. *The Literary Criticism of Henry James*. Athens: Ohio University Press.

Downs, M. Catherine. 1999. *Becoming Modern: Willa Cather's Journalism*. Selinsgrove, PA: Susquehanna University Press.

Freedman, Jonathan. 1990. *Professions of Taste: Henry James, British Aestheticism, and Commodity Culture*. Stanford, CA: Stanford University Press.

James, Henry. 1884/1948. "The Art of Fiction." In *The Art of Fiction and Other Essays*. New York: Oxford University Press.

Hoover, Sharon, ed. 2002. *Willa Cather Remembered*. Compiled by L. Brent Bohlke and Sharon Hoover. Lincoln: University of Nebraska Press.

Lutes, Jean Marie. 2006. *Front Page Girls: Women Journalists in American Culture and Fiction, 1880–1930*. Ithaca: Cornell University Press.

Middleton, Jo Ann. 1990. *Willa Cather's Modernism: A Study of Style and Technique*. Rutherford, NJ: Fairleigh Dickinson University Press.

Moseley, Ann. 2009. "Editing the Scholarly Edition of *The Song of the Lark*: The Legacy of Cather's Journalism in the Social and Literary History of the Novel." *American Literary Realism* 41 (2): 133–53.

O'Brien, Sharon. 1987. *Willa Cather: The Emerging Voice*. New York: Oxford University Press.

Skaggs, Merrill Maguire. 2007a. *Axes: Willa Cather and William Faulkner*. Lincoln: University of Nebraska Press.

———. 2007b. "Cather's Violent Assimilation of Henry James's Art." In *Violence, the Arts, and Willa Cather*, edited by Joseph R. Urgo and Merrill Maguire Skaggs, 160–72. Madison, NJ: Fairleigh Dickinson University Press.

Slote, Bernice. 1966a. "First Principles: The Kingdom of Art." In *The Kingdom of Art: Willa Cather's First Principles and Critical Statements 1893–1896*, edited by Bernice Slote, 31–112. Lincoln: University of Nebraska Press.

Slote, Bernice, ed. 1966b. *The Kingdom of Art: Willa Cather's First Principles and Critical Statements 1893–1896*. Lincoln: University of Nebraska Press.

Stout, Janis, ed. 2002. *A Calendar of the Letters of Willa Cather*. Lincoln: University of Nebraska Press.

Summers, Claude J. 1990. "'A Losing Game in the End': Aestheticism and Homosexuality in Cather's 'Paul's Case.'" *Modern Fiction Studies* 36, no. 1 (Spring): 103–19.

Woodress, James. 1987. *Willa Cather: A Literary Life*. Lincoln: University of Nebraska Press.

Part IV

ART AND RELIGION

Chapter 14

Willa Cather's Sheltering Art

Cather's Cathedral and the Adams Factor

John J. Murphy

In her most definitive statement on fiction, "The Novel Démeublé" (1922), Willa Cather articulates her artistic credo:

> Whatever is felt upon the page without being specifically named there—that, one might say, is created. It is the inexplicable presence of the thing not named, of the overtone divined by the ear but not heard by it, the verbal mood, the emotional aura of the fact, or the thing or the deed, that gives high quality to the novel or the drama, as well as to poetry itself. (1922/1962, 41–42)

If an essay or lecture can communicate things not specifically named, my essay will imply, I hope, that in the fiction of her major phase, Cather distanced herself from her earlier, Nebraska novels—*O Pioneers!* (1913), *My Ántonia* (1918), and *A Lost Lady* (1923)—and took her place among the major writers of the twentieth century.[1] This lecture will also set *Death Comes for the Archbishop* (1927) within a world context rather than a New Mexican one and demonstrate that this novel was neither a putdown of the local culture nor a vindictive portrayal of certain dubious local heroes—the defensive view of some New Mexicans. Rather, writing the *Archbishop* represented for Cather "a happy vacation from life" and "return to childhood" (1927/1962, 11), an escape from the disillusionment evident in *The Professor's House* (1925) and in her essay "Nebraska: The End of the First Cycle" (1923), a putdown, clearly, and a jeremiadic one, of Americanization, materialism, and the collapse of liberal arts education.

197

My attempt here is to explore the alternative Cather created in several subsequent works, the *Archbishop* among them, as a solution, perhaps, as well as escape for herself and sympathetic readers.

I. STRATEGY

A youthful declaration that Willa Cather made in her 1891 essay on Thomas Carlyle that "Art is an exacting master, more so even than Jehovah . . . [, and] accept[s] only human sacrifices" (1891/1966, 423) falters at face value when we consider her later fiction. It is, at least, an inadequate support for her biographer Mildred Bennett's claim that this "was Willa's religion and she told friends she was going to devote her life to the worship of Art and would probably follow her creed to a place much hotter than Pittsburgh" (1961, 219), where she was at the time teaching school and editing magazines. Bennett's idea of Cather's "religion of art" (225) contradicts Professor St. Peter's claim in *The Professor's House* that "Art and religion . . . are the same thing, in the end . . ." (Cather 1925/1990, 55). Not only are the two construed as the same by St. Peter, but in his examples of Moses "invent[ing] elaborate ceremonials" and the Christian theologians "getting splendid effects through excision" of "the books of the Law" (55–56), religion becomes art. The synthesis is strategic for understanding the direction of Cather's career. As her first biographer E. K. Brown explains, the apparent "shift" in that career in *The Professor's House* "is not a weakening in Willa Cather's belief in the primacy of art, but a bracketing of religion with art" (1953, 247).

The clearest way to understand the significance of this bracketing is to rearrange Cather's "religious fiction"—*The Professor's House, My Mortal Enemy* (1926), *Death Comes for the Archbishop, Shadows on the Rock* (1931), and the Avignon story, "Hard Punishments," left unfinished at Cather's death in 1947—more or less according to historical setting, beginning with *Shadows* (a seventeenth-century setting) and the Avignon fragment (a fourteenth-century setting) and concluding with the 1925 and 1926 novels (both twentieth-century settings). A rather rigid faith sustains the worlds of the Avignon story and *Shadows*, yet, in *Archbishop*, Father Latour understands that this faith construct must become organic to survive and to propagate in an alien environment. The conflict underlying this series of works then becomes evident, as the world created by the "great artists" of religion (as described by Cather's history professor), in which "every man and woman who crowded into the cathedrals on Easter Sunday was a principal in a gorgeous drama with God" (Cather 1925/1990, 56, 55) confronts the adversarial forces of twentieth-century science, materialism, and secularism. This celebration of art and religion as an antidote or escape seems somewhat strained in the post–World War I struggles of Professor St. Peter, an agnostic who nevertheless despairs at the emptiness of life without an enriching religious construct and accuses contemporary science of destroying it. "I don't think much of science as a phase of human development," he tells one of his students. "It has given us a lot of ingenious toys; they take our attention away from the real problems. . . . But the fact is, the human mind . . . has always been made more interesting by dwelling on the old riddles . . . Science hasn't given us any new amazements, except of the superficial kind. . . . It hasn't given us any richer pleasures, . . . nor any new sins—not one! Indeed, it takes our old ones away. It's the laboratory, not the Lamb of God, that taketh away the sins of the world" (54–55).

The conflict is essentially a clash of rival fictions, as Raymond Carney explains in his introduction to Henry Adams's *Mont Saint Michel and Chartres* (1904): "There is no refuge from fiction in [Adams's work], no intelligible human 'truth' or 'reality' that exempts itself from its own fictionality. We cannot lever ourselves outside of our own systems of knowledge and understanding, and there is no alternative to such systems that is not another equally arbitrary and tentative fictional system" (1986, xv). Professor St. Peter's argument with modern science is that it impoverishes our lives by destroying a medieval system of "miracles and great temptations and revelations" that makes life "a rich thing" (Cather 1925/1990, 55). However, like Adams's, St. Peter's nostalgia for the thirteenth century is ambivalent. "On the one hand," continues Carney on Adams, "it is obvious that [Adams] would have given almost anything to have lived in an age as 'very beautiful and very true' as the thirteenth century, and yet . . . his characterization of it as 'very childlike [and] very foolish' reveals his doubts about whether it would . . . have satisfied him . . ." (xiii). Adams fought in vain almost his entire life for a science of history to keep pace with the unleashing of new energies. "The new philosophy of radiation and electricity required higher powers of mind and more elasticity of thought than had been imagined in any previous age," he wrote (Samuels 1989, 413). A unifying principle had to be applied to the multiplicity of forces, something other than the "gold-bug" spirit of American capitalism with its "foolish optimism about the unique destiny of the American people, as if they were exempt from the laws of historical development" (Samuels, 414). "Science hesitates, more visibly than the Church ever did," Adams insisted, "to decide once for all whether Unity or Diversity is ultimate law; whether order or chaos is the governing rule of the Universe, if Universe there is" (Adams 1904/1986, 275). Yet Adams was forced to admit in a letter to a friend that "[t]he assumption of unity which was the mark of human thought in the middle ages has yielded very slowly to the proofs of complexity" (Samuels, 376).

To an extent, such ambivalence applies to Cather, whose early enthusiasm for Adams's book had obviously developed into an influence during the writing of *The Professor's House*. In a 1914 letter to Ferris Greenslet, her editor at Houghton-Mifflin, Cather thanks him for a new trade edition of Adams's book and claims she has been telling her friends about it. *Mont Saint Michel and Chartres* is definitely a helpful resource for understanding Cather's bracketing of religion and art as a tentative and personal response to the crises of her time, one to which I refer throughout this essay.

II. CREATION

"Hard Punishments" (the working title for the Avignon fragment) and *Shadows on the Rock* provided refuge for Cather and for readers who, like Professor St. Peter, felt smothered by a spiritually impoverished contemporary world. Her companion Edith Lewis reports that during their visit to Paris in 1920, Cather declared that she "wanted to live in the Middle Ages" (1953, 119), a desire including her in what Ernest Samuels describes in his biography of Adams as "the intellectual counterrevolution that had declared war upon the materialist values of the modern age, a war whose main strategy was an aggressive retreat from the present," and for some "disenchanted idealists" involved "the escape to the Middle Ages" (1989, 334–35). While it is "undeniable," acknowledges Carney, that such a desire reflects "nostalgia for an era before the modernist insight, for a time before truths were discredited as 'truths' and rendered relative," he adds this disclaimer: "On the other hand, there is a feeling of joy and potential liberation in the new situation. . . . Freed from enslavement to . . . any one fiction, the self is freed to become an aesthetic eclectic" (1986, xvi), which amounts to saying one can create one's own world—or recreate a historical one, as Adams and Cather do in their books. Indeed, as Samuels explains, the student of history "must rub his eyes in astonishment" at the world that lies behind the created ideal: "The apparent unity of the world of art and religious imagination is belied at every turn by the fact of discord and tension" (1989, 358). Adams concludes his meditation on the Middle Ages with an elaborate metaphor celebrating Thomas Aquinas as the master architect of "thirteenth-century unity." Modernist license begets compound art: Aquinas is distinguished as the creator of this integrated world and is himself re-created in fashioning it according to Adams's own needs. As Carney observes, Adams "bends and twists Aquinas' arguments . . . by making him over into a kind of American Romantic (descended . . . from the double tradition of seventeenth-century meditative prose and poetry and nineteenth-century Wordsworthian

Romanticism" (xxxi). The aggregate resembles Cather's collage method in her "Catholic novels," bits and pieces of factual stuff interwoven with fiction to produce an inventive historical tapestry.

The challenge for Thomas Aquinas in the mid-thirteenth century was to make Aristotle's philosophy compatible with Christian doctrine, to give reason and natural science a new role in Catholic tradition. According to Charles Freeman, Aquinas achieved this with such mastery "that in some areas of thought Aristotelianism and Catholicism become virtually indistinguishable" (2005, 327). Adams poeticizes this achievement by depicting Aquinas negotiating a series of architectural hurdles to create a cathedral of the Trinity in which humanity is linked to God and placed at the center of the universe. God as "an intelligent, fixed Prime Motor" and "concrete fact" (1904/1986, 332) becomes the foundation, the unity behind creation's multiplicity. Adams uses the Chartres cathedral south belfry tower to illustrate the solution to the greatest of Aquinas's many architectural challenges, defining human free will within the context of divine determinism: "The square foundation-tower, the expression of God's power in act,—his creation,—rose to the level of the church façade as part of the normal unity of God's energy; and then, suddenly, without show of effort, without break, without logical violence, became a many-sided, voluntary vanishing soul [/spire]" (356). The entire process involves art and religion, and the ensuing edifice accommodates the Cather novels considered here.

Clearly, in his lecture, Professor St. Peter tries to define a world in which humanity and human behavior are so connected to God as to possess significance and mystery. However, the professor's own world has fled the cathedral, and that is his lament. For Adams, too, the structure has been abandoned for any use other than his aesthetic pleasure. He concludes his chapters on Chartres emphatically so: "We have done with Chartres. . . and can safely leave the Virgin in her Majesty . . . looking down from a deserted heaven, into an empty church, on a dead faith" (186). The characters in *Shadows on the Rock* and the Avignon story, on the other hand, exist securely if not always comfortably within this cathedral. The nuns in *Shadows* who left France for Canada continue to live "in their accustomed place in the world of the mind," an integrated place in which all the lines converge. Whether in Quebec or Dieppe or Tours,

> they had the same well-ordered universe about them: this all-important earth, created by God for a great purpose, the sun . . . to light it by day, the moon . . . to light it by night,—and the stars . . . to beautify the vault of heaven like frescoes. And in this safe, lovingly arranged universe . . . the drama of man went on . . . and the Sisters played their accustomed part in it. (Cather 1931b/1995, 78)

The reference to frescoes emphasizes the role of art in creating a shelter-ing space, "congenial" and "not too vast" (78). The individual items—sun, moon, stars—suggest church decorations like those in the Arena Chapel in Padua, where Giotto painted the Christian story, from the lives of the Virgin's parents to a Last Judgment crowned with angels peeling away these depictions to uncover the final cosmic mystery. *Shadows* is primarily an attempt to contain life within a shelter and to defend what sociolo-gist Peter Berger refers to as the sacred canopy, "man's ultimate shield against the terror of anomy. To be in a 'right' relationship with the sacred cosmos," he continues, "is to be protected against the nightmare threats of chaos" (1967/1990, 26). The creative nature of that protection at once intrigued and comforted Cather and Adams, and probably Thomas Aqui-nas and Giotto as well.

Cather explains in her essay "Light on Adobe Walls" that while the artist should avoid "wrangling with abstractions or creeds" (n.d./1962, 126), he cannot avoid establishing "barriers and limitations," deciding on "a certain relation of creatures or objects to each other. . . . Nobody can paint the sun . . . or what it does to forms. He . . . can only paint . . . some man-made arrangement . . . that happens to give him personal delight" (123–24). In rendering the contained world of her "Catholic" novels, com-fort and delight more than belief motivated Cather; and these qualities are especially evident throughout the text of *Shadows on the Rock*, as in the description of Quebec on a June morning introducing the fourth book:

> When the sun came up over the Ile d'Orleans, the rock of Kebec stood gleam-ing above the river like an altar with many candles, or like a holy city in an old legend, shriven, sinless, washed in gold. The quickening of all life and hope . . . had reached the far North at last. (Cather 1931b/1995, 137)

The phrase "toy village" rather than "holy city" was Cather's first choice, as indicated in an earlier version of this description (c. 1930). Like T. S. Eliot in the first part of *Ash Wednesday*, "Because I do not hope to turn again," Cather felt compelled during difficult times "to construct some-thing / Upon which to rejoice" (Eliot 1963, 85, lines 24–25). Edith Lewis speculates that the "great pleasure" Cather took in Quebec "came from finding a sort of continuation . . . of the Catholic theme which had ab-sorbed her" in writing *Death Comes for the Archbishop*, and that she under-took *Shadows* from "a reluctance to leave that world of Catholic feeling and tradition in which she had lived so happily for so long" (Lewis 1953, 155). In a June 1931 letter to Dorothy Canfield Fisher, Cather communi-cates the reprieve she felt in writing *Shadows* during her mother's fatal illness, comparing the process to weaving a tapestry tent she could unfold in hotels and sanatoriums, picking it up and putting it down during the chaos of life in transit (Cather 1931a).

III. DEFENSE

Cather's Quebec is a fortress church much like Adams's Mont St. Michel crowned by its abbey and the Archangel. Adams rhapsodizes that prior to the Reformation this grand pile in Normandy had "solved the whole problem of the universe": "One looks back on it all as a picture; a symbol of unity; an assertion of God and Man in a bolder, stronger, closer union than ever was expressed by other art" (1904/1986, 46–47). *Shadows on the Rock* opens with apothecary Euclide Auclair looking down on the Quebec settlement from the highest point of the rock upon which it is set, "a mountain rock, cunningly built over with churches, convents, fortifications . . . following the natural irregularities of the headland on which they stood" (Cather 1931b/1995, 4). At its base, the broad St. Lawrence, the counterpart of the Gulf of St. Malo encircling Mont St. Michel, rushes toward the Atlantic. Cather's narrator observes that "[t]hese heavy grey buildings . . . steep-pitched and dormered, with spires and slated roofs, were roughly Norman Gothic in effect, made by people from the north of France who knew no other way of building" (5)—rough examples of that architecture Adams declared "makes even Raphael vulgar" (Samuels 1989, 307). The settlement is a sanctuary of order surrounded by the chaos of a newly discovered continent, "the dead, sealed world of . . . interlocking trees . . . strangling each other. . . . The forest was suffocation, annihilation; there European man was quickly swallowed up" (Cather 1931b/1995, 5–6). The fortifications, earthworks, and ramparts also suggest political and religious foes: the English and their Iroquois allies to the south.

The military and religious aspects of this fortress church coalesce in the altar of Notre Dame de la Victoire, a humble church in Quebec's Lower Town so named after the repulsion in 1690 of an attack by the English under Sir William Phips (fig. 14.1). When Cécile Auclair and Jacques Gaux, the neglected child Cather's young heroine befriends, seek shelter in this church, they marvel at its high altar, a miniature fortified castle: "The outer wall was low and thick, with many battlements," and contained an "arched gateway . . . [where] the Host [Sacrament] was kept" (64). The wall within has many windows and rises into three towers, on the tallest of which "the Blessed Mother and Child stood high up among the shadows" (65). Not only does this altar duplicate the settlement as a defense of the Real Presence and the cult of the Virgin, but it also typifies the theological or sacred canopy transported to Canada from France. The children regard the altar as a faithful "reproduction" of the Kingdom of Heaven "made in France by people who knew" (64). The city as altar or church reappears later, in the description (quoted above) opening the fourth book, and earlier, during winter, when "Quebec seemed shrunk to a mere

Figure 14.1.   John J. Murphy, Altar of Quebec City's Notre Dame des Victoires Church, formerly Notre Dame de la Victoire, inspiring Cather's description in *Shadows on the Rock*. (Courtesy of the author.)

group of shivering spires; the whole rock looked like one great white church, above the frozen river" (110). In this church, order and regularity reign. Old Bishop Laval rises early each morning to ring the bell for mass, and the Auclairs dine ritualistically each evening on a linen-covered table set with silver candlesticks and decanters of wine. In the epilogue, Bishop Saint-Vallier, who returns after years of exile in England, congratulates Auclair for remaining in Quebec, "where nothing changes"; and in the novel's final sentence, the apothecary reflects that "he was indeed fortunate to spend his old age here where nothing changed" (228–29).

This "holy city" (or "toy village") is an efficacious setting for miracles, religious mystery, and mystics. Miracles dominate the novel's third book. The bleak winter is relieved by news from Montreal that the famous recluse Jeanne Le Ber, who lives in a cell behind the tabernacle in a convent chapel, has been visited by angels who repaired her spinning-wheel. Outside the context of this novel, Jeanne could be dismissed as a seventeenth-century religious hysteric, but here she bequeaths to the community "an incomparable gift":

> [T]he story of Jeanne Le Ber's spinning-wheel was told and retold . . . during that severe winter . . . as if the recluse herself had sent to all those families . . . a blooming rose-tree. . . . The people have loved miracles . . . because they are the actual flowering of desire. In them the vague worship and devotion of the simple-hearted assumes a form . . . and can be bequeathed to another. (110–11)

This miracle occurs during Epiphany, the feast of divine manifestation, along with another, less spectacular miracle depending for validity on what Father Latour in *Archbishop* calls "human vision corrected by divine love" (Cather 1927/1990, 50). Woodsman Antoine Frichette relates to the Auclairs how he and the missionary Father Hector made their way through a blizzard to bring the Sacrament to Frichette's dying brother-in-law. On the fourth day of their journey, lost and out of food, the travelers happen upon a friendly Indian carrying two freshly shot hares, which he cooks for them before leading them to the dying man. Earlier, when Frichette is about to give up hope, Father Hector, referring to the Sacrament they are transporting, tells him, "never fear . . . while we carry that, Someone is watching over us. Tomorrow will bring better luck" (Cather 1931b/1995, 116). Indeed it does, but, within this context, more than mere "luck." Later, during his visit to the Auclairs, Father Hector alerts them to the challenges facing this sheltering world of divine manifestation. He concludes his story of the Jesuit martyr Noel Chabanel, a rhetoric professor like himself whose suffering and sacrifice as a missionary in Canada has inspired his own decision to continue working among the Hurons, with a question: "How can there be men in France this day who doubt the existence of God, when for the love of Him weak human beings have been able to endure so much?" Cécile asks in turn, "Are there such men, Father?" He responds, "There are, my child,—but it is the better for you if you have never heard of them" (124).

IV. KEYSTONE

The second book of *Shadows* and the four surviving paragraphs of the Avignon story portray the great miracle and mystery housed within Aquinas's cathedral: God made human in Christ. In *Shadows*, Cécile unpacks the Christmas crèche from France. The individual pieces are detailed: the "rosy and naked" Infant; the Virgin, "a country girl . . . seated on a stool"; Joseph, a bald old man with "wrinkled brow" (87). While placing these figures, Cécile recounts the Nativity story to Jacques. In the "Hard Punishments" (Avignon) fragment, set during Christmas mass in the "Old Chapel" of Benedict XII in Avignon's Papal Palace, the building which, according to Edith Lewis, "stirred [Cather] as no building in the world had ever done" (1953, 190), Cather approaches the essence of the Christian story. Two boys mutilated for crimes against the theocracy and their old blind priest mentor experience "release from bondage" extending "to all the generations of the future" (c. 1941). The scene in the Papal Palace resembles one in Samuels's biography of Adams, when "[o]n a journey into Normandy to visit its cathedrals . . . in the late summer of 1895 Adams experienced a sudden illumination like that of [Walter] Pater's Marius, who discovered the beauty of the Mass 'amid a deep sense of the vacuity of life'" (Samuels 1989, 306).

In *Shadows*, Cather illustrates the ongoing springing of Aquinas's cathedral through the localization of Christmas. The Holy Family is placed beneath "a little *cabine* of branches," like those under which the first missionaries to Quebec "used to say mass" (1931b/1995, 87), and Jacques contributes his toy beaver to the animals of the crèche, with the approval of a wise old neighbor, who declares, "Our Lord died for Canada as well as for the world over there [in Europe], and the beaver is our very special animal" (90). Quebec itself becomes a New World Bethlehem. Auclair constructs a shelf below a windowsill, so "the [crèche] scene could be arranged in two terraces, as was customary at home [in France]" (86). These shelves duplicate Quebec's Upper and Lower Towns and recall the opening description of the city, Auclair's comparison of the settlement to an elaborate *santon* crib display such as Cather would have seen during several visits to Provence:

> Auclair thought this rock-set town like . . . one of those little artificial mountains . . . made in the churches at home to present a theatric scene of the

Nativity; cardboard mountains, broken up into cliffs and ledges and hollows to accommodate groups of figures on their way to the manger. (4)

Book Two closes with groups of faithful Quebecers moving across snow-covered ledges toward the cathedral for mass at midnight.

The surviving paragraphs of the Avignon story,[2] most likely its climax according to Edith Lewis's outline of the plot, depict such a mass, involving André, a "spirited, intelligent, well-born" boy whose tongue has been torn out for blasphemy and subversive activities; Pierre, a "simple, childlike" peasant boy whose hands have been ruined for thievery; and Father Ambrose, "André's friend and confessor," who "comforts . . . and absolves" André and is able to restore his life "on a new plane," turning disability into challenge by making the poor peasant boy Pierre "a part of this challenge" (Kates 1956/1992, 482–84). In the four paragraphs, probably a flashback, rebirth in Christ is dramatized through light, darkness, and sound imagery in an interior monologue from Father Ambrose's perspective, leaving the theology, according to the aesthetic principle articulated in "The Novel Démeublé," to be "felt upon the page without being specifically named there" (Cather 1922/1962, 41). Cather's theme embraces the priest's renewal of faith and the transformation of the boys, particularly André. Upon hearing the choir and deciphering the candlelight, Father Ambrose senses "something more beautiful" than either, "the kindling of emotion, faith, belief, imagination" in the people around him. "At Christmas Mass," Ambrose believes, "something is born in thousands of unlikely people" (Cather c. 1941). Thomas Aquinas's faith theology, evident throughout the fragment, illuminates this four-part cluster, which probably has its source in Hugh Pope's "Faith" entry in the *Catholic Encyclopedia* Cather began consulting during the writing of *Archbishop*. In beginning this list with emotion, Cather is reflecting Augustine's view that the act of faith is "motivated by charity or love of God" (Pope 1909–1913, 5: 757), which the priest compares to "a heart beating under his hand." Closing this list with imagination, the power to apprehend the unseen, as Ambrose closes his blind eyes, also echoes Augustine: "You ought not to see in order to believe, you ought to believe in order to see; you ought to believe so long as you do not see, lest when you do see you may be put to the blush" (Pope, 757). The "kindling" Ambrose senses as taking place around him is Christ's rebirth in each of the faithful during the mass. The experience is "more beautiful" than candlelight because candles merely symbolize the actual occurrence of Christ in this place. The theme of the traditional Nativity masses is repeated in Cather's text in "*is born*" and then its Latin equivalent, "*Natus est*" (Cather c. 1941). The prayer introducing the first chapter of John's Gospel celebrates this "sanctified day . . . a great light hath descended upon the earth" (*St. John's* 1950, 147).

In the longest and most complex of the four Avignon paragraphs, Father Ambrose grapples with the "wonder" generated by this rebirth he senses within him and in those around him. Cather uses the image of a "wave" to suggest an emotional experience equated with "humility," "exaltation," and "triumph." The priest now contemplates "wonderment," the human ability to experience awe, the power of "littleness" to "rejoice" in "immensity," but then encounters a dilemma. God's wonderment and rejoicing in creation would amount to "self-worship," but the inability to wonder and worship would seem to reduce "any being," even God, to "a stone," to eternal "blindness" and dumbness. The priest's solution is to separate "great creators" (artists) from other beings and to allow them to be "satisfied partly" with their creations, but "not admiring." At this point, Cather introduces in Latin the recurring phrase from the first chapter of Genesis, "*Et vidit Deus quod esset bonum*"—"And God saw that it was good" (Cather c. 1941). This entire speculation has its source in the *Hexameron, or Six Days of Creation*, a fourth-century series of homilies by St. Ambrose (which explains Cather's choice of Father Ambrose's name). Addressing Creation as a cooperative act of the Father and the Son, the historical Ambrose writes,

> And so . . . "God spoke" and "God created," . . . both Father and Son are honored with the same name of majesty. "And God saw that it was good." He spoke as if . . . to one who knew all the wishes of His Father. He saw as if He knew all that His Son had accomplished, acting with him in community of operation. . . . He did not, of course, recognize that of which He was ignorant. Rather, His approval was given to what gave Him pleasure. (Ambrose 1961, 63)

In other words, due to foreknowledge, God was not astonished at what He created, nor did He (to use Cather's words) "rejoice" or experience "wonder"; he merely approved, "satisfied—partly."

The final paragraph of the Avignon fragment dramatizes the direct communication between God and humanity achieved by Adams's Aquinas in vaulting the nave of his cathedral. "He swept away the horizontal lines," writes Adams. "The whole weight of the arches fell . . . down to the church-floor. In Thomas's creation nothing intervened between God and his world. . . . Every individual . . . was created by the same instantaneous act, for all time. . . . [E]very individual is a part of the direct act" (Adams 1904/1986, 334–37). Cather's first sentence repeats "is born" in Latin, and the fourth sentence explicitly applies it to Christ—"He" who "made" the blind see, the lame walk, and the dumb speak. His birth occurs both "among" and "within" the people at mass and is confirmed by Father Ambrose's testimony: Ambrose knew it "[i]n his heart" (Cather c. 1941). The climax of the paragraph (indeed, of the entire fragment) is the "shudder" the priest senses running through André. Like St. Ambrose, who instructed Augustine during his conversion, Cather's Ambrose directs a sinner toward conversion. André's shudder and Pierre's moan suggest that they, like the others at Christmas mass, are each sharing an experience involving will and intellect that Adams puts in mechanical terms in discussing human free will as reflex action: "an increase of energy from the Prime Motor [God], which enables [the conductor—in this case André] to attain the object aimed at [God]" (Adams 1904/1986, 352). The priest interprets the process as "release" and extends it from the lowly, "unlikely people" gathered here to "all . . . generations" in the "future" (Cather c. 1941). Christ, he concludes, has bequeathed time ("hours") for each soul to escape its "bondage" (social as well as sinful) and enjoy its "moment" of birth into the light of faith. This, indeed, is the "gorgeous drama with God" envisioned by Professor St. Peter as an opportunity for every man and woman to be happy "believing in the mystery and importance of their own little individual lives" (Cather 1925/1990, 55).

V. CORUSCATION

Cather claims in "Light on Adobe Walls" that "Art . . . is no good . . . unless it is let alone to be . . . a game of make-believe, of reproduction, very exciting and delightful to people who have an eye . . . or an ear for it" (1949/1962, 125). In the fiction of the 1930s and 1940s I've been discussing (*Shadows* and the Avignon story), make-believe and historical reproduction have particular significance as comforting, almost therapeutic, escape tactics; however, *Death Comes for the Archbishop* (1927) is a watershed book, using such reproductive tactics not only to bridge the social criticism and despair evident in *The Professor's House* and the resistance to change evident in *Shadows on the Rock* but to accommodate the ordered world of the latter to the modern situation. Writing *Death Comes for the Archbishop* offered Cather what she described as "a happy vacation from life" (1949/1962, 11) but also seriously involved her in an alien system of values and traditions she would use to present a spiritual alternative to the materialistic, consumer-driven future she envisioned for the society of her time. Like Adams, she "had found a source of strength with which to oppose the gold-bug" (Samuels 1989, 306).

In a letter to *The Commonweal*, Cather explains that the "story of the Church and the Spanish missionaries was always what most interested me [in the Southwest]; but I hadn't the most remote idea of trying to write about it. . . . [A]ny story of the Church in the Southwest was entirely the business of some Catholic writer, and not mine at all" (1927/1962, 6–7). Gradually, though, Archbishop Jean Lamy (fig. 14.2) of Santa Fe,

Figure 14.2.   John J. Murphy, Statue of Archbishop Jean Baptiste Lamy, prototype for Cather's Archbishop Jean Marie Latour, at St. Francis Cathedral in Santa Fe. (Courtesy of the author.)

prototype of her Jean Latour, provided the link. He was a Frenchman and she a Francophile, and he had been an outsider in New Mexico as she was in the Church. Discovering a copy of Father William Howlett's 1908 biography of Denver's Bishop Joseph Machebeuf, prototype of her Father Joseph Vaillant, "I found out," she writes, "how the country and the people of New Mexico seemed to those first missionary priests from France" (1927/1962, 8). The novel offered several artistic challenges: "to do something in the style of legend," in which "all human experiences" would be measured "against one supreme spiritual experience," and to do so "without accent," without "hold[ing] the note, not [using] an incident for all there is in it—but to touch and pass on" (9). Cather achieved in what she preferred to define as "a narrative" (12) rather than a novel a fluid pattern of incidents gleaned from various historical sources and arranged to invite comparison and juxtaposition and to reveal what she defined elsewhere as the "presence of the thing not named" (1922/1962, 41). The incidents are held together by the missionary routine of her priests and framed by the life of Archbishop Latour, whose death provides the closure. A similar structural principle would be followed in *Shadows*.

The *Archbishop* enabled Cather to be an apologist of sorts for the well-ordered universe of her priests, while fashioning an ideal churchman to rebuild a corrupt and abusive institution to serve as a buffer to the materialism and racism of Anglo-American culture. The world of this Church is not far away in Canada or France, or distant in time; it is set two states away from Nebraska and set just a few decades earlier than the opening book of Cather's popular prairie novel *My Ántonia*. As an apologist, Cather demonstrates prophetic powers, anticipating reforms still existing in potency in the documents of the Second Vatican Council, the Catholic Church's attempt to engage the modern world. Jean Marie Latour, introduced as "a priest in a thousand" with "a fine intelligence" and also "generous, reflective, . . . brave, sensitive, courteous" (Cather 1927/1990, 18–19), is Cather's candidate to oversee the rebuilding she symbolizes in the fulfillment of his dream of a cathedral in Santa Fe. When Father Vaillant wonders why a man of such "scholarship" and "delicate perceptions" as Latour had been placed where one of "much rougher type would have served God well enough," the speculation remains inconclusive: "But God has his reasons . . . Perhaps it pleased Him to grace the beginning of a new era and a vast diocese by a fine personality" (251–52). What needs to be negotiated with such elegance involves clerical reform, ecumenical tolerance, and social justice. The Church emerging from these achievements and represented for Cather in the building of Santa Fe's cathedral incorporates the maternal benevolence, clemency, and inclusiveness highlighted by Henry Adams in his fantasy of the cathedral at Chartres.

Latour's efforts at clerical reform focus on three influential New Mexican priests who represent "the old order" (153)—the native Church developed between the expulsion of the Spanish clergy in 1827 and the ceding of New Mexico to the United States in 1848. Padre Gallegos, the aristocrat of the three, has amassed great wealth from gambling and exploiting his parishioners. He neglects unprofitable pastoral duties, especially the Indian missions, for pleasurable flirtations with a rich Mexican widow. Padre Antonio José Martínez represents a cluster of abuses issuing from his position as "ruler in temporal as well as spiritual affairs" in Taos. As "dictator to all the parishes in northern New Mexico" (139), Martínez resents the authority of both Washington and Rome and is implicated in the beheading of American Governor Charles Bent. He is accused by some of having "debauched" a "Mexican girl who aspired to be a nun" (157), and Kit Carson claims "he's got children and grandchildren in almost every settlement around" (76). The third padre, Marino Lucero, functions as a foil for the other two. "He had the lust for money as Martínez had for women" (161), and unlike Gallegos, he hoarded it and lived in dire poverty. He "takes everything a poor man's got to give him a Christian burial" (76), Carson tells Latour. Of the three, Gallegos is dispatched with the least trouble, suspended and replaced in Albuquerque by Father Vaillant. Martínez and Lucero prove difficult to dislodge, are excommunicated, and organize a schismatic Church before they die.

All three priests are rustic counterparts of the three cardinals in "Prologue. At Rome," the novel's opening scene, and the destiny of all six is grotesquely intimated in "The Legend of Fray Baltazar," a tale told to Bishop Latour during his return from Ácoma in the third book. The scene in Rome depicts American missionary Bishop Ferrand pleading over dinner with the cardinals for an apostolic vicarate in New Mexico and the proper man to head it. The setting is an elegant villa in the Sabine hills, a stark contrast to the mission field. In their crimson-accented cassocks, these "princes" of the Church betray the relative indifference and self-absorption of the prepotent: "Their interest . . . was tepid, and had to be continually revived by the missionary . . ." (4). The owner of the villa, Cardinal de Allande, a Spanish aristocrat, is the most talkative and authoritative of the three. He had been "the most influential man at the Vatican" (5) under the late Gregory XVI, a notorious archconservative, and shared his boss's opposition to the Free Italy movement and the spirit of revolution everywhere. Neither the missionary bishop's argument that the scandalous state of affairs in New Mexico will further prejudice an already anti-Catholic American government nor his emphasis on the "momentous things" (6) a new bishop might accomplish sways de Allande's instinct to go with the status quo and assign the territory to the vicar of the Bishop of Durango, Mexico, under whose jurisdiction conditions have deteriorated. More contemptible is this cardinal's lack of interest in the Native peoples making up a large percentage of New Mexico's Catholic population. Not only does he boast that his knowledge of Indians, whom he refers to as "scalp-takers" (12), is "chiefly drawn from the romances of Fenimore Cooper" (10), but when informed that Pueblo culture is different, he responds, "No matter . . . I see your redskins through Fenimore Cooper, and I like them so" (13). This playboy aristocrat, obviously more interested in tennis than in evangelizing, and his cardinal companions are as much a part of "the old order" as Martinez, Lucero, and Gallegos, "something picturesque" and "left over from the past" (141). All six co-exist not named in Cather's portrait of Fray Baltazar.

Set some fifty years after the 1680 Pueblo Revolt, "The Legend of Fray Baltazar" of Ácoma, which has strategic similarities to both the prologue and the corrupt New Mexican padres, is Cather's silent little game of ridding her toy Church of corruption. In the legend, the division between secular and ecclesiastical authority is blurred. Baltazar is a tyrant as well as a notorious sensualist, exploiting the Ácoma people to recreate the comfortable life he left behind in Spain, using his position to enrich his kitchen and garden and embellish his cloister. He controls his people largely through the superstition that a picture of St. Joseph given them by the King of Spain will prevent drought and famine. The core of his corruption is neglect of priestly duties, sending his runners on errands "seldom of an ecclesiastical nature," forgetting his breviary for days at a time. "It was clear," the narrator concludes, "that the Friar of Ácoma lived more after the flesh than after the spirit" (105). The upshot of this perversion is his killing of a stable-boy during a dinner he gives for neighboring missionaries. It is the ultimate act of his betrayal of his people and ministry.

Both the dinner at Ácoma and the one in Rome opening the novel are provided with details that associate them and allow the prologue to anticipate the legend that echoes it. In Rome, as at Ácoma, the clerics are situated on a rock with the landscape spread beneath them. De Allande's villa is a showplace, and its food and vintages excellent. The excellence of the Ácoma feast matches its European counterpart, and Baltazar's lavish accommodations, enhanced by plans for a cloister fountain, are shown off to generate envy. However, beneath the extravagance are the grumblings of those exploited to sustain it: "Baltazar's tyranny grew little by little, and the Ácoma people were sometimes at the point of revolt" (106). At Rome, the churchmen "avoided politics, as men are apt to do in dangerous times" (13). When the stable-boy accidentally spills gravy on one of the padre's guests and Baltazar loses his temper and flings the heavy pewter mug that kills the boy, machinery is set in motion that will quickly rid the rock of its tyrant. When the new pope, Pius IX, vetoes his parliament's attempt to liberate the Papal States, his prime minister is assassinated, and the pope is forced to flee Rome. A strategic sentence in the opening paragraph of the prologue—"Beyond the balustrade was a drop in the air" (3)— is echoed in the execution of Ácoma's tyrant: "The executioners took him up . . . and, after a few feints, dropped him in mid-air" (113). Here Cather reveals herself, although silently, to be the kind of anarchist Adams boasted to a friend that he was—"[t]he Virgin and St. Thomas . . . my vehicles of anarchism" (Samuels 1989, 354). Her book, like his, employed the spiritual energy of the Thomistic cathedral and the unorthodox compassion of the Marian cult to confound both contemporary and traditional establishments.

However, Latour, Cather's "priest in a thousand," is both a compassionate and aesthetic rationalist, and the Church Cather has him build in New Mexico is, in a positive sense, Janus-faced, inspired by earlier models but qualified by progressive principles. While Latour is determined to reform what Martínez defends as "a living Church, . . . not a dead arm of the European Church" (1927/1990, 146), by curbing the violent rites of the Penitentes, suspending priests who have violated celibacy, and restraining theatrical subservience to the clergy and idolatrous practices, he will do so cautiously, heeding the advice of Kit Carson's wife: "The old people have need of their old customs; the young will go with the times" (155). When the less discreet Vaillant prods him to remove Martínez because the man's life is "an open scandal," Bishop Latour is firm in his refusal. "It is not expedient to interfere," he insists. "I do not wish to lose the parish of Taos in order to punish its priest" (156–57). The Church Martínez denigrates as "a dead arm" must be revived and integrated with care. It will then blossom into "a thick coruscation of growth" like the cottonwoods Latour observes during his retreat at the home of his friend Eusabio in the Navajo country; "they seemed to be of old dead, dry wood," yet "at the end of a preposterous length of twisted bough, would burst a faint bouquet of delicate green leaves" (222).

Nevertheless, because Latour is attempting to revive a transplant, not a native growth, accommodation to new territory requires cultural expansion as well as discipline. Thus Cather provides her ecclesiastical artist with a genius for universalizing. He shocks Father Vaillant by explaining that the fourteenth-century silver-alloy bell discovered in an old mission church, and supposedly pledged to St. Joseph during the Moorish wars in Spain, would be indebted to the Moors, who taught the Spanish all they knew about working silver, knowledge then passed down through the Mexicans to the Navajos. In fact, the European custom of bell-ringing to announce religious services and the Angelus prayer is, Latour continues, "really an adaptation of a Moslem custom" (45). Rather than regarding Native culture with scorn, he readily admits being at a loss, "convinced that neither the white man nor the Mexicans in Santa Fe understood anything about Indian beliefs or the workings of the Indian mind" (133). During the mass at Ácoma, for example, he feels so remote from the congregation of turtle-like, "ante-diluvian creatures" that he suspects the sacrifice on Calvary could hardly reach back so far" (100). His respect for the Indian is ever present in his relationship with his Pecos guide, Jacinto, and with his Navajo Christian friend, Eusabio, and he increasingly detects correspondences between Catholicism and Indian belief.

As early as his Ácoma visit, he compares that great rock stronghold to the Church and to the Hebrew concept of God:

> The rock . . . was the utmost expression of human need, . . . the highest comparison in love and friendship. Christ Himself had used the comparison for the disciple to whom He gave the keys of His Church. And the Hebrews of the Old Testament, . . . their rock was an idea of God, the only thing their conquerors could not take from them. . . .The Ácomas . . . had their idea in substance. They actually lived upon their Rock. (98)

This common bond between belief and landscape prompts Latour to appreciate Indian accommodation to the earth, the meditative influence of the desert, and the Navajo creation myth materialized in Shiprock and Canyon de Chelly, where the pastoral fields between towering sandstone walls become "an Indian Garden of Eden" (295). As he pauses to contemplate his cathedral for the last time when returning to die in Santa Fe, the old archbishop recognizes that while it fulfills "the European's desire to 'master' nature, to arrange and re-create" (233), it also accommodates itself to the landscape, "is part of a place, . . . that kinship is there" (270). Latour is wrapped in his Indian blankets in this scene, almost as if in liturgical garb.

Cather places her most defining scene for this "priest in a thousand" in the middle of the seventh book and resolves his fitful struggle to respect Mexican life and faith. Titled "December Night," it is his meeting with Sada, the bond-woman of a Protestant family that forbids her to attend church. Before the encounter, Latour is lying in bed, anguishing over his failure to lure the Indians from pagan practices and to discipline the Mexicans, who "were children who played with their religion." Getting up from what has become "a bed of thorns" (211) to pray in the church, he discovers Sada crouching in the snowy courtyard and weeping. He watches as she falls to her knees in the Lady Chapel, kisses the floor and the feet of the Virgin; then, as they pray together, he "behold[s]" as never before "such a deep experience of the holy joy of religion." Kneeling beside her, he experiences anew the mystery of "the Cross that took away indignity from suffering and made pain and poverty a means of fellowship with Christ," and the comfort of having "a Kind Woman in heaven, . . . a Woman, divine, [who] could know all a woman can suffer.

. . . The beautiful concept of Mary pierced the priest's heart like a sword" (216–17).

This scene is charged with many implications. Certainly, Sada is no child playing with her religion. Thus, the Bishop's reservations about the seriousness of Mexicans are nullified. Also, his insight into the feminine component of the Deity overrides orthodox sexism. In fact, Cather has her priest and her slave woman exchange roles. Not only does Latour realize from this experience that "[t]his church was Sada's house, and he was a servant in it" (217) but also that she has been an example for him, his teacher, his priest. The Church he rebuilds and embodies in stone in his cathedral will emphasize the Virgin, equalize her with the Father, Son, and Holy Spirit. This is, perhaps, the tactical parallel between *Death Comes for the Archbishop* and Adams's book. According to Adams, the construction of Chartres cathedral reflected that, by the twelfth century, Mary "began to overshadow the Trinity itself" (1904/1986, 90). The Santa Fe cathedral is named for St. Francis of Assisi but is never named as such in Cather's text. By custom, since it is a French cathedral, it would be named for the Virgin. So, let it be named—Our Lady of Santa Fe, or, if you will, Nuestra Signora de Santa Fé. "Chartres represents," claims Adams, "not the Trinity, but the identity of the Mother and Son. The Son represents the Trinity, which is thus absorbed in the Mother. The idea is not orthodox, but this is no affair of ours" (100).

Cather shares such modernist license, reflecting Adams's "logic" in her opening book. Latour is wandering through a landscape of triangular shapes that "begin to suggest the mystical number of the spirit and the Trinity itself" (Stouck 1975, 136). In his thirst, he recalls the Passion of Jesus, which he is contemplating when he sees the cruciform tree, dismounts, and kneels at its foot with "a kind of courtesy toward . . . the God whom he was addressing" (Cather 1927/1990, 19). However, this first chapter ends with a greeting of the Virgin, "*Ave María Purísima*," at Hidden Water, and we learn in the next chapter that it was "the Holy Mother, to whom he had addressed himself before the cruciform tree" (29). In the eighth book there is a stronger echo of Adams, when Latour returns to his study after bidding farewell to Vaillant. Instead of the loneliness he expects to feel, he is surrounded by the graces of "the Queen of Heaven: *le rêve suprême de la chair* [the highest ideal of the flesh]" (254). The bishop then contemplates the Marian tradition in art, the great masters who made paintings of her and music for her, and built cathedrals for her: "Long before Her years on earth, in the long twilight between the Fall and the Redemption, the pagan sculptors were always trying to achieve the image of a goddess who should be a woman" (255). Cather may have remembered the following passage in Adams, which lists "Astarte, Isis, Aphrodite, and the last and greatest deity of all, the Virgin," and affirms that the "study of Our Lady, as shown by the art of Chartres, leads directly back to Eve" (Adams 1904/1986, 187). And Adams constructs her cathedral at Chartres, "a toy-house to please the Queen of Heaven . . . to charm her till she smiled" (88), as antithetical to twentieth-century materialism: "The scientific mind is atrophied," he writes, "and suffers under inherited cerebral weakness when it comes in contact with the eternal woman" (187). In Latour's own church in Santa Fe, the "little wooden figure" of *La Conquistadora*, for which the women create an elaborate wardrobe, is the "doll" as well as "queen" of the people, "something to fondle and something to adore, as Mary's Son must have been to Her" (Cather 1927/1990, 254–55).

The cathedral in *Death Comes for the Archbishop* might well be read as Cather's counterpart to Adams's Chartres transported to the American Southwest, but Romanesque rather than Gothic because it is "of the South" (269). "Midi Romanesque is the right style for this country" (240), declares Latour in defending the cathedral project to Father Vaillant. Indeed, the meaning of the Santa Fe cathedral in the novel duplicates the progress of the Church being rebuilt in the new territory. Initially it seems a self-indulgent clerical project: "such a building might be a continuation of [the bishop] himself, . . . a physical body full of his aspirations after he had passed from the scene" (175). But eventually, struggling with such apparent extravagance in so poor a country, the cathedral is depersonalized; it "is not for us," he tells his skeptical vicar. "We build for the future . . ." (241). Finally, to the dying archbishop, the cathedral becomes a "harbour," a "golden face," an "honest building . . . start[ing] directly out of . . . rose-coloured hills—with a purpose so strong it was like action" (269–71). If we juxtapose Adams's version of the western rose window of Chartres and Nuestra Signora de Santa Fé "leap[ing] out" of the "intense rose-carnelian" (270) Sangre de Cristos, we get some sense of this universalizing purpose. Adams compares the rose window to a jewel "placed upon the breast of [the Virgin's] Church—which symbolized herself" to affect "the men who feared, and the women who adored her," and "infidels, Moors and heretics" (1904/1986, 137) as well. At the center of "this gorgeous combination of all the hues of Paradise," Christ sits in judgment, displaying his five bleeding wounds. It is "a Last Judgment as . . . never seen before or since . . . Never . . . has one of us looked up at this Rose [window] without feeling it to be Our Lady's promise of Paradise" (138). In a circle above Christ, Abraham rocks the souls of the blessed in his bosom. Mercy and inclusiveness rather than terror and damnation are the message, the inclusiveness suggested in the final paragraph of Cather's text, when the bell tolls at the archbishop's death: "the Mexican population . . . fell on their knees, and all American Catholics as well. Many others who did not kneel prayed in their hearts. Eusabio [the

Navajo] and the Tesuque boys went quietly away to tell their people"
(1927/1990, 297).

CODA

In the two novels prior to her achievement of this fictionalized, sheltering Church, Cather depicts the collapse of religion in the late nineteenth
and early twentieth centuries. The earlier in historical setting, *My Mortal
Enemy*, concerns a spoiled, self-centered woman who rejects in youth and
embraces in age a Catholicism corrupted by materialism and sentimentality. In *The Professor's House*, an intellectual lacking religious connection
despairs at the acceptance of science and material goods as panaceas for
moral vacuity after the Great War. The religious components in both novels function as equivocal alternatives to the predominant contemporary
fictions of modernism. We cannot quite conclude from either book, as Adams does in his, that the Virgin and her prophets are now "looking down
from a deserted heaven, into an empty church, on a dead faith"; however,
Cather's fictionalized Church (if we arrange these novels according to historical setting) has, indeed, been vacated, although the greater emptiness
is the lives of these protagonists.

Myra Henshawe's mistake in *My Mortal Enemy* was choosing mortal
love over divine, rather than developing one as the foil of the other, as
her religion should have taught her to do. Partially in an act of defiance,
she eloped with Oswald Henshawe, whose Ulster Protestant father was
detestable to her Irish Catholic uncle, John Driscoll. Subsequently, she is
haunted by having married outside the Church, although that condition
seems self-imposed. She volunteers to narrator Nellie Birdseye, "I went
before a justice of the peace, and married without gloves, so to speak,"
to which she adds a pseudo disclaimer: "Yes, I broke with the Church
when I . . . ran away with a German free-thinker [Oswald's mother was
German]; but I believe in holy words and holy rites all the same" (Cather
1926/1990, 69–70). However, Oswald later confides to Nellie, "It is one
of her delusions that I separated her from the Church. I never meant
to" (80). The Church and God Himself are confused in her mind with
Driscoll, a self-made entrepreneur who amassed a fortune by exploiting
workers in the Missouri swamps and whose concept of God is defined
by money: "It's better to be a stray dog in this world than a man without
money," he warns Myra before she elopes. "A poor man stinks, and God
hates him" (13). Her disappointment with the modest conditions Oswald
can provide soon causes insane resentment—"the rich and powerful ir-
ritate her"—and she confesses to Nellie, "it's very nasty being poor!"
(33–34).

When Myra is dying in poverty she dismisses Oswald as her "mortal enemy" (78) and laments her split with Driscoll: "I should have stayed with my uncle. It was money I needed" (62). Not being able to make amends with him—"if he'd lived till now," she declares, "I'd go back to him and ask his pardon" (67), her recourse is to return to the Church. Although she confesses and takes the Sacrament before she dies, her histrionics and bitterness prove her to be self-obsessed until the end. During the final stage of her illness, when Nellie takes up her crucifix to adjust her sheets, Myra testily reaches out to demand it back: "Give it to me. It means nothing to people who haven't suffered" (75).

In *The Professor's House*, Godfrey St. Peter's religious inheritance is ignorance rather than distortion. As he tells Augusta, the devout Catholic seamstress whose worldview anticipates Cather's "Catholic novels," "there was no Catholic church in our town in Kansas, and I guess my father forgot his religion" (Cather 1925/1990, 83). Augusta is amazed at the primary nature of his questions about the Virgin and his confusion of her Litany with the Magnificat. "Did you receive *no* religious instruction at all?" she asks. "I always think of you as knowing everything, Doctor St. Peter!" His response should alert the reader: "And you're always finding out how little I know" (83–84). Indeed, we too are amazed that a historian whose specialty is the Spanish colonization of the Americas and who lectures his students on religion and art should be so uninformed. His lack of awareness characterizes his marriage and family life as well. His longtime aloofness from his family and community and his guarded idealization of his late student, Tom Outland, during a time of changing values he cannot share have contributed to the rift between himself, his wife, and two daughters contending over material possessions, as well as to the lapse of his university into a business school. This cluster of problems defines the novel's crisis: "The university, his new house, his old house, everything around him seemed insupportable" (131). St. Peter loses any desire to live and considers asphyxiation when he awakens from a nap to discover his gas heater has failed, an act that would amount to surrendering to what he finds "insupportable." Augusta, who rescues him, is "embarrassed by . . . the condition in which she had found him" (254), yet she becomes his hope. We are left with a survivor who faces an uncertain future but senses beside him the "solid earth," Augusta with "her little religious book. . . . If he had thought of Augusta sooner, he would have got up from the couch sooner" (255–56).

We will never know what or how much Willa Cather believed. Her 1922 confirmation with her parents in the Episcopal church in Red Cloud, Nebraska, was assuredly a symbolic act—but of what? Was it a statement of belief or primarily one of family solidarity and cultural traditionalism? The only claim I would make is the one she made for the dying Count

Frontenac near the end of *Shadows*, that there is an elusive component in human nature that demanded submission:

> He would die here, in this room, and his spirit would go before God to be judged. He believed this, because he had been taught it in childhood, and because he knew there was something in himself and in other men that this world did not explain. Even the Indians had *to make a story* to account for something in their lives that did not come out of their appetites: conceptions of courage, duty, honour. The Indians had these, in their own fashion. These ideas came from some unknown source, and they were not the least part of life. (1931b/1995, 200–1, emphasis added)

Cather turned from the emptiness of her time to the Middle Ages for a foundation upon which to build a sheltering art. Hers was an aesthetic project, but not necessarily not religious. As Flannery O'Connor commented to a friend about a fourteenth-century statue of a laughing Virgin and Child she "was greatly taken with" at The Cloisters in New York, "Back then their religious sense was not cut off from their artistic sense" (1980, 523, 529).

NOTES

This article was first presented as a Santa Fe 400th Anniversary Worrell Lecture at St. John's College, March 5, 2010.

1. While this lecture contains material condensed from two earlier essays (cited below), "Building the House of Faith" (2002) and "Prophecy, Violence, and the Old Order in the *Archbishop*" (2007), it combines, develops, and complements this material in the most complete argument on Cather, art, and religion I have published thus far.

2. Subsequent to the writing of this lecture, additional fragments of the Avignon story were discovered at the University of Nebraska among the papers of the late Charles E. Cather, Willa Cather's nephew. They help flesh out the outline of the story provided by Edith Lewis, although in no way alter the significance of the fragments in the Alderman Library referred to here. These are discussed in my essay "Toward completing a Triptych: The 'Hard Punishments' Fragments."

WORKS CITED

Adams, Henry. 1904/1986. *Mont Saint Michel and Chartres*. New York: Penguin.

Ambrose, Saint. 1961. *Hexameron, or Six Days of Creation*, translated by John J. Savage. In *The Fathers of the Church*. Vol. 42, 3–283. New York: Fathers of the Church.

Bennett, Mildred R. 1961. *The World of Willa Cather*. Lincoln: University of Nebraska Press.

Berger, Peter L. 1967/1990. *The Sacred Canopy: Elements of a Sociological Theory of Religion*. New York: Anchor.

Brown, E. K. 1953. *Willa Cather: A Critical Biography*. New York: Knopf.

Carney, Raymond. 1986. "Introduction." In *Mont Saint Michel and Chartres* by Henry Adams, ix–xxxvii. New York: Penguin.

Cather, Willa. 1891/1966. "Concerning Thomas Carlyle." In *The Kingdom of Art: Willa Cather's First Principles and Critical Statements 1893–1896*, edited by Bernice Slote, 421–25. Lincoln: University of Nebraska Press.

———. 1914. Letter to Ferris Greenslet. 12 January. Houghton Library, Harvard University, Cambridge, MA.

———. 1922/1962. "The Novel Démeublé." In *On Writing: Critical Studies on Writing as an Art*, 35–43. New York: Knopf.

———. 1923. "Nebraska: The End of the First Cycle." *The Nation*, September 5, 236–38.

———. 1925/1990. *The Professor's House*. New York: Vintage.

———. 1926/1990. *My Mortal Enemy*. New York: Vintage.

———. 1927/1962. "On *Death Comes for the Archbishop*." In *On Writing: Critical Studies on Writing as an Art*, 3–13. New York: Knopf.

———. 1927/1990. *Death Comes for the Archbishop*. New York: Vintage.

———. c. 1930. Typescript page of *Shadows on the Rock* with Cather's corrections. Philip L. and Helen Cather Southwick Collection, University of Nebraska—Lincoln Libraries, Archives and Special Collections.

———. 1931a. Letter to Dorothy Canfield Fisher. June. Bailey-Howe Library, University of Vermont, Burlington.

———. 1931b/1995. *Shadows on the Rock*. New York: Vintage.

———. c. 1941. Avignon. Manuscript with typescripts. Special Collections Department/Rare Books, Alderman Library, University of Virginia Library, Charlottesville.

———. 1949/1962. "Light on Adobe Walls." In *On Writing*, 123-26.

———. 1949/1962. *On Writing: Critical Studies on Writing as an Art*. New York: Knopf.

———. 1966. *The Kingdom of Art: Willa Cather's First Principles and Critical Statements 1893–1896*, edited by Bernice Slote. Lincoln: University of Nebraska Press.

Eliot, T. S. 1963. *Collected Poems 1909–1962*. New York: Harcourt Brace.

Freeman, Charles. 2005. *The Closing of the Western Mind: The Rise of Faith and the Fall of Reason*. New York: Vintage.

Howlett, W. J. 1908/1987. *Life of the Right Reverend Joseph P. Machebeuf, D.D.* Denver, CO: Regis College.

Kates, George N. 1956/1992. "Willa Cather's Unfinished Avignon Story." In *Collected Stories* by Willa Cather, 464–93. New York: Vintage.

Lewis, Edith. 1953. *Willa Cather Living: A Personal Record*. New York: Knopf.

Murphy, John J. 2002. "Building the House of Faith: 'Hard Punishments,' the Plan and the Fragment." *Literature and Belief* 22: 202–27.

———. 2007. "Prophecy, Violence, and the Old Order in the *Archbishop*." In *Violence, the Arts, and Willa Cather*, edited by Joseph R. Urgo and Merrill Maguire Skaggs, 282–94. Madison, NJ: Fairleigh Dickinson University Press.

——. 2011. "Toward Completing a Triptych: The 'Hard Punishments' Fragments." *Willa Cather Newsletter and Review* 55: 208.

O'Connor, Flannery. 1980. *The Habit of Being: Letters of Flannery O'Connor*. Edited by Sally Fitzgerald. New York: Vintage.

Pope, Hugh. 1909–1913. "Faith." In *The Catholic Encyclopedia: An International Work of Reference*, edited by Charles G. Hebermann et al. Vol. 5, 756–59. New York: Encyclopedia Press.

St. John's Missal for Every-Day. 1950. New York: Brepols' Catholic Press.

Samuels, Ernest. 1989. *Henry Adams*. Cambridge, MA: Harvard University Press.

Stouck, David. 1975. *Willa Cather's Imagination*. Lincoln: University of Nebraska Press.

Index

223

About the Editors and Contributors

Sarah Cheney Watson is professor of English and chair of the Department of Languages and Literature at East Texas Baptist University, where she teaches American literature, composition, adolescent literature, and linguistics. She holds the Doctor of Education degree from Texas A&M–Commerce, where she wrote her dissertation under the direction of Ann Moseley. Entitled *Servant of Beauty: Willa Cather and the Aesthetic Movement*, it examines the influence of the Aesthetic movement on the development of Willa Cather's artistic vision. Watson has presented papers at several Cather conferences, often focusing on Cather's relationship to the movement. Her essay "Parsifal Lost in the Wasteland: The Modernist Grail Quest in Cather and Fitzgerald" appears in *Critical Insights: Willa Cather* by Salem Press (2011). She is co-editor of *Willa Cather and Aestheticism*.

Ann Moseley is William L. Mayo Professor and Professor of Literature and Languages Emerita at Texas A&M University–Commerce. She is the historical editor for the Scholarly Edition of *The Song of the Lark* (2012). She has made numerous presentations on Cather and other topics in American literature, children's literature, and composition and has published essays on Cather in *Willa Cather Newsletter and Review*, *Cather Studies*, *Literature and Belief*, *Western American Literature*, *American Literary Realism* and other journals. Her most recent essays appear in the collections *Teaching the Works of Willa Cather* (2009), *Willa Cather's* The Song of the Lark (2010), and *Willa Cather: A Writer's Worlds* (2010). Coeditor of the present volume, Moseley is also the author of *Ole Rölvaag* (1987) and the coauthor of the 2004–2007 bibliographic essay "Wharton and Cather" in *American Literary Scholarship* and the composition textbook *Interactions: A Thematic Reader*, now in its eighth edition.

Olga Aksakalova holds a Ph.D. from the Graduate School and University Center of the City University of New York. She is the director of Writing and Communication Center and lecturer in the English Department at the New Economic School in Moscow, Russia. Her research interests include twentieth-century literature, film, autobiography, and writing pedagogy.

Peter Betjemann is associate professor and coordinator of the M.A. program in English at Oregon State University, where he specializes in American literature and material culture of the late nineteenth and early twentieth centuries. He is the author of *Talking Shop: The Language of Craft in an Age of Consumption* (2011) and has published in *American Literary Realism, The Journal of Design History, Word and Image,* and other journals. He is currently working on a book that examines how the decorative arts provided progressive-era writers with ready metaphors for describing political and social systems.

Timothy W. Bintrim is assistant professor of English at Saint Francis University in Loretto, PA. He co-directed a centennial observance of Cather's arrival in Pittsburgh at Duquesne University, where he completed his dissertation on Cather's Pittsburgh writings. In 2008, he helped found a summer retreat for the study of Western Pennsylvania Women Writers (including Cather) at Saint Francis University. He is a contributor to the Cather Journalism Project at The Cather Archive, has published in the journals *Willa Cather Newsletter and Review, The Mowers' Tree,* and *Teaching Cather* and in the essay collections *Violence, the Arts, and Cather* (2007) and *Willa Cather: Facts, New Glimpses, Revisions* (2008).

Nicholas Birns teaches British, American, and postcolonial literature as well as literary theory at Eugene Lang College, the New School, in New York. He is the author of *Understanding Anthony Powell* (2004), *A Companion to Australian Literature Since 1900* (2007), and *Theory After Theory: An Intellectual History of Literary Theory from 1950 to the early 21st century* (2010). He has published on Willa Cather in *Religion and the Arts, The Anglican,* and *The Willa Cather Newsletter.* In addition, he has published many essays in general and academic journals such as *The New York Times Book Review, National Forum, The Hollins Critic, Arizona Quarterly,* and *Studies in Romanticism.* He served as a Visiting Research Fellow at the University of Wollongong in Australia in 2008.

Angela Conrad is professor of English and women's studies at Bloomfield College, where she heads the English program. At Bloomfield College, she led the Teaching and Learning Center of faculty development. She holds a Ph.D. from Drew University, where she was program director of the 1998 "Willa Cather in New York" International Colloquium. In 2000, she published *The Wayward Nun of Amherst: Emily Dickinson and Medieval Mystical Women*. She contributed entries on feminism, Jean Rhys, Edwidge Danticat, and others to the *Encyclopedia of Caribbean Literature* (2005). She also served for five years as a trustee of the New Jersey Humanities Council.

Mark Facknitz is professor of English at James Madison University. The 1989 winner of the Virginia Prize for fiction, his creative work has appeared in *The Georgia Review, Shenandoah, Story Quarterly, The Iowa Review,* and numerous other journals. His essays on Raymond Carver, Anthony Powell, Henry Green, Joseph Conrad, Michel Tournier, and others have appeared in *Studies in Short Fiction, CEA Critic, The Journal of Modern Literature, Twentieth-Century Literature, The Journal of Narrative Technique,* and other publications. Facknitz has given papers at several Cather conferences, and his essay "Character, Compromise, and Idealism in Willa Cather's Gardens" appeared in *Cather Studies 5: Willa Cather's Ecological Imagination* (2003) and "Changing Trains: Metaphors of Transfer in Willa Cather" in *Cather Studies 9: Willa Cather and Modern Cultures* (2011).

Jacqueline H. Harris is a Ph.D. student in English at The University of Nebraska–Lincoln and is also employed as a graduate instructor. With an emphasis on nineteenth-century British literature, Jacqueline has additional specializations in nineteenth-century studies and women's and gender studies, and enjoys interdisciplinary and cultural studies as well as art, writing fiction, and creative nonfiction. Her current work focuses on female coming-of-age literature.

Robert Lee Lynch Jr. is associate professor of English at Longwood University in Farmville, Virginia, He earned his Ph.D. in American literature from Indiana University–Bloomington. His dissertation examines the American historical epos of Ezra Pound and William Carlos Williams. He has presented at the International Cather Seminar (2005, 2009), and his work has appeared in *American National Biography* (1999), *American Literature: A Prentice-Hall Anthology* (2001), and *American History Through Literature, 1870–1920* (2006). With his wife Sonja Froiland Lynch, he is working on a book-length study of impressionism in Willa Cather's fiction.

Sonja Froiland Lynch is associate professor of English and director of writing across the curriculum at Wartburg College in Waverly, IA. She earned her Ph.D. from Indiana University–Bloomington in American literature. Her doctoral dissertation examines American literary impressionism in the works of several major American authors. She has presented at the International Cather Seminar (2005, 2009) and the 20th Century Literature and Culture Conference (2007), and her work has appeared in *American History Through Literature, 1870–1920* (2006). With her husband Robert Lee Lynch, Jr., she is working on a book-length study of impressionism in Willa Cather's fiction.

Jo Ann Middleton is affiliate associate professor of English literature and founding director of the Medical Humanities Program, Casperson School of Graduate Studies, Drew University. She is the author of *Willa Cather's Modernism: A Study of Style and Technique* (1990). She has presented numerous papers on Cather at national and international conferences, and her essays on Cather have appeared in *Literature and Belief* and the *Willa Cather Newsletter and Review*. She authored the annual bibliographical essay "Fiction: 1900 to the 1930s" in *American Literary Scholarship* from 1992 to 1998.

John J. Murphy is professor emeritus of American literature, Brigham Young University, Utah, and the former editor of *Literature and Belief* and of the *Willa Cather Newsletter and Review*. He serves on the editorial board of the Willa Cather Scholarly Edition, University of Nebraska Press, and is volume editor of the scholarly editions of *Death Comes for the Archbishop* (1999) and *Shadows on the Rock* (2005). He is also the author of *My Ántonia: The Road Home* (1989) and more than sixty journal articles and book chapters on Cather and other American writers, including the annual bibliographical essay "Fiction: 1900 to the 1930s" in *American Literary Scholarship* (1980–87). He is the editor of *Critical Essays on Willa Cather* (1984); *Willa Cather: Family, Community, and History* (1990); *Flannery O'Connor and the Christian Mystery* (1997); *Willa Cather: New Facts, New Glimpses, Revisions* (2008); and *Willa Cather: A Writer's Worlds–Cather Studies 8* (2010), as well as the Penguin *My Ántonia* (1994).

Joseph C. Murphy is associate professor of English at Fu Jen Catholic University, Taipei, where he teaches graduate and undergraduate courses in American literature and edits *Fu Jen Studies: Literature and Linguistics*. His recent work on Cather appears in *Cather Studies 7* and *8*, the *Willa Cather Newsletter and Review*, and *Violence, the Arts, and Willa Cather* (2007). He has also published essays on Henry Adams, Benjamin Franklin, Cormac McCarthy, Flannery O'Connor, and Walt Whitman.

Leona Ann Sevick is associate provost and associate professor of English at Mount St. Mary's University. In addition to American literature, her teaching and scholarly interests include world literature and poetry. Her published writing focuses on Cather and *antimodernism,* a term that explores Cather's complex responses to masculinity, arts and crafts, and spiritualism. She has published essays on *Death Comes for the Archbishop,* including a chapter in the *Cambridge Companion to Willa Cather* on neurasthenia and modernism, and she is a published poet.

Janis P. Stout is professor emerita of English and dean of faculties/associate provost emerita of Texas A&M University. She is the author of numerous books and essays on American literature, among them *Willa Cather: The Writer and Her World* (2000), *A Calendar of the Letters of Willa Cather* (2002), *Coming Out of War: Poetry, Grieving, and the Culture of the World Wars* (2005), and *Picturing a Different West: Vision, Illustration, and the Tradition of Cather and Austin* (2007). She has also edited the collection of essays entitled *Willa Cather and Material Culture: Real-World Writing and Writing the Real World* (2004). At present, she and Andrew Jewell are preparing a volume of selected letters of Willa Cather.

CPSIA information can be obtained at www.ICGtesting.com
Printed in the USA
BVOW070815070612

291797BV00001B/3/P